28-1837 HB884.5 89-38870 CIP
Donaldson, Peter J. **Nature against us: the United States and the world
population crisis, 1965-1980**. North Carolina, 1990. 207p bibl index
ISBN 0-8078-1905-0, $29.95

In this book Donaldson discusses the role of the US in dealing with the world
population crisis. The author has extensive experience in Third World population
policy. His materials come from archives for AID, the CIA, the FBI, and the Population Council, and also from interviews with many persons who were influential
in US international population policy. Unfortunately, the book's scope is too
broad for an adequate treatment of the topic. One chapter documents American
concern with overpopulation; the next one discusses postwar foreign policy. Four
chapters deal with the evolution of AID's international program. The world's reaction—essentially positions taken by various international organizations and two
international population conferences—is summarized in one brief chapter. A case
study of the Population Council's activities in South Korea and an analysis of the
relation between modernization and contraceptive use close the discussion. References to the mainstream demographic literature are somewhat skimpy. Most likely users: upper-division undergraduates, graduate students, and faculty in public
policy.—*J. De Vries, Carleton University*

NATURE AGAINST US

NATURE AGAINST US

THE UNITED STATES AND THE WORLD POPULATION CRISIS, 1965–1980

PETER J. DONALDSON

677157

THE UNIVERSITY OF NORTH CAROLINA
Chapel Hill and London

Portions of Chapter 1 appeared in somewhat different form in Peter J.
Donaldson, "American Catholicism and the International Family Planning
Movement," *Population Studies* 42 (1988): 367–73.

Portions of Chapter 7 appeared in somewhat different form in P. J.
Donaldson and C. B. Keely, "Population and Family Planning: An International Perspective," *Family Planning Perspectives* 20, no. 6 (Nov.–Dec.
1988): 307–20. © The Alan Guttmacher Institute.

Portions of Chapter 9 appeared in somewhat different form in Peter J.
Donaldson, "Modernizing Family Planning," *Society* 25, no. 5 (1988): 11–17.
Published by permission of Transaction Publishers, © 1988 by
Transaction Publishers.

The paper in this book meets the guidelines for permanence and durability
of the Committee on Production Guidelines for Book Longevity of the
Council on Library Resources.

94 93 92 91 90   5 4 3 2 1

Library of Congress Cataloging-in-Publication Data

Donaldson, Peter J.
Nature against us : the United States and
the world population crisis,
1965–1980 / Peter J. Donaldson.
p.   cm.
Includes bibliographical references.
ISBN 0-8078-1905-0 (alk. paper)
1. Population assistance, American
—Developing countries.
I. Title.
HB884.5.D66   1990
363.9—dc20
89-38870
CIP

FOR THE WOMEN IN MY LIFE

Rose, Rita, Phyllis, Katharine, Mary,
Nancy, Jean, and Marie, and

FOR JOHN

CONTENTS

Preface

This book investigates the origins, implementation, and impact of the American effort—both private and government—to regulate fertility and thus to slow population growth throughout the developing world. I examine why and with what effect the United States decided to promote the regulation of childbearing around the world. I try to highlight aspects of the design and conduct of America's international population programs, such as their links to fundamental American values, that other authors have missed. I do not devote much attention to reviewing the consequences of rapid population growth or to examining the dynamics of population change. Rather, my interest is in what the effort to slow population growth tells us about the United States and its place in the world.

My research is different from most other studies of public policy related to the demography of the developing world because of the type of data I employ. I have relied heavily on information collected from the archives of the Agency for International Development and, less extensively, from the files of the Population Council and the archives of several federal agencies. I have also interviewed policy makers, program managers, providers of family planning services, and population researchers both in the United States and overseas. A detailed review of the sources of data used in this analysis is presented in an appendix.

Many people believe that rapid growth of the world's population is among the most serious dangers we face. For years American political leaders ranked population growth behind nuclear war as the second most important threat to the world. Efforts to control population growth merit serious consideration, and the programs of the U.S. government and of private American organizations are of special historical interest. Between 1965 and 1980, the United States contributed more than half of all international assistance for population and family planning and underwrote numerous Third World family planning programs. In the past decade the formulation of policy and the leadership of important programs have shifted away from the United States, and so now is a good time to examine exactly what the country's efforts have accomplished. The United States sought to change the behavior and values of governments and, more importantly, of millions of families across the globe. America's international population program thus represents an important instance of U.S. global power and involvement in the lives of people around the world.

Few, if any, of the remarkable and far-reaching social changes that have taken place in the latter half of the twentieth century are as little noted or as poorly understood as the contraceptive revolution that American aid helped ignite. Twenty-five years ago only a small number of the world's women controlled their childbearing effectively—now, thanks to what can legitimately be called a contraceptive revolution, approximately half a billion women, or their partners, regularly use a contraceptive. This change in contraceptive practice is the most visible element in the modernization of family life and in the institutionalization of government involvement in the family.

This book deals with both government and private efforts to bring the problem of rapid population growth to the public's attention and to implement programs to slow that growth. Too often, students of population policy concentrate on government agencies and programs and ignore the influence of private organizations on the formulation and execution of public policies. One of the central features of the evolution of America's international population policy has been the extent to which experts within the government and at private organizations have worked together on the design and implementation of that policy.

The changes that have taken place in the regulation of fertility and the sociology of childbearing trouble some people. Birth control is frequently seen as challenging valued sexual ideals. Sometimes, as illustrated by the Comstock laws or the more militant tactics of the "right-to-life" movement, a crusade may be mounted to get people to follow certain sexual ideals that family planning is seen to threaten. Opponents of birth control have blamed family planning for a variety of ills—lower sexual standards, promiscuity (especially among adolescents), and increased family breakups being among the most frequently cited.

In the 1830s, the American physician Charles Knowlton published *Fruits of Philosophy or the Private Companion of Adult People*, the first text devoted wholly to family planning. In the most concise way possible, Knowlton summarized the moral stance against tampering with childbearing when he noted that people object to birth control because it leads to "illegal intercourse" or because it is "against nature." In the case of human reproduction, however, nature may be against us—in that the biology of human reproduction makes dangerously high fertility more likely than low levels of human reproduction. The nature of our social life makes sex and reproduction among the best-regulated aspects of human existence and, thus, among the most difficult issues for individuals to deal with on their own. In both traditional and modern societies all sorts of people, from parents to politicians, feel able to help women decide when they should have children and how many children they should have.

Too little attention has been paid to these issues. Few historians, political scientists, sociologists, or demographers have expressed interest in the impact of foreign involvement on Third World population and family planning programs. In addition, it has been taken for granted that modern contraceptive methods and new delivery systems supported by foreign aid are better suited to the needs of the developing countries than are traditional technology and delivery systems. The agencies providing assistance for population and family planning activities overseas have also supported most of the research that has been carried out on the topic. These groups have shown little interest in outside evaluation of their impact. There have been a small number of studies, but not as many as the issues involved merit. A host of serious questions about the demographic, social, political, and economic effects of population- and family-planning-related foreign assistance have been ignored. The best way to preserve the quality and integrity of government and private population-related foreign assistance programs is to have more knowledgeable analysis and discussion of them.

Acknowledgments

Many people helped with the preparation of this book. I am grateful to those I interviewed, all of whom were generous with their time and gracious in allowing me to question them. Some wished to remain anonymous. Those who did not, include: Daya Abeywickrema, William Bair, Leona Baumgartner, David Bell, Donald Bogue, Gerald Bowers, Philander Claxton, Jarrett Clinton, Ronald Freedman, Moye Freyman, Duff Gillespie, Charles Gurney, Oscar Harkavy, Sam Keeny, John Knodel, Philip Lee, Sander Levin, Parker Mauldin, Frank Notestein, Allan Rosenfield, Roberto Rivera, Hamid Rushwan, Sheldon Segal, Steven Sinding, John Sullivan, Somsak Varakamin, Benjamin Viel, George Worth, and Jae Mo Yang.

I also appreciate the encouragement and criticism provided by Malcolm Potts, president of Family Health International. J. Joseph Speidel, former deputy director of the Agency for International Development's Office of Population, offered many valuable leads and a great deal of support for telling AID's story "warts and all," as he once put it. Reimert T. Ravenholt, the head of AID's population program for most of its history, was generous with his time and his willingness to be cross-examined about his tenure at AID. William A. Campbell helped with several Freedom of Information Act requests and provided office space when it was needed for quiet work. John O. G. Billy was a source of thoughtful advice on methodological problems. Catherine Cameron, Jason Finkle, Michael Goldstein, Charles B. Keely, Clifford Pease, Malcolm Potts, Ronald R. Rindfuss, Warren C. Robinson, J. Joseph Speidel, and Terence P. Thornberry read drafts of the book and made numerous suggestions that contributed greatly to the quality of this account. I am particularly grateful to Paul Betz, W. Parker Mauldin, and Amy Ong Tsui for reading and commenting on several versions of the manuscript. Debbie Wade, Cheryl Hailey, Sarah DeLoach, and Diane Goldman typed and retyped the manuscript and did numerous other odd jobs required to complete the book. I am very grateful for their help.

NATURE AGAINST US

1

The Roots of American Concern

In the fall of 1976, the American naturalist and writer Peter Matthiessen recorded his impressions of a remote village in one of Asia's poorest countries. "The village creaks to the soft rhythm of an ancient rice treadle, and under the windows babies sway in wicker baskets. In the serene and indiscriminate domesticity of these sunny villages, sow and piglet, cow and calf, mother and infant, hen and chick, nanny and kid commingle in a common pulse of being" (Matthiessen 1979, p. 29).

Matthiessen calls attention to the integrity of village life, the metaphysical nature of existence fully understood and explained by village culture. Living things share a "common pulse of being" and, as such, are accepted and taken for granted. In most such villages, women who remain childless are not just a curiosity; they are pitied because the bearing and rearing of children are essential elements in the identity of adult women, in their own eyes and in the eyes of their fellow villagers.

An adolescent girl soon to get married has little choice about whether or not to have children. Because all the other married women in her village have had children, the young bride's options are clearly defined and set out. They are not matters to be puzzled over. Moreover, because universal childbearing will have been the accepted pattern for several generations, newly married women will be socialized to believe, should anyone bother to ask them, that not having children is wrong. They will not think very much about this because it will be self-evident. Since everyone in the village will also believe that married women should have children, the correctness of this view is "proved" by the attitudes and behavior of other villagers.

If the young bride remains unpersuaded about the value of childbearing, gossip, ridicule, and perhaps more threatening forms of social control will be used against her. If she can free herself from her surroundings and think about the costs and benefits of children in the most hard-nosed terms, she will almost surely decide that having children is a good idea because in traditional villages children are assets.

Margery Wolf spells out what this complex of attitudes has meant in rural Taiwan, at a time when it was typical of much of the developing world:

> Until a young woman becomes the mother of one of the family's sons, she feels very insecure. . . . She wants to become pregnant, and if she is married to the eldest son, she is made to feel she must become pregnant. Her mother-in-law begins asking embarrassingly blunt questions about her menstrual cycle and allows her to overhear the disgusting comments she makes to her friends. The watchful eyes of village women with few other interests take note of any swelling of her breasts or expanding of her waistline and as months go by comment questioningly on the absence of such symptoms. (Wolf 1972, p. 149)

The high birth rates promoted by these traditional attitudes toward childbearing assured that populations replaced themselves, even if high death rates kept them from growing quickly. For most of history, the human race grew very slowly because death rates were high. The risk of death, particularly among infants and children, was astronomical by today's standards. Although women had many children, in most communities there was a rough balance between a large number of births and a large number of deaths that over time led to only modest population growth. It took until the first decades of the nineteenth century for the world's population to reach one billion. A second billion people had been added by the 1930s. The next billion came by the 1960s, and in less than twenty years a fourth billion was added. A million years were needed before the world population reached one billion people, but less than twenty years were required to jump from three to four billion people. Indeed, the net increase in human beings between 1960 and 1983, nearly 90 percent of which occurred in developing countries, equaled the total world population at the beginning of this century (Demeny 1983, p. 3). The world reached five billion people early in 1988, and given the current rate of global population growth (an estimated 1.7 percent per year), it is clear that by the end of the twentieth century the world's population will be over six billion.

The rate of population increase in the developing world has been especially rapid in our own time mainly because death rates have become so low. A young woman is much more likely to live through her reproductive period, and many more of her children will also survive than ever before. Beginning in the middle of the 1930s, public health programs began a steady improvement, immunization became widespread, and sulfa drugs were introduced in developed countries and in the urban areas of many underdeveloped countries; these events had a significant impact on mortality. The war years saw increased attention given to public health, in particular to the prevention of malaria. During the 1940s, new antibiotics came into widespread use and were disseminated among medical practitioners even faster than sulfa had been. These antibiotics both supplemented and replaced sulfa drugs in the treatment of many infections. Following World War II, a greater use of antibiotics, more widespread immunization, and spraying against malaria spread quickly throughout the developing world. As a consequence, death rates, which had been declining slowly for some time, fell even more rapidly (Omran 1971). In some countries, death rates after World War II were probably only one-half, perhaps even less, of what they had been in the prewar period. On the other hand, there was little or no reduction in birth rates; thus, the rate of growth and the size of the population increased quickly.

The mortality reduction was accelerated because a host of social changes improved living conditions in the Third World and increased the effectiveness of the new medical technologies. For the first time, many countries enjoyed proper hospitals and public health services. The number of trained practitioners increased. More women enjoyed at least some medical attention during pregnancy and childbirth, a change that probably contributed to lowering maternal and neonatal mortality. Railroads, roads, and other means of mass transportation and communication increased, making it easier for government health workers to reach rural areas and for villagers to get food, medicine, soap, insecticide, and other supplies on a regular basis. Finally, many developing countries started on the slow road toward economic progress that led to increases in per capita income, growth in agricultural production, and improvements in living conditions.

Most of these changes spread quickly because they encountered very little resistance. Everyone wants to live longer and better. Hospitals and television stations are almost universally welcomed. Moreover, many of the most important changes did not require the cooperation of the man-in-the-street. Nobody asked the rural villagers in the developing world whether or not they wanted a railroad, or if it was all right to spray DDT.

Sri Lanka is many demographers' favorite example of the impact of quickly declining death rates. In 1945, Sri Lanka's crude death rate (the number of deaths per 1,000 population) was 24; by 1950 it had dropped to 12 per 1,000. Sri Lanka's birth rate was 38 per 1,000 in both 1945 and 1950. The arithmetic is straightforward: assuming that migration had no impact, when the birth rate was 38 and the death rate was 24, the rate of population increase was 14 per 1,000, or 1.4 percent per year; when the death rate declined but the birth rate did not, the rate of increase jumped to 2.6 percent per year, sufficiently fast to cause the population to double in less than thirty years. This scenario has been repeated in numerous countries.

Some scholars argue that the eradication of malaria was the major reason for the decline of mortality in Sri Lanka; another group believes the change was caused by improvements in health services; a third group claims the shift was due to economic development and better nutrition. The debate, which has been carried out in academic journals, has become impossible for the casual reader to follow (for a representative example, see Gray 1974). Whatever the precise importance of different factors for the decline in Sri Lanka's death rate (most likely a wide variety of changes contributed to it), it is easy to see why development specialists became concerned that rapid population growth represented a new and potentially serious barrier to the modernization of the Third World and to the stability of the world system.

The level of population growth experienced by many countries between 1950 and 1980 was astronomical. Consider the case of any of the Asian giants—China, for example. Between 1950 and 1980, China's population increased by 82 percent, going from an estimated 547 million to more than 1 billion. Remarkable increases took place in other parts of the world too. Mexico's population increased two and a half times between 1950 and 1980, going from 27 to 68 million people. Nigeria grew from 33 million in 1950 to 77 million in 1980 (U.S. Bureau of the Census 1981, pp. 36, 61, 121). This dramatic population growth encouraged scholars and policy makers to examine the relationship between population increase and economic modernization.

Scholars and policy makers, however, were not the only ones to reevaluate the consequences of traditional patterns of childbearing. People had difficulty stretching the "common pulse of being" to include all that was required to gain a toehold on the modern age. Modernization requires the acceptance of new values and new definitions of appropriate behavior. Thus, values, attitudes, and behavior changed to fit the new circumstances. People have become less fatalistic and more self-interested and goal-oriented. The sequence and tempo of these changes is very difficult to decipher, but gradually over several years first one element changed, and then another, until a new pattern was pervasive. In the process, school enrollments and literacy rates increased. Jobs changed; more people became professional and technical workers, and there was a corresponding growth in hospitals, television stations, and domestic air transportation. Modernization also meant bigger cities and greater inequality between rural and urban populations—between those working in traditional occupations, such as farming, and those employed in modern-sector jobs. Government policy changed as well: today, as a matter of government policy, China, Mexico, and Nigeria, together with numerous other developing countries, are encouraging women (with different amounts of energy and impact, to be sure) to have fewer children.

Childbearing practices changed in developing countries not only because, thanks to new birth control techniques, those who wanted fewer children had effective and convenient ways to control fertility, but also because people's views of sex, marriage, and the family were transformed. Etienne Van de Walle and John Knodel (1980, p. 34) refer to "the spread of a new mentality—an openness to the idea of manipulating reproduction" as a decisive element in the transition from high to low birth rates in Europe. A similar process occurred in the developing world. No longer did the village girl find marriage and children her only option—a move to a nearby city or town to continue school or to find a job also made sense and, in many cases, was welcomed by family members.

The idea of manipulating reproduction spread in the developing world because controlled childbearing fit better with the demands for a mobile, well-educated, and independent labor force that are characteristic of modern societies—and, in a lesser way, of societies on their way to becoming modern. In addition, fertility control became an important social movement. Throughout the developing world, family planning activists and organizations played a central role in breaking up the old understanding of childbearing and in legitimating new rules for the bearing of one's offspring.

In the mid-1960s, the U.S. government officially joined the movement to slow population growth. Many politicians and federal bureaucrats thought the United States should avoid becoming involved in family planning in developing countries, and most Americans had no idea their tax dollars were being spent to promote fertility control. But the campaign "to do something about population" had deep roots and influential supporters in the United States and abroad.

Why the United States tried to change the "pulse of being" in villages around the world and what its efforts produced are key issues for understanding America's place in the world.

Fertility Control and Foreign Policy

I once heard Charles Kuralt, the CBS television journalist, address a luncheon sponsored by the Charlotte chapter of the North Carolina Planned Parenthood Association to honor his father, who that day received the group's Margaret Sanger Award. Kuralt said his travels around America had convinced him that one of the country's most valuable national virtues was an eagerness to solve problems, to try to make things better. He argued that history would remember more the changes caused by thousands of citizens joining together to do something to help those who needed it than all but a very few of the people and events that made the front page of the *New York Times* or got time on the CBS evening news. Among those who tried to make life better, Kuralt mentioned his parents and others who worked to provide contraceptive choices to the women of western North Carolina.

Observers traveling in the developing world have had similar impressions of Americans' eagerness to try to improve things. As John C. Sommer, for example, describes it: "Traveling along the ruttiest dirt trail, across mountains, deserts, or swamps, miles from the beaten track, one is constantly struck to find there some isolated American doing his or her bit to help other people. There seems no place too remote and no cause too marginal to deter these missionaries for modernity. In fact, the more difficult the assignment the greater their commitment. The countries of the Third World have in a sense become the new frontier. . . . Problems to be solved? Americans are there" (Sommer 1977, p. 1). The American enthusiasm for making things better has been a crucial ingredient in the country's international population program. Many, perhaps most, of those involved in the American effort to control population growth around the world felt they were tackling one of the twentieth century's most important problems and, in the process, improving life for the majority of mankind.

The rough-and-ready optimism that underpins much of the nation's foreign aid assumes that things can be improved. Non-Americans often find this view naive and meddling. Likewise, the American conviction that individuals can make a difference is frequently seen as foolish and quite pompous. Others recognize that an impatience to do something can compound problems better left alone. In a society where the group is all-important and the value of change is not taken for granted, Americans, busy encouraging individuals to develop new ways of doing things without sufficient concern for the consequences of the new style, frequently seem misguided and self-ish. Change in such places is often seen, not as a step toward a better life, but as a disruptive force upsetting valued ways of behaving.

Although it is self-interested and can be self-righteous and paternalistic as well, the American approach to the problems of development is rarely mean-spirited. The U.S. effort to control population growth was, in part, rooted in a concern about how best to preserve U.S. interests around the world in the context of the very rapid growth of the poorest countries. But in reviewing thousands of pages of documents from federal and private organizations, including personal files and official correspondence, and in interviewing several dozen people, I encountered only one person who used racist language to describe those whose growth the United States tried to slow—and even in this case, the racial slurs were used to shock me and distance the subject from the "bleeding hearts" he claimed were too much involved in the population movement. To properly understand why the United States tried to slow population growth, it is necessary to understand what thoughtful people saw as the consequences of rapid population growth.

Growth's Consequences

The modern consensus finds rapid population growth of the sort experienced by many poor countries (3 percent per year, doubling population size in less than thirty years) to be a hindrance to long-term economic improvement (National Research Council 1986). While some research (Boserup 1981; Simon 1981; Simon and Gobin 1980) concludes that economic progress seems to require the stimulus of population growth, or that high population density, or the growth of the labor force or of the consumer population, can help development, most other research indicates that population growth does not automatically stimulate progress and that today's rapid increases make most development problems more difficult to solve. This is not the same as saying that slowing growth will bring development—a host of other conditions must be met before a country will modernize successfully. But it seemed clear to politicians and policy analysts in Washington and to foundation officials in New York that all the world's present population could not live like Americans, and that larger numbers did nothing to increase the prospects of the good life for the poor majority.

In addition to the contribution that slower population growth makes to economic development, the practice of family planning was seen as enabling women to avoid unwanted pregnancy. It is difficult to capture the particular importance of easily available contraception to the lives of families outside the developed world. One aspect of being poor anywhere, but most especially in poor countries, is a lack of choice. Family planning programs provide that choice in one important area of life, and then help to provide the means for the newly modernized segments of the population to exercise choice with regard to family formation. Malcolm Potts provides a sense of what such services may mean when he describes a scene that has moved him and many others: "Old Dacca is not a nice place, but it is no different than a hundred other cities on the Indian subcontinent. People living in abject poverty, with no sense of personal value, want, and need, these services. They rarely get them. Concerned Women for Family Planning has set up a model of service delivery that is succeeding. Field workers trudge through the slums every day delivering oral contraceptives, providing information, conducting classes, offering choices, and providing . . . hope" (Potts 1980b, p. 2).

Some Americans supported the idea of international family planning because they thought increased contraceptive use and fewer high-risk pregnancies would improve health. Family planning programs around the world tried to reduce the number of births to older women who already had a large number of children and to encourage all women to increase the interval between births. In many places, these women were eager to practice contraception. Reducing births, especially high-risk births, and increasing the interval between births saved lives: fewer mothers died in childbirth and fewer children died as well (National Research Council 1989). In Chile during the late 1960s and early 1970s, when the use of contraception increased from less than 5 percent to roughly 25 percent, not only did fertility decline, but infant deaths also declined by 60 percent and deaths to women during pregnancy and childbirth fell by 70 percent (Maine 1981, p. 7). The historian Edward Shorter argues cogently that much of the traditional lower status of women throughout the world was caused by their overwhelming physical disadvantage in relation to men, which effective birth control, together with better health care and safe abortions, helped correct (1982, p. 285).

Emphasizing the need to increase the availability of contraceptive services sometimes led to overly aggressive campaigns to distribute contraceptives. Many observers have been troubled by the level of incentive payments provided to contraceptive accepters by some family planning programs in developing countries. For a poor family in a poor country, the need for money may push people to accept a contraceptive they later wish they had rejected (Chomitz and Birdsall 1985). In a few cases, in programs opposed by most U.S. family planners, compulsory measures have been used to force contraceptive acceptance—India's sterilization program during Indira Gandhi's emergency, and the zealous promotion of one-child families and abortion in China, being two particularly well-known examples. But more often, family planning was a model of appropriate assistance in that governments provided a service people wanted and could not otherwise obtain. Thus, the provision of family planning services, while not the most complicated undertaking, did demonstrate government interest and commitment—a rare opportunity for Third World governments. By promoting choice and enabling couples to choose the number and spacing of their children, government-supplied family planning services certainly increased the private welfare of families with very little cost and probably with substantial benefit to the society at large.

Government efforts to lower fertility and thereby slow population growth have also contributed to modernization by providing a model of how to plan, budget, and implement a large-scale program of deliberate social change. Understanding the importance of such planning, faculty at the Harvard Business School recently incorporated material on the implementation of a specialized contraceptive distribution scheme in one of the school's courses (Rangan 1985).

Efforts to slow population growth are properly seen as a useful means of increasing the likelihood that poor countries, as well as the families and individual citizens who populate those countries, will become better off. Circumstances (in terms of people's education, economic well-being, and eagerness to change) must be right before government intervention will help change reproductive behavior—but then circumstances must be right for most government policies to be effective.

American Catholicism and Family Planning

A large measure of the success of America's international population control movement was due to its appeal to diverse constituencies having very different political orientations, but nevertheless sharing the belief that the control of rapid growth and the support of contraceptive services would aid a valued goal. The near-universal appeal of international population control is well illustrated by the actions of American Catholics. Despite strong theological opposition to contraception, Catholics, at least during the early years of America's international population program, had a uniquely American reaction to family planning. The American Catholic response to growing government involvement in the provision of contraceptives tells us much about why the U.S. population program became successful.

Most people who have examined the history of America's international population and family planning program have concluded that the influence of the Catholic church was a principal reason why the acceptance of government efforts to slow population growth around the world did not increase faster. The standard histories are especially clear on the matter. In their history of the United Nations' treatment of the population question, Richard Symonds and Michael Carder note that "the Roman Catholic Church . . . put pressure on governments to prevent any resolutions or action by international agencies which might encourage the practice of what were regarded as illicit methods of birth control" (1973, p. xvi). Phyllis Piotrow writes about the role played by "the attack of the Catholic Bishops" in slowing acceptance of the 1959 Draper Committee's recommendation that the U.S. government move to slow population growth, and she cites "declining official Catholic opposition" as a key factor enabling American political leaders to cautiously support greater attention to controlling population growth by America's foreign assistance program (1973, p. xii). Malcolm Potts and Peter Selman claim the Catholic church was behind what they call "a willful act of community self-mutilation" that brought Latin America its population problems; they argue that, ". . . while [papal encyclical] *Humanae Vitae* made no difference to the behavior of individuals in their homes and abortions continued to rise among the middle classes, it denied desperately needed services to the poor" (1979, p. 311). Reimert T. Ravenholt, former director of the Office of Population of the Agency for International Development (AID), blames efforts to dismiss him and to moderate AID's family planning effort on a "right-to-life religious connection" of midwestern Catholics, including the late Milwaukee congressman Clement Zablocki, then-AID administrator and former Ohio governor John J. Gilligan, and Gilligan's assistant administrator for Asia and former Zablocki assistant John H. Sullivan, who together with other "reactionary elements of certain religious . . . disciplines have long opposed direct action toward solution of problems of excess fertility and population growth" (Ravenholt 1980, pp. 12, 18).

Government-backed contraceptive services were strongly opposed by the Catholic church. In a typical case in the late 1940s, New York's Francis Cardinal Spellman lobbied against Rockefeller Foundation involvement in international population work, and helped to slow the Rockefeller Foundation's entry into the field (Notestein 1971, p. 79). A decade earlier, a family planning project in Puerto Rico had been stopped because of the protests of Spellman's predecessor, Patrick Cardinal Hayes (de Arellano and Seipp 1983, p. 86). Catholic spokesmen denounced as pessimists those who promoted birth control as an aid to development; church leaders insisted that with a new, more equitable economic order, the world could support a much larger population. This was basically the same position that representatives of Communist states offered, thus making the Catholics and the Communists strange bedfellows (Jones 1979, pp. 216–21). (At the United Nations, the Marxists of Eastern Europe and the Soviet Union defined Western Protestant concern for population growth in the developing world as neo-Malthusian reactionary politics.) Most observers have focused on the church's historical condemnation of the so-called artificial means of fertility control, but only part of the Catholic resistance to publicly supported birth control services was due to worries about the licitness of the methods themselves. There were several other important reasons why the church was particularly leery of government-supported family planning services.

First, the involvement of the government in fertility control, whether in the United States or in the developing world, was an involvement in family life. Children, after all, are born into and reared by families. Family life is a central concern of the church. Even among nonpracticing Catholics, the key life-cycle events—birth, marriage, and death—demand an appearance in church. Objections were raised not only because of the details of what the government proposed, but also because church leaders saw the government as usurping an area of special competence for the church.

Second, early advocates of birth control both in the United States and in Europe—think of Clarence Gamble in Boston (Reed 1978, p. 227) and Marie Stopes in London (Soloway 1982, p. 219)—wanted to increase births among the upper classes (said to be "well-bred"), but to reduce the number of working-class children, who were disproportionately Catholic in religious affiliation. As mostly Catholic Irish and Italian immigrants flooded the cities of the northeastern United States in the first decades of the twentieth century, the well-established citizens became alarmed about being displaced by the newcomers with whom they seemed to have so little in common. President Herbert Hoover, in phrasing characteristic of the period, once told Italian political rival Fiorello La Guardia, "like a lot of other foreign spawn, you do not appreciate the country which supports and tolerates you" (quoted in Hirschman 1983, p. 397).

Piotrow has nicely captured the Irish reaction to the promotion of birth control:

> Not altogether welcome in their new home and led by priests and bishops who equated English origins with Irish subjection, the Irish were Catholic in culture and politics as well as in religion.

When the ladies of Planned Parenthood tried to offer help, the Black Irish reaction was "what business do those thin-lipped Boston Brahmins have telling us how to behave in bed?" When Harvard graduates argued for repeal of the nineteenth-century Massachusetts and Connecticut Comstock laws in order to prop-agate birth control, the Irish and Italian Catholics voted "no" at the polls even if they practiced a measure of birth control at home. The emotional revulsion that contraception aroused among Catholics was often an ethnic revulsion against the peo-ple who were promoting it. (Piotrow 1973, p. 10)

Priests and bishops charged with safeguarding the spiritual life of the faithful also worried about their temporal well-being and were concerned that birth control efforts represented a move to reduce the size of the working class without increasing welfare measures or opportunities. This concern was echoed in the genocide charges made by American Black leaders in the late 1960s and early 1970s (Littlewood 1977, p. 71). Using birth control has been everybody's affair; promoting it has been an upper-class preoccupation.

There are other reasons for the particularly hostile reaction that contraception, especially the pill, intrauterine devices (IUDs), and sterilization, received from the hierarchy of the Catholic church. Members of the Catholic hierarchy became, in Garry Wills's term, "prisoners of sex" (Wills 1971, pp. 174–87). Wills claims that the "tortuous intellectual exercises" that went into the encyclical *Humanae Vitae*, which restated papal condemnation of birth control, were "at the service of one unvarying thing—the fear of sex; a sense that constantly thinking of babies is the only means for rescuing those who engage in sex from the charge of bestial concupiscence" (ibid., p. 183). He argues that the "very top rungs of the hierarchy" have become "obsessive old men who have risked all credibility, order, and good will within the church to uphold their animus against human intercourse" (ibid., p. 186).

Wills is correct but not complete in his analysis. The encyclical and the orientation it manifests were oblivious to the joys and sufferings of children and sex, to the playfulness of both, and to the rack of either gone bad. ("True playfulness," Robert Wilson says, "is the common element in lover and saint. . . . Play's entrancing charm lies precisely in the fact that it is good for nothing. That is, nothing in our traditional vocabulary; it is good only for itself, and accordingly good for everything" [1981, p. 300].) The continuing ban on contraception and the inability to rethink the theology of family formulation were also due in part to a view of women sharply at odds with their circumstances in the latter half of the twentieth century. John T. Noonan, Jr., notes that in twenty centuries no Catholic woman had written about contraception. Moreover, "the emancipation of women in the late nineteenth century was particularly resisted by some Catholic churchmen who identified a given social structure with the gospel; as late as 1930 a portion of *Casti Connubii* [the encyclical that first condemned contraception] gave a caricature of feminine emancipation and deplored the consequences" (Noonan 1965, p. 580).

The birth control movement was further opposed by the institutionalized church because so much was seen to depend on a complete and unquestioning acceptance of the church's position. Especially during the 1960s, any change in the position on birth control must have been viewed as a threat to the entire structure of Catholic thinking on marriage and the family, as well as to the nature and governance of the church itself. The birth control movement alarmed the hierarchy because it challenged their sphere of influence in both secular and sacred society. If bishops did not adjust their views to the new biology of the pill and the increasing secularization of their flocks, they would lose influence in the city of man; but if they altered their understanding of human sex, man's world and its concerns would soil the city of God. After all, there will be no problem of population growth in heaven. Indeed, for some traditionalists, population growth on earth meant more souls to glorify God in heaven.

Humanae Vitae (1968) upheld the church's traditional stand against most birth control methods. As a result, the church lost influence, as well as priests and parishioners. Nevertheless, despite their church's formal opposition to family planning, American Catholics were less of a barrier to the development and implementation of America's international population program than most people believe. *Humanae Vitae* presented the church's official position—but individual Catholics often held vastly different positions.

Catholics in the United States caused fewer delays and forced fewer compromises in the implementation of the American effort to control population growth in the developing world than one would expect from a religious group with a large membership (20 percent of all Americans regard themselves as Catholics), considerable political influence (until recently, Catholics were overwhelmingly urban and Democratic), money (Catholics are now more prosperous than members of most denominations), a tradition of social activism, and a strongly held point of view (Greeley 1977). A comparison of the Catholic opposition to birth control in the United States throughout the 1960s, and the right-to-life movement of the 1980s, in which the resources, talents, and appeal of evangelical Protestantism have been joined by conservative Catholic support, suggests that American Catholics played only a limited negative role in the effort to slow population growth. The American Catholic church produced no Jerry Falwell during the 1960s; the Catholics' heroes were President John F. Kennedy and Pope John XXIII. The strength of Catholic opposition to birth control in America can also be judged by a comparison with other societies where religious opposition to government fertility control programs is widespread: American Catholics represented far less trouble for the process of political compromise and accommodation with respect to contraceptive practice than have religious zealots in other countries. The reasons for this are rooted in the American political tradition and the Catholic reaction to it.

It was not an accident, or a misjudgment of the importance of the issue, or a lack of adequate information that led American Catholics, their clergy, and their bishops to treat the government's growing support for birth control as a serious but not overwhelming threat. Immediately before the release of *Humanae Vitae*, a careful reading of the theological tea leaves had led many Catholics to believe that a revision of the old prohibition was likely to be forthcoming. The Papal Commission of bishops, theologians, and lay experts appointed to review the church's position had concluded, not unanimously but with a strong majority, that the church's teaching on family building, and thus the practice of family limitation, needed revision (Northcott 1965). Privately, priests were advising couples that one way to judge the sinfulness of contraceptive practice was to examine the practice as an expression of the will of the people of God: if so many well-meaning people who were trying to live good lives, following what they understood to be God's will, saw the practice of family planning as acceptable, it was unlikely that this expression of the will of the people of God was sinful. The roots of this theology were in John Henry Newman's 1859 essay, "On Consulting the Faithful in Matters of Doctrine."

When the faithful were consulted by default in confession, it was evident that contraception was widely practiced. Studies of the Catholic response to *Humanae Vitae* confirmed what Catholics themselves and their clergy already knew—namely, that few of the American faithful took the church's position very seriously. Surveys of contraceptive practice carried out before and after the encyclical found that fewer women endorsed or conformed to the church's law after the encyclical than before its release. Not only did the pope not reverse the widespread practice of nonapproved methods of birth control, his announcement did not even slow the trend toward greater Catholic use of those methods (Westoff and Ryder 1970). By 1965, the majority of married Catholic women were using proscribed methods of fertility control. This trend has continued, as has the convergence in contraceptive practice among different religious groups (Mosher and Goldscheider 1984).

The most important key to the Catholic reaction to the government's moves to expand support for family planning services is not found in the behavior of Catholic couples, or even in the theology of marriage. American Catholics had come to accept a political and social philosophy that promoted accommodation and compromise rather than confrontation. The architect of the understanding that guided most American Catholics throughout the 1960s and early 1970s was a New York Jesuit named John Courtney Murray. It was Father Murray who helped write John F. Kennedy's famous campaign speech to Houston's ministers that explained how the would-be president's religion would influence his politics. The words were speechwriter Ted Sorensen's, but the ideas were Murray's (Schlesinger 1965, p. 108; Sorensen 1965, p. 190).

Murray defended the separation of church and state by arguing that Catholics were not dominated by the church's teachings, but only formed and informed by them. When Murray argued for pluralism, he understood exactly what the consequences were: "coexistence within the one political community of groups who hold divergent and incompatible views with regard to religious questions" (1960, p. 4). Catholics had certain moral principles, but so did people of any belief—or indeed, those without belief. Former Jesuit Garry Wills summarizes the thinking this way:

> The only authority is that of personal commitment to the right, as one sees the right—yet to admit this principle is to allow for other men's commitment as they see the right, and, therefore, to allow for open debate and discussion of these differing views on what is right. Church authority in political matters could not, consequently, be a matter of group or episcopal command. The only sanction was internal, and that required a proviso for the inner rights of other men. Where such consciences meet, but do not agree, they compromise, or allow for alternatives within a neutral framework. That is the essence of pluralism. (Wills 1971, pp. 83–84)

The approach of the American Catholic hierarchy to the birth control issue was political. There were behind-the-scenes lobbying and threats, but the possibility, indeed the desirability, of compromise was always present. Thomas B. Littlewood describes one such negotiating session:

> The place is the Petroleum Club in Shreveport, Louisiana. Over a sumptuous dinner of the finest Chateaubriand, Joseph Diehl Beasley, doctor of medicine, is engaged comfortably in conversation with Msgr. Marvin Bordelon representing the bishops of the Catholic Dioceses of Louisiana. In that unlikely setting, the charismatic young crusader from coastal Georgia and the clergyman from French Louisiana are discussing the new Politics of Population. To be more precise, they are negotiating the conditions under which the church would permit Beasley to begin providing tax-financed birth control services to low-income residents of the state. (Littlewood 1977, p. 88)

Throughout its evolution, Congressman Zablocki tried to slow AID's population program. He challenged every expansion of the program (see, for example, Zablocki to Dutton, May 13, 1964, 286-73A-974 [for an explanation of AID citations, see the Appendix]), but as a Catholic and a politician he was ready to compromise; he did, and the program prospered. As New York City Health Commissioner, Leona Baumgartner had to deal with Cardinal Spellman's objections to public support for family planning in New York City; she did (by agreeing not to encourage Catholic women to use contraception), and family planning services were made available (author's interview).

A final element in the peculiar American Catholic reaction to birth control was Catholic social philosophy. Like the particularly American compromise that Catholics in the United States made when faced with the implications of the separation of church and state, the social philosophy of the Catholic church fit with prevailing values. Two encyclicals widely known among Catholics at the time outlined this philosophy. The first was the 1891 letter of Leo XIII, *Rerum Novarum*; the second was *Quadragesimo Anno*, Pius XI's letter marking the fortieth anniversary of Pope Leo's encyclical. These encyclicals argued for greater attention to the condition of the working classes and to a concern for the abuses of industrial capitalism—child labor, lack of a decent minimum wage, monopolistic practices, loss of individual and community values. The program outlined in the encyclicals became identified by many Catholics with the Democratic party platform and the work of the American labor movement. The encyclicals were landmarks of the church's involvement in the world and of using

Catholic principles to criticize economic and political arrangements without demanding a particularly Catholic, or indeed religious, solution. These social teachings were continued by John XXIII, who criticized both capitalist and communist development strategies for not respecting individual dignity and freedom. Papal endorsement of involvement in the affairs of the world led, in the 1960s, to Catholic activism—including that of Michael Harrington, author of *The Other America* (1962), the book that moved Kennedy to approve the war on poverty, and of Philip and Daniel Berrigan, priest-brothers who were influential anti–Vietnam War activists. The activist orientation fit easily with American values. Catholics involved in development work accepted contraception, first as a by-product of the world's pluralism and later as a reasonable adjunct to a comprehensive development program.

Even conservative Catholics accepted this point of view. In 1982, Catholic Undersecretary of State for Security Assistance, Science and Technology James Buckley served as point man in the fight to save the AID population budget from cuts threatened by the Office of Management and Budget. Buckley says he saved his department's budget, not AID's population program, which he consistently denigrated while at the State Department (author's interview). But most Catholics approved using foreign aid to promote population control (Segal 1984).

Religious opponents to birth control in the 1980s, even when Catholic, are different in orientation from the Catholics of the 1960s. The differences are not only theological but also political and social. The fundamentalist thinking on which the right-to-life movement and the more general opposition to government support of family planning are based has concluded that John Courtney Murray's understanding of the separation between church and state was wrong. The theologians of the new right believe that the church and the people of God should try to mold the state to their view; that faith and reason should not work separately. Pluralism is not a value if it allows evil. The notion that there is something profoundly incompatible between religious faith and the modern world is at odds with the concept of political accommodation that first allowed the United States' population program to prosper.

2

Population Growth and Foreign Policy

In 1944, demographer Dudley Kirk neatly summarized the rationale for America's international population program: "We will probably be serving our own ultimate political interests by speeding the social evolution that will bring about slower population growth. Most important of all, we shall lead all humanity to new possibilities of life for the common man freed from degrading influences of hunger and grinding poverty" (Kirk 1944, p. 35). Slowing population growth, serving the political interests of the United States, and improving human welfare were thus linked in the basic argument that would be used for the next forty years to justify American involvement in the control of population growth in the developing world. Kirk's analysis had deep roots in American history and far-reaching implications for the developing world.

This chapter reviews the origins of American policy with respect to the control of rapid population growth in the developing world. I argue that American involvement in the population policies and programs of developing countries was motivated primarily by pessimistic or conservative sentiments about the potential dangers of rapid population growth and their impact on U.S. interests around the world. But U.S. efforts to slow growth were also encouraged by an optimism about the development prospects of poor countries and a hope for a better life for the people in those countries.

Thomas Jefferson himself embodied the concern with population size and growth that has troubled Americans since the country's independence. Jefferson argued against increasing immigration to Virginia because the contribution of immigrants in helping Virginia to reach what he saw as the desirable demographic goal of six to seven million inhabitants was not worth the risk that the newcomers, inexperienced in self-rule, might jeopardize the "temperate liberty" achieved in America and threaten the government's peace and durability. The happiness that the Declaration of Independence said all men had a right to pursue was seen by Jefferson as a measurable public happiness, the amount of which could be forecast on the basis of population size, and potentially diminished by too many foreign-born residents. Jefferson asked, "Suppose 20 million of republican Americans thrown all of a sudden into France, what would be the condition of that kingdom? It would be more turbulent, less happy, less strong, we may believe that the addition of half a million of foreigners to our present numbers would produce a similar effect here" (quoted in Wills 1979, p. 164).

Jefferson and the Declaration of Independence also represent a second element in the American character that propelled us into the business of population control. We share what Garry Wills calls "a belief in our extraordinary birth, outside the process of time" that "has led us to think of ourselves as a nation apart, with a special destiny, the hope of all those outside America's shores" (1979, p. xix). In the 1830s, Alexis de Tocqueville saw the same thing in us: "They have an immensely high opinion of themselves and are not far from believing that they form a species apart from the rest of the human race" (quoted in Reeves 1982, p. E15). Our national self-confidence that we could solve whatever problems we encountered was as strong as ever in our history when Lyndon Johnson became president and America officially began to encourage the control of population growth in the developing world. Charles Morris calls it a time of "rationalist omnicompetence" in government when almost all problems, including those related to the regulation of childbearing among the rural poor of the Third World, were seen as merely technical or administrative (1980, p. 37).

Since Thomas Jefferson, a great many people have argued that the level and pattern of demographic change were important factors in national development and relations among nations. Michael S. Teitelbaum and Jay M. Winter document the extent to which what they term "strategic demography" was not just an American worry but also a concern of European leaders, especially during the years between the world wars. Even in today's high-technology environment, the number of troops or potential troops is frequently considered a crucial, and sometimes a decisive, factor by military leaders (1985, pp. 13–43).

The Old Understanding

Dudley Kirk not only represents America's increasing postwar involvement in the demography of the Third World, his work also symbolized a significant shift in thinking about the consequences of different patterns of human reproduction. Kirk and other postwar leaders of the population field moved from a focus on differential reproduction by race or class for reasons of its supposed biological impact, to a concern for the social, economic, and environmental consequences of different rates of reproduction.

Gone from Kirk's paper, and from all but a tiny fraction of subsequent discussions of the topic, was an explicit concern with racial or ethnic homogeneity of the sort that fired an earlier generation of eugenicists and birth controllers. World War II put an end to most public expressions of racist sentiments with respect to population control. Instead, attention shifted to anxiety over the impact of the rapid growth of those who had not been properly socialized, whether they were a poor minority in an American urban area or the "Asiatic masses" whose potential impact on the United States Kirk analyzed.

Two decades before Kirk published his 1944 analysis of the effects of rapid population growth, Margaret Sanger, the well-known American supporter of birth control, had worried openly about the "menace of the feebleminded" and promoted family planning to allay it (Sanger 1922, p. 240). The American attitude toward population growth in the 1920s and 1930s is well documented in James Reed's fine history of the birth control movement in the United States, *Private Vice to Public Virtue* (1978). Reed points out that in America, interest in birth control was closely tied to worries about the high level of childbearing among the immigrant population. The American upper class thought that the less-well-off should learn from their betters and control their fertility. By the late 1930s, few argued with the idea that those who were dependent on charity did not have a right to bear children.

In the United States, the rapid growth of certain groups caused particular concern among social scientists who were quick to point out the dangerous long-term consequences of the uneven pattern of human reproduction. The Population Association of America was founded in 1931 with Henry Pratt Fairchild, a New York University sociologist, serving as its first president. Reed calls Fairchild "the leading academic racist of the 1930s" (1978, p. 204), and Anders Lunde, in a history of the Population Association, notes Fairchild's interest in "preservation of the nation's ethnic homogeneity" (Lorimer 1981, p. 489).

In 1936, sociologist Norman E. Himes published a now-classic history of contraception that included a summary of the latest thinking on the demography of the United States. Among Himes's conclusions was his "hunch" that "Catholic stocks in the United States, taken as a whole," are "genetically inferior . . . to non-Catholic stocks in general." He argued that if "the differences in genetic endowment" and "the differentials in net productivity" were real, then the higher fertility of American Catholics was "anti-social, perhaps gravely so" (Himes [1936] 1963, p. 413).

Fairchild and Himes represented a well-established school of thought that included Harvard's Pitirim Sorokin, one of the leading figures in early twentieth-century American sociology, and numerous other social scientists of the day. As Howard Becker and Harry Elmer Barnes put it: "Hankins, Fairchild, Bossard, Sorokin, and Himes are among those who hold that present population tendencies make for the deterioration of the innate capacities of the population because the upper classes, who are presumably more intelligent, fail to keep pace with the survival rate of the lower" (Becker and Barnes 1961, p. 995).

In 1939 Frank Notestein, the distinguished American demographer who in a long career helped establish three institutions of far-reaching influence in the population field—the Office of Population Research at Princeton University, the Population Division of the United Nations, and the Population Council—spelled out the unhappy consequences of existing class differences in reproduction. But as a leader of a new generation of scientists working in this field, Notestein highlighted the social causes and consequences of differential growth, not the biological: "If . . . we continue a permanent recruiting of our population from groups with the least economic opportunity serious damage may be done. . . . Few thoughtful people are happy at the prospect of drawing our population heavily from families whose incomes provide inadequately for the healthy development and education of their children" (Notestein 1939, p. 123).

By the late 1930s, the birth control movement in Britain and America aimed at providing contraceptives to the largest number at the lowest cost. Clarence Gamble, heir to the Procter and Gamble fortune and a graduate of Harvard Medical School, was among those who feverishly pursued the goal of fewer births for the poor at the lowest possible cost. Gamble founded the Pathfinder Fund, a Boston foundation that still supports family planning projects in the developing world. He also supported the population studies program at Harvard. Over the years, Gamble's fervor caused problems with less militant family planners, leading in one case to an effort to cut him off from his source of contraceptives, which, it was said by more moderate physicians, he was distributing improperly (Williams and Williams 1978, pp. 367–68).

Gamble was intolerant of those whose enthusiasm did not match his own. His enthusiasm was derived from the belief that the rapid growth of certain populations was a danger to the social order. He also worried about the low fertility of America's college graduates. Reed summarizes Gamble's view of birth control this way: "For Gamble birth control was a reform that went beyond the palliatives of New Dealers and struck at a fundamental source of social disorder, differential fertility between classes. His mission was to make the world safe for his kind of people, the frugal, hard-working, and prosperous leaders of American society" (Reed 1978, p. 227).

The population control movement was not transformed when the first-generation leaders died or retired. The tension between the desire to control the threat that rapid population growth represents to the order of everyday life, and the eagerness to enhance individual freedom and to promote health and development, continued. A few extremists in the population movement even continued to stress the racial aspects of rapid growth.

The geopolitical implications of rapid population growth in the developing world have also long been apparent to American demographers. In 1929, American demographer Warren Thompson argued that population growth in Japan, Germany, and Italy was creating pressures that would lead to a major war. Throughout the 1940s, American demographers explained population growth by referring to the colonial rule of the European powers. Dudley Kirk, Frank Notestein, Kingsley Davis, and Thompson himself all cited colonial influences on demographic behavior. Dennis Hodgson summarizes their point of view as follows: "In promoting their colonies as sources of raw materials, mother countries consistently introduced certain socioeconomic changes: the rationalization and commercialization of agriculture, the maintenance of internal order, improvements in transportation and communication, and implementation of public health innovations. Mortality declined as famine and epidemics were brought under control. But because, in promoting their colonies as markets for their own industrial goods, mother countries prevented or failed to foster industrialization, fertility remained high" (Hodgson 1983, pp. 8–9).

Dudley Kirk's 1944 analysis of the "typical colonial situation" that was creating a pattern of rapid growth included as examples the British in India, the Dutch in Java, the Japanese in Korea, and the United States in the Philippines. Kirk explained the implications of this growth for the United States: "Increase of population, and the very mass of the Asiatic population itself, could be ignored in the past as unimportant in the balance of world power. But with the prospect that the Asiatic masses will ultimately learn to forge the tools that will give them power, the differential population trends may become of very great importance" (Kirk 1944, p. 35).

American demographers were not the only ones who worried about the consequences of rapid population growth. A particularly important figure in the evolution of America's international population program was William H. Draper, Jr., an investment banker and a World War II general who played a key role in the administration of U.S. postwar assistance to Germany and then served as undersecretary of war, and later as undersecretary of the army. Draper ended his career as chairman of the Population Crisis Committee, and as a lobbyist responsible for promoting funding for population control activities in Congress and encouraging greater interest in the problem of rapid population growth at the State Department and the United Nations.

In 1958–59, Draper chaired the President's Committee to Study the United States' Military Assistance Program. R. R. Adams prepared a committee report entitled "The Population Explosion." Basing his discussion on the then-recently-published book by economists Ansley Coale and Edgar M. Hoover (1958), Adams argued that rapid growth meant that resources accumulated by poor countries could not be invested in economic growth; with quickly expanding populations, any extra had to be used for maintaining the level of goods and services already available in the community. Adams's report concluded that "population growth is rapidly becoming a major problem of our age." He recommended that the United States "encourage those countries in which it is cooperating in economic development programs to formulate programs designed to deal effectively with the problem of excessive population growth" (Adams 1959, p. 1).

The impact of population growth on economic development was worrisome because the Draper committee began its work "from the basic premise that the threat (political, economic, military, and subversive) to the free world by communist dictatorships was greater than ever" (Eisenhower Library 1977, p. 2). Improving development was considered essential to winning the cold war against communism, the era's key political danger. Adams's report raised the specter of political instability and "international class war" if rapid growth continued. "Unless population trends are reversed . . . grave political disorganization must be anticipated in many areas of the world," Adams said (1959, p. 12).

Many of those who have identified population growth as a problem have had a vision of a world dominated by the United States and her Western allies in which capitalist trading is the source of vast wealth. This vision is challenged by the inability of poor countries to participate in the developed world system and by threats from indigenous forces unfriendly to the West. One population control organization has spelled out the danger of the rapid growth of the Third World in this way:

> Most experts agree that widespread and chronic famines will inevitably occur if present growth rates go unchecked. Apart from the suffering of those who die . . . we can expect to see racial and class strife, large-scale terrorism, economic upheaval, abrupt decline of raw materials production, . . . and sporadic wars of survival. . . . [T]he more democratic governments will doubtless be the first to crumble, and the net weight of harsh authoritarianism in the world (presumably on the pro-Communist side) will sharply increase. . . . [S]uch a situation will confront the U.S. with dangerous military vortexes and booby-traps of the Vietnam type. . . . [W]e shall face the loss of vital raw materials that keep our industrial economy going." (Population Services International, n.d., p. 7)

Former Population Council vice-president Paul Demeny sees the danger to the West of rapid population growth among the poor in evolutionary terms: "In the domain of evolutionary theory, the consequence of any sustained difference between the rates of growth of two populations occupying the same ecological niche is straightforward: the eventual complete displacement of the slower growing population by the faster growing one" (1982, p. 8). Demeny points out that in 1950 Canada and the United States were bigger than Latin America, but that today Latin America and the Caribbean are larger. Because they are still growing, they may have as many as 267 million more people in the year 2000 than Canada and the United States. He notes that the appeal of population growth control in such an environment "lies in the hoped for result of greater political tranquility in friendly countries, greater stability of international relations, security of export markets and sources of needed imports, and reduced pressures for unilateral international wealth transfers from developed to developing countries" (ibid., p. 18).

At least since the time of the Draper Committee, many of the architects of the United States' foreign policy have believed that an economic interdependence existed between the United States and the Third World. To preserve the Third World as a source of sales and raw materials was in America's interest, and this meant that America had to preserve order and, thus, control population growth. America would also provide the capital to develop resources and to help developing countries channel their nationalist impulses in directions compatible with American interests. This vision helped define the American response to the population problem.

The importance of the Third World has grown substantially since the Eisenhower administration. Oil has made this clearer than anything else in recent years, but America buys many other vital raw materials from Third World nations and sells more to the Third World than to the European Common Market or Japan. Exports account for a larger share of America's gross national product today than they did in the 1960s—10.7 percent in 1980, versus 6.1 percent in 1965. Part of the growth of Third World imports is attributable to increases in credits provided by U.S. banks. But high interest rates in the United States and lower demand for Third World exports have sharply increased the Third World's debt, leading to serious problems for the world financial system.

For these reasons, the Population Crisis Committee (PCC), which William Draper founded, continues to argue that America's economy and national security require support for fertility control programs. One of the "talking points" included in a 1981 PCC document on the increased funding needed for population assistance sounded the familiar theme: "Some 30 developing countries are sources of oil, minerals, and other natural resources essential to the U.S. economy and defense, or they occupy important strategic locations. The populations of these countries are doubling every 20–35 years. . . . Two-thirds of the urban populations are under age 25, many of them unemployed, thus forming the potential for urban crime and political violence which threaten the stability of Third World governments" (Camp and Green 1981, p. 1).

In 1983, the Population Crisis Committee issued a briefing paper entitled "World Population Growth and Global Security," which reasoned, "the Third World's high population growth rate . . . puts additional strains on economic and political institutions . . . helps create new sources of conflict between nations . . . ," and may be, therefore, "as important a long-term factor in global security as the proliferation of military technology" (Population Crisis Committee 1983, p. 1).

It is not just population control lobbyists who see rapid growth as a security concern. The list of senior American officials who have pushed population control as an important ingredient in our foreign policy begins with Draper and includes every secretary of state from Dean Rusk to George Schultz—who thinks "rampant population growth . . . poses a major long-term threat to political stability and our planet's resource base" (Schultz 1983, p. 105). In 1980 the National Security Council's Ad Hoc Group on Population Policy concluded that rapid population growth in developing countries presents "a growing potential for social unrest, political instability, mass migrations and possible international conflicts over control of land and resources. . . . The near certainty of at least a doubling of the populations of most developing countries within the next two to three decades has particular significance for the United States, which has been the goal of so many of the world's emigrants and refugees" (National Security Council 1980, p. 510).

Richard N. Gardner, who as a Kennedy administration official announced the official U.S. interest in population, argued that rapid growth "may threaten . . . the very foundations of civilized society" (1973, pp. 334–35). John D. Rockefeller III, founder of the Population Council and long-time advocate of public support for family planning, thought that population growth "fosters social unrest and political instability" (1966, p. 2). In a confidential memo to President Richard Nixon, then–Secretary of State William P. Rogers and Agency for International Development Administrator John A. Hannah concluded that population growth contributed to "crime, banditry and civil unrest in many developing countries" (November 14, 1969, 286-73A-716, p. 7). The Central Intelligence Agency (CIA) saw population growth and concurrent food shortages leading to a worst-case scenario in which "nuclear blackmail is not inconceivable," as "militarily powerful, but nonetheless hungry, nations" try to move into new territory or get enough food (CIA 1974).

This aspect of America's interest in the control of population growth is recognized by those receiving assistance. Rafael Salas, the late executive director of the United Nations Fund for Population Activities, once remarked that he thought "the main reason why the United States has supported population policy for the past 15 years [was] to promote stability and reduce conflict" (Salas 1985). Salas and the United Nations accept American money, but others are more cautious. From time to time, a small number of developing-country governments have refused American population aid because of concern that superpower involvement would jeopardize family planning activities by opening them to political attacks (for one such example, see American Embassy/Bamako to Secretary of State, May 5, 1972, 286-76-286).

Much of what Americans in the international family planning movement tried to do was based on a belief in the fundamentally disruptive effect of too many children being born of the wrong women in the wrong places. Women having children out of proportion to what Western, developed-country people thought proper, raised questions about the validity and security of the well-ordered middle-class world. Even today, although we no longer rush to sterilize incompetents and half-castes, we push the practice of family planning, worried about our failure to do otherwise. Many people, maybe most of us, see the right to bear children as limited by the ability to support them.

A classic example of this view is the following quote by Reimert T. Ravenholt, a physician and former director of the U.S. Agency for International Development's Office of Population, the group responsible for implementing the American government's international population policy: "No one should reproduce beyond their capacity to care for their offspring. If a poor family wishes to place having children and raising children ahead of many other considerations I certainly think that's their prerogative as long as they'll care for them. But I'm very strongly opposed to poor people sort of willy nilly reproducing beyond their capacity and then turning to their neighbors and saying, 'you have to take care of these offspring because I can't' " (author's interview).

Dr. Ravenholt devoted thirteen years of his career and a substantial share of his incredible energy to ensuring that poor people would have access to the means to control their fertility. This was one way to reduce the danger of the poor reproducing beyond their capacity to care for their children. Ravenholt's motivation was only partly based on the idea that too many children made people poor, or that high fertility was a health hazard for mothers and their offspring, or that rapid population growth slowed economic development and used scarce resources. All these beliefs formed a basis for Ravenholt's work, but so also did the idea that uncontrolled reproduction threatened those with the good sense not to have more children than they could afford.

Most descriptions of the population problem assume not only a particular set of demographic circumstances but also a certain structure of economic and social relations. To say that the world's poor should limit their reproduction to ensure their capacity to care for their offspring avoids the issue of major changes in existing social and economic relationships, or the control of resources. Talking about "their capacity" represents an implicit justification of the existing social structure.

It is easy to dismiss people like Ravenholt or to count them as representatives of a particularly ardent group within the population movement. But they represent a worldview that has found numerous expressions in the modern history of population control. People concede the bigotry of the older generation (and are embarrassed by residual contemporary expressions of it), but they avoid the pervasiveness of control and order as motives for America's support for international family planning. As a consequence, important questions have been side-stepped. In 1968, when family planning was deemed a human right by the United Nations, the question never arose as to whether having ten children was to that right what yelling "Fire!" in a crowded theater was to the right of free speech.

In many respects, we have failed to face up to the core issue of the contemporary demographic dilemma, namely, the conflict between the demographic goals of individuals and the collective impact of these individual decisions. It is this troublesome lack of harmony between what individuals perceive to be in their benefit and the high rates of population growth that may result when individuals take only self-interest into account in childbearing decisions that creates the need for government attention to fertility. To date, only a few countries—and then only for a time and only under particular circumstances—have decided that individual decisions so threaten the social order that fertility must be forcefully controlled. But numerous other countries have found the impact of individual reproductive decisions to be detrimental enough that they have implemented programs to encourage the control of childbearing.

Conclusion

A variety of motives have moved those who devoted themselves to the control of fertility and the reduction of population growth in the developing world. For a very few people the motive was an ugly racism, but most others had more complex sentiments. Population control was seen as contributing to national and international stability. High fertility and rapid population growth have an important impact on health and on economic development, and a concern about this has been a central aspect of the population movement. For many people, spreading better contraceptive services and campaigning to get people to use them was part of America's effort to civilize the developing world. Family planning programs represented prudence, foresight, restraint, and self-reliance. Socialized to these virtues, the world's poor would be better able to improve their lives.

Access to family planning services is now regarded as a basic human right, but as McGeorge Bundy has noted, "there are many basic human rights . . . whose fulfillment around the world we do not undertake to pay for from the United States Treasury" (1984, pp. 5–6). It is the wish for stability that motivates both the reformer who wants to make contraceptives more available to promote responsible parenthood or to enhance development prospects, and the security analyst who supports population control because it contributes to a reduction in international tension or urban unrest. From the American perspective, proper health is viewed as a prerequisite for full participation in society. Sickness is destabilizing; thus, the effort to improve health fits with the interest in maintaining stability. This is especially clear in the case of public health measures aimed at stopping widespread contagion, but it includes family planning as well (Parsons 1972).

The importance of these themes waxes and wanes, but each persists in our own time. Given one's perspective, arguments from another perspective can be embarrassing. Those who think the greatest danger of rapid population growth is its impact on American national security find arguments about the health effects of high fertility softhearted and ultimately damaging, because they define the problem in a way that limits the resources likely to be made available for population control. Likewise, those who support family planning because it gives women new choices do not like to have the eugenics perspective brought up, because it makes their individually liberating justification for helping others appear soiled and in the service of less-acceptable goals.

In all societies, there is a tendency toward what sociologists call system maintenance—the inclination to follow the existing ways of doing things and to resist changes that seem likely to upset established patterns of thinking, feeling, and behaving. Things do change, of course, and sometimes radically, but the change must always be defined in a socially acceptable way. This accounts for the sometimes schizophrenic justification for American support of developing-world family planning programs—such programs fit with our values of free choice, control of one's environment, and self-determination, and with our wishes for a better life for those less fortunate than ourselves; at the same time, they serve our interest in maintaining the dominance of American interests and orientation around the world. The belief that a certain demographic balance is an essential feature of a properly ordered social life has been everywhere evident in discussions of the population problem. American supporters of family planning wanted not only a more prosperous poor, but a less numerous poor.

The British journalist William Shawcross has argued that the United States places "order before justice." Someone with a broader view of our history and a kinder reaction to our foreign policy might have said instead that Americans recognize that order is a prerequisite for justice. Population is an important element in that order.

Richard Nixon (helped by Daniel Patrick Moynihan) may have said it best: "population growth is a world problem which no country can ignore, whether it is moved by the narrowest perception of national self-interest or the widest vision of a common humanity" (Nixon 1969, p. 2). Americans never forgot their self-interest, but neither did they completely lose their wider vision.

3

Evolution and Implementation

A key stage in the evolution of the population movement occurred when fertility control was transformed from the preoccupation of a band of enthusiasts to the day-to-day business of the federal bureaucracy and, through federal grants and contracts, to a concern for major American universities and nonprofit organizations. The success and character of this change, which occurred during the late 1960s and early 1970s, tells us a great deal. The shift from small local programs to a large international undertaking required a growth in personnel and budget, both in the United States and overseas. Such a change also required a product—in this case, an approach or solution to the problem of rapid population growth—that could be mass-produced and used everywhere, as well as an increasing management and program-development capacity and a clearer separation between policy making and program implementation.

Previous chapters analyzed the values as well as the political and economic orientations underlying America's attention to population growth in the developing world. This and the following three chapters trace the evolution of the official American international population program within the Agency for International Development (AID).

The American government's involvement in organized efforts to slow population growth in the developing world began in the early 1960s. Perhaps more then than ever before or since, Americans felt able to address their own and the world's problems. In some ways, the nation was transformed in the 1960s as it had been only a few times in its history. Encouraged in part by an outburst of urban riots, America turned to reform and began a frenzy of government spending. The effect was visible to most people in new domestic programs: the War on Poverty, Model Cities, Medicare, and Medicaid. But the rush of new programs also had an impact on foreign affairs and defense. In the latter case, spending declined from its traditional dominant position in the federal budget as spending on domestic programs grew.

The country's industrial strength and military power, together with the success of the Marshall Plan in helping to rebuild Europe, encouraged the belief that the United States could solve the developing world's problems. Many people, both in and out of government, thought that American money and advice could promote social and economic progress. At the same time, worries about the Soviet Union and the possibility of Communist-inspired revolutions in the Third World were widespread in government and foreign-policy circles. Foreign aid was promoted as one means of checking the spread of communism (Bolling and Smith 1982). Nowhere can the activist disposition characteristic of American foreign policy in the 1960s be seen more clearly than in the AID program in Vietnam.

From 1960 to 1968, Agency for International Development staff increased by 4,112. In Vietnam, AID staff increased from 195 to almost 2,000 Americans and 3,100 Vietnamese during the same period (AID 1977). Many of those who were hired were directly involved in the war effort, but others served in support positions of one sort or another; there were agricultural experts, hospital administrators, education specialists, and, of course, population and family planning experts. Each group of specialists saw Vietnam's problems and their solution from their own point of view. For example, a report from two Census Bureau technicians concluded that "the Republic of Vietnam should celebrate the cessation of hostilities and the attainment of post-war stability by taking its first modern census of population and housing" (Galt and George, report notes, September 1970, 286-76-304). While AID did not support a census in Vietnam, it did conduct so-called hamlet evaluation surveys, which examined "facets of the pacification program (security, morale of the population), [and] effectiveness of government services . . . " (Town to Brackett, December 18, 1972, 286-76-304). As American troops increased, the AID mission grew. Many of the experts the agency employed in Vietnam thought that the United States could not only win the war but remake society. The result, according to Frances FitzGerald, was that "land reform, education, 'motivational research'—every possible 'solution' turned up at least once in the roulette wheel of priorities" (1972, p. 260).

Duff Gillespie, current director of AID's Office of Population, spells out some of Vietnam's impact on AID this way: "Vietnam had a tremendous impact on the Agency. . . . They were hiring people left and right to ship them over to Vietnam. . . . God knows what they were doing. You also had the Office of Public Safety which was a front for, among other things, the CIA. . . . People who were here during the height of it say it was simply madness. You still have a lot of people carried over from the Vietnam days who weren't technically qualified who have a very strong notion of what AID's about. It had an impact and I think it was a bad impact" (author's interview).

As AID's support for family planning and population control was growing, the agency dramatically increased its work and staff in Vietnam. But AID's involvement in Vietnam in support of the U.S. war effort caused a loss of credibility for AID's development programs in Vietnam and poisoned many analyses of the agency's other activities. Even AID staff themselves tried to get the administrator to transfer security assistance activities to the State Department. Development assistance personnel were uncomfortable supporting police and military overseas, especially when they had little direct control over program operations that were typically handled by staff from other agencies, including the CIA (Stern, Birnbaum, and Arndt to Hannah, December 13, 1971, p. 3, gift file).

The Evolution of AID's Program

The story of American involvement in Vietnam and in the population affairs of developing countries begins in the early days of the Kennedy administration. In December 1961, Secretary of State Dean Rusk appointed Robert Barnett, at that time a State Department counselor in Belgium, as the department's population advisor. Six months later, Barnett sent a memo to Rusk suggesting an increase in behind-the-scenes support for population, in particular "maximum support to activities in the population field by the UN." Moreover, Barnett argued that the United States should "in one or two countries like Formosa or Korea where a problem is known to exist, the government is known to be willing to act, and where foreign assistance has already been sought . . . quietly explore possibilities for responding to requests for U.S. Government help" (Barnett to the Secretary, May 8, 1962, no source). He also encouraged close contact between the State Department and private organizations active in the population field. Barnett himself met regularly with General Draper, the lobbyist for population control who had first tried to awaken official Washington to the dangers of rapid population growth, as well as with staff of the Population Council, the Ford Foundation, and the Planned Parenthood Federation.

At the same time that Barnett was urging the administration to become more active in the population field, Kennedy was reorganizing America's foreign assistance program. In 1961, the Agency for International Development was created from the International Cooperation Administration. In December 1962 David Bell, a Harvard-trained economist and former director of the Bureau of the Budget, was named AID administrator. Bell left three and one-half years later "broke and bushed" ("Administration Bell's Toll," 1966), but having helped population gain an important role in America's development assistance program.

Bell was not as militant as those who worried most about the impact of rapid growth would have wished, but he believed that rapid population growth hampered development and he worked quietly to see that population issues were considered by program planners at AID and the State Department. Like most economists, Bell saw economic development as depending primarily on things other than the rate of population growth. Moreover, he worried that moving ahead too quickly with American efforts to control population growth would subvert the rest of AID's development program by alienating the public, members of Congress, and leaders of developing countries.

When Bell was first at AID, development specialists were less sure of the effect of high fertility and rapid population growth than they are today. The impact of high fertility on the health of mothers and their children was not nearly as clear nor as well documented. The pill and the IUD—contraceptive methods on which developing-country national family planning programs came to depend—had just been introduced: the Lippes loop, for a time the world's most popular IUD, was introduced in 1962 (Lippes and Zielezny 1975), and the birth control pill was approved in the United States in May 1960 (Reed 1978, p. 364). This new technology made national population control policies and family planning programs much more practical than they had been.

Throughout the Kennedy administration, senior officials, eager to protect the president and uncertain of where the passion of the population control enthusiasts would lead, moved gingerly, claiming that developing countries themselves should take the initiative before the United States considered increasing its support for international population control efforts. Major growth in AID's population program was still a few years away. Senior AID and State Department officials had yet to conclude that population control was so important that the United States had to encourage countries to review the impact of population on their economic prospects, and it was a few years after that before the United States began to insist that developing countries receiving American foreign assistance take the level and pattern of population growth into account in their development planning.

A new American policy with respect to population growth required a new understanding of appropriate American involvement in developing countries. In late 1962 Richard N. Gardner, deputy assistant secretary of state for international organizations, speaking at the United Nations, announced U.S. support for research on the impact of population growth. Gardner's speech was the first official recognition by the U.S. government that population growth was an important issue on the development agenda. Leona Baumgartner, former New York City health commissioner, who was serving as assistant administrator at AID, had copies of Gardner's speech sent to AID missions overseas to stimulate an interest in population projects (Piotrow 1973, p. 68), and in a cable sent to all AID missions at the same time, David Bell said that Secretary Gardner's speech "defines U.S. policy on population growth and economic development" (AIDTO A-173, December 4, 1962, 286-73-474). In that speech, Gardner said that "the United States will not suggest to any other government what its attitudes or policies should be as they relate to population . . . we will not advocate any specific policy measures regarding population growth to another country" (Gardner, December 10, 1962, 286-73-474).

A similar point of view was put forward at about the same time by Fowler Hamilton, Bell's immediate predecessor as administrator of the federal foreign assistance program. In November 1962, Hamilton told Dr. Baumgartner that AID did not "support or advocate any policy or measures" with respect to population. "Nevertheless," Hamilton went on, "increase or decrease of population, changes in geographic or age distribution and related population problems are obviously relevant to the economic and social development in less-developed countries and AID must therefore take account of them. AID recognizes that the measures any country decides to take with respect to the population problem are its own affair." Hamilton referred to "measures for the ordering of pregnancies," but noted "it is not the business of AID to advocate any of these" (for Baumgartner from Hamilton, TOAID 116, November 21, 1962, no source).

In the summer of 1963, in an effort to demonstrate his own and more widespread congressional concern about the problems associated with rapid population growth, Senator J. William Fulbright (Democrat-Arkansas) added an amendment to the Foreign Assistance Act that allowed "funds made available to carry out this section [of the Foreign Assistance Act] [to] be used to conduct research into the problems of population growth." Fulbright wanted to give AID a mandate to provide assistance to countries trying to control population growth, but Catholic Congressman Clement Zablocki (Democrat-Wisconsin) insisted the language be changed before he supported the bill (Piotrow 1973, p. 78). Piotrow argues that although "AID already possessed full legal power to do everything in the amendment and more besides . . . there was a hortatory purpose to be served by specific Congressional endorsement in such a sensitive area. Then, as later, AID's refusal to support the amendment confirmed Fulbright's conviction that additional pressure was necessary" (Piotrow 1973, p. 79). But AID was probably not as indifferent as Piotrow and other critics thought. David Bell, for example, remembers that even with Fulbright's endorsement, congressional opposition to greater U.S. involvement in population control activities overseas was widespread, as were misgivings within the agency and elsewhere in the administration about becoming too active. Bell was not a zealot of the sort the population control lobby would find praiseworthy. Still, unlike Piotrow, I find no evidence of his having slowed Leona Baumgartner, a highly regarded public health physician who was trying to promote family planning projects at AID. Twenty years after they were at AID, both claim to have worked easily together. Baumgartner, for her part, remembers Bell supporting her efforts to get population issues taken more seriously (author's interviews).

Bell's support for increasing U.S. government involvement in population control, and the hesitancy of some of the administration's other senior foreign policy staff about even discussing the potential problems associated with rapid population growth, are nicely illustrated by an incident that took place two days before President Kennedy was assassinated in November 1963. Teodoro Moscoso, assistant secretary for the Alliance for Progress, cautioned Bell about sending books on population and family planning to AID missions in Latin America. (Included were *Family Planning, Sterility and Population Growth*, by Freedman, Whelpton, and Campbell [1959]; *The Time Has Come: A Catholic Doctor's Proposals to End the Battle over Birth Control*, by John Rock [1963]; and *The Population Dilemma*, by Philip Hauser [1963].) After reviewing the list, Moscoso wrote Bell: "Isn't this a bit more forthcoming than you want to be at this stage? At the proper time, I would recommend that we go further than this, but right now we have to be careful even with the titles of books we send to our missions" (Moscoso to Bell, November 20, 1963, 286-73A-474). In a handwritten note, Bell replied: "Ted, in view of adoption of the Fulbright amendment, I think this is probably okay now" (Bell to Moscoso, December 13, 1963, 286-73A-474). The books were important because they represented a first step in the development of an interest in population and a competency to analyze the impact of growth and ways to control it.

Still, it was one thing for Kennedy's international activism to express itself in the Peace Corps, or in advisors in Vietnam, and quite another for the United States government to tell people they were having too many children. What business could the U.S. government possibly have trying to alter the family-building practices of citizens not their own? Unless there was a compelling reason for such intervention, the United States had little justification for becoming involved in an effort to slow population growth.

Justifying AID's Program

Justification for the American support of population control was forthcoming in two forms. First, advocates of stronger support for population control and family planning pointed out that women around the world *wanted* to limit their fertility. A very large number of mothers died each year trying to end unwanted pregnancies through self-induced or illegally obtained abortions—in the process, providing tragic testimony of how widespread and how deeply held was the desire to control fertility.

This argument was joined by a second: Excessive population growth slowed development, and development and increasing prosperity were the *sine qua non* of the tranquil world that American officials wanted. Population growth was identified as a barrier to modernization and a threat to the international social order. The specifics differed among analysts. Some thought growth would drain natural resources; others saw in rapid growth and urban concentrations the roots of difficult-to-control civil unrest; some worried over the hereditarian consequences of a world overwhelmed with a non-European underdeveloped majority. But it was only after the consequences of this rapid growth for America's interest became clear, that support was forthcoming. It was not just an awareness of population growth that mattered, it was a sense that this growth was potentially dangerous for the United States (not just harmful for those directly involved), and that America could and should do something about it.

New data on population growth came in a small but steady stream throughout the early 1960s. Staff from the Population Council, researchers from population centers at Johns Hopkins and Columbia and the universities of Michigan, North Carolina, and California, and experts from other organizations wrote articles about women's favorable view of family planning and the growing recognition by Third World government officials that population was an important variable in the development process. The Population Council began its widely cited periodical, *Studies in Family Planning*, in July 1963. Council President Frank Notestein noted in the initial issue that, "in their travels throughout the world in the past few years, staff members of the Population Council have been impressed with the rapidly developing interest in population problems" (1963, p. 1). And in an early issue, Bernard Berelson, who would follow Notestein as Council president, outlined the other basic tenet of the family planning movement: ". . . results of fertility surveys carried out in a variety of countries—i.e., studies of people's information about family planning, their attitudes, and their practices . . . naturally vary in outcome, not to mention validity, but typically they reveal more interest in and approval of family planning than government and medical leaders expect or perceive. In this sense, the people are usually ahead of the leadership" (Berelson 1964, p. 2). He went on to note that the target for family planning services included the 40 to 60 percent of all women with three children who, he said, wanted no more.

Another essential ingredient in the evolution of America's population policy was Lyndon Johnson's willingness to add the birth rate of the world's poor to his agenda of social conditions that had to be changed. In fact, some official accounts date America's entry into the international population control movement from January 1965, when President Johnson announced in his State of the Union message that he would "seek new ways to use our knowledge to help deal with the explosion in world population and the growing scarcity in world resources" (Guidelines . . . , August 7, 1967, 286-73A-474; also Piotrow 1973, pp. 89, 93). The president's message was followed by an AID announcement that technical assistance in family planning would be available to countries requesting it. Barely two years earlier, Richard Gardner had withheld American endorsement for the United Nations' providing technical assistance to developing-world family planning programs.

A series of congressional hearings chaired by Senator Ernest Gruening (Democrat-Alaska) were particularly useful in increasing official awareness of the population problem. Gruening was a medical doctor who had been promoting birth control since his student days in Boston early in the century. During the depression, he had served as administrator of the Puerto Rico Reconstruction Administration and, until he was slowed to a standstill by opposition from the Catholic church, he tried to support a birth control program at the island's public health clinics (de Arellano and Seipp 1983, pp. 42–43). Gruening chaired a Senate subcommittee on Foreign Aid Expenditures. Beginning in June 1965, and lasting on and off until February 1968, Gruening's committee held hearings on the rapid growth of the developing world, during which a steady parade of politicians, population experts, priests, public health physicians, and professors made the problems of rapid population growth more visible to Congress and more acceptable for public discussion. Piotrow (1973, p. 107) argues that Gruening's hearings moved analysis of the appropriateness of U.S. government support for birth control in developing countries from the question of how one could justify government aid for a program many taxpayers considered wrong to a question of how one could withhold family planning from the poor who so clearly needed and wanted it. The hearings provided a platform for the supporters of greater U.S. involvement in international population control efforts to argue their case, but they did not significantly affect the management of AID's population programs.

The three and one-half years of Bell's administration of AID were characterized by steady behind-the-scenes promotion of the agency's population program, never overwhelming in its enthusiasm, but consistently supportive. Bell encouraged the members of the General Advisory Committee on Foreign Assistance Programs, which included Eugene R. Black, William R. Hewlett, David Rockefeller, and William Zellerbach, to review the impact of rapid population growth on the economic development of poor countries. At a luncheon meeting of the committee in the fall of 1965, members were asked what concerned them most about the U.S. foreign aid program. Franklin Murphy, chancellor of UCLA and chairman of the board of the Times Mirror Co., argued that the problem for him was "how to make a tougher, more sophisticated utilization of our aid resources to achieve U.S. objectives overseas." Almost all the participants agreed. David Rockefeller, for example, suggested giving more consideration to foreign assistance to small countries, because "a program of $1 million in one small country might, in certain circumstances, be more important to U.S. interests than a program of $100 million in another country." Josephine Young Case summed up by saying that "with a little finesse and subtlety, our influence can be exercised in ways the receiving government will like. Sometimes governments need and are grateful for a little push which helps them undertake activities which they feel will be wise and constructive." She then argued that she would like to see the committee's planned review of the foreign aid program "come up with a recommendation to expand and develop work on population control." She remarked that "other aid activities don't make much sense without a successful effort to deal with the population explosion." She reported that on a recent trip to South America, she had found "enthusiasm . . . for doing something in this field and the readiness of people there to go ahead aggressively." At the meeting's end, David Bell suggested that the next Advisory Committee meeting take up the topic of population control (GAC Minutes, October 12, 1965, no source).

The pattern of Third World population growth visible in Washington and other Western capitals was also apparent in the capitals of many developing countries themselves. Government planners became alert to the rapid growth of population and wondered about the wisdom of traditional policies encouraging such growth. Most important in many places, including the United States, was a food crisis that reached famine proportions by the mid-1960s. Piotrow has described its impact as follows:

> The triggering event that moved Washington and raised the population problem to higher priority and new urgency . . . was a world food shortage. Caused in part by bad weather, in part by inattention to agriculture in the developing countries, and certainly aggravated by population increase, the food deficit reached public notice by the summer of 1965. Then in the autumn of 1965 the monsoon rains failed in India; again, in unprecedented repetition, the monsoon failed in 1966. Floods and drought plagued other food producing areas. For the first time in two centuries statisticians could document what birth control supporters described as a genuine Malthusian crisis. (Piotrow 1973, p. 112)

Clearly, one way to help was to reduce future demand for food by slowing population. In November 1966, the president's General Advisory Committee on Foreign Assistance Programs concluded that population control was the first step in alleviating food shortages. In the words of a committee report, "the widening imbalance between world population increase and food production is a worsening situation that can become catastrophic." To solve the world's food problem, the committee recommended that the president first "exercise his leadership in the community of nations . . . to ensure that population restraint is adopted in the world" (Perkins 1966, p. 1).

Seven weeks later, following the committee's recommendation, President Johnson in his State of the Union address said that, "next to the pursuit of peace, the really greatest challenge to the human family is the race between food supply and population increase. That race . . . is being lost." Shortly after Johnson's address—against the wishes of most senior AID officials, who wanted to maintain control of the agency's program themselves—Congress moved to earmark funds for AID's population control efforts. America's international population policy received a mammoth increase in funds, beginning a fifteen-year trend of growing support and increasing budgets.

Of course, not everyone involved in the nation's foreign assistance program agreed that population growth was a problem that could or should be tackled by the United States. Indeed, even the letter trans-

mitting copies of the Advisory Committee report to committee members reminded them "to make sure that the existence of this report
does not become known to the press or the public" (Wood to Committee Members, December 7, 1966, no source). Part of the worry involved the implications of the report for domestic farm policy, but
much concern also focused on what the report referred to as the
"personal sensitivity of birth control."

Despite its strong language and clear conclusions, the Advisory
Committee's report was not as forceful as the Washington supporters
of population control thought it should be. A draft copy was sent to
Philander Claxton, who had been appointed early in 1966 as special
assistant for population matters to the secretary of state. Claxton
revised the report to include a recommendation that the United States
work to "persuade other nations to start full-scale population control programs." The committee itself had stopped short of such a
strong recommendation. Committee member Joseph Beirne objected
to Claxton's revision, saying, "AID's role should be limited to urging
developing countries to face the population problem squarely . . .
giving full support to those nations which elect to begin birth control
programs" (Douglas to Andreas, September 9, 1966, 286-73-159).
Beirne's more cautious formulation was used in the final draft of the
committee report.

Although the orientation of those in the population control movement became better understood and more widely shared throughout
the early 1960s, supporters of a more interventionist role for the U.S.
government remained disappointed by the limited concern that the
problem of rapid population growth caused among senior AID officials. Four days before President Johnson's pronouncement that the
race between food production and population growth was being lost,
William S. Gaud, who had replaced David Bell as AID administrator
in June 1966, wrote to Senator Gruening regarding AID's prohibition
against supplying contraceptives to developing countries—a policy
that Gruening was working to reverse and a practice that would in
time become the centerpiece of the AID program:

> The policy prohibiting the financing of contraceptives under
> the Foreign Assistance Program has been in existence since 1948,
> when the ineligible commodities list was first established.
>
> We have recently reviewed this policy in terms of its effect on
> the family planning programs of the developing countries. Most
> of the AID staff—especially our overseas mission directors—feel
> that it has not had an adverse effect on these population pro-
> grams. . . .

For this reason, we have decided to let the policy against contraceptives stand for the time being. However, we are aware that a number of countries are now considering the possible use of the more expensive oral contraceptives. . . . I am prepared, therefore, to review the policy again when and if a particular case comes up where a country cannot meet the costs of contraceptives for its family planning programs and requests our help. (Gaud to Gruening, January 6, 1967, 286-72A-7553)

Less than six months later, when the president's General Advisory Committee on Foreign Assistance Programs met again to discuss the world food situation, Gaud was still very cautious about the appropriate role for the United States in the population control movement. The minutes of the committee meeting recall his hesitation: Gaud "underline[d] the fact that the population field is particularly delicate. It is very easy for AID to try to go too far, too fast." Gaud was particularly worried about congressional proposals to earmark funds for population. According to the minutes, ". . . efforts by some Senators to earmark funds in the AID bill to be used only for family planning causes him great concern. This creates an untrue impression that family planning programs are compulsory . . . in many countries we must move very slowly" (GAC Minutes, June 21, 1967, 286-73-159).

There are few signs in the records of AID that Gaud was in principle against increasing the agency's work in the population field. In fact, after he left AID, he became head of the Population Crisis Committee. Gaud wanted to control AID's resources himself and, according to Piotrow (1973, p. 134), was being encouraged to move slowly by David Bell, who one assumes was already hearing from his colleagues at the Ford Foundation (where he had become a vice-president) of the recently appointed director of AID's population program, Dr. Reimert Ravenholt. Ravenholt, together with Claxton and General Draper, was lobbying for earmarked funds for population control on the grounds that they were essential if AID was to respond as the Congress wanted to the crisis caused by rapid population growth.

The Early Program

The Agency for International Development had started to support demographic research as early as 1965. One of the reasons for this support was a hoped-for change in policy, or at least a new awareness of the population problem, on the part of developing-world leaders. But often other motives played a role in these early programs. For example, confidential AID documents indicate that the agency's support for the Centro para el Desarrollo Económico y Social de América Latina (DESAL) in Chile was encouraged in part by the close ties of the leadership of DESAL with Chile's Christian Democratic Party.

It was not until the late 1960s that AID staff began seriously to consider how to motivate the governments of developing countries to address the problems of rapid population growth. By late 1967, some American officials were encouraging their counterparts in foreign governments to begin family planning programs. For example, State Department officials met to discuss "the area of maneuver available to us in influencing Thai attitudes and in light of these considerations to work out a course of action with regard to family planning in Thailand"; they favored what they termed "indirect working level approaches" and suggested that AID officials in Bangkok develop a research project to make Thailand's top "political leaders . . . more aware of the social and economic costs of rapid population growth" (Barnett to Claxton, October 5, 1967; Barnett to Bullitt, August 4, 1967; Bell memo, March 10, 1965; 286-76-286).

The congressional earmarking of funds for population control activities in 1967 accelerated the involvement of American government officials stationed in the Third World in the development of local family planning activities. The White House staff was assured by AID that "U.S. Missions abroad will be instructed to proceed upon the assumption that lack of funds should never be a reason for governments to postpone or neglect effective programs in the field of family planning." A significant change in orientation had taken place. No longer would the United States simply answer requests for help with support for research: now AID set out "to use as appropriate our influence" to get political leaders in the developing world to recognize and address "the adverse impact of rapid population growth on economic developments" (Read to Rostow, June 14, 1967, 286-70A-2036). With congressional funding now available, AID Administrator Gaud "directed that lack of funds is not to be the reason for failure to carry forward any sensible project in this field." Indeed, early in 1968, AID staff did not have a sufficient number of programs in need of "sound and imaginative assistance efforts" to spend the $35 million that Congress had set aside for population and family planning (AID Circular X3309, 286-70A-2036).

By January 1968, AID's population program had passed an important landmark. No longer simply the controversial interest of a few private citizens, the effort to control population growth in the developing world had become official U.S. government policy, well funded by Congress, accepted by the public, and endorsed by the incumbent president as well as by two out of three of his immediate predecessors and by the man who was to follow him in office. The program was being implemented by a group of energetic professionals. It grew steadily in size, range of operations, and the number of countries and institutions requesting support.

President Nixon was as supportive of AID's providing population assistance to developing countries as Lyndon Johnson had been. Nixon appointed former Michigan State University president John Hannah as administrator of the Agency for International Development. Hannah brought to his new job a belief in technical assistance and in partnerships between federal agencies and private and state institutions. There was a history of looking outside AID for help in implementing the population program because so few individuals skilled and experienced in population worked at the agency during the early days of its involvement in family planning activities. Moreover, funding other organizations to carry out population and family planning projects overseas distanced AID and the United States from these still-controversial activities. Hannah's model fit well with the way the Office of Population worked, and this further enhanced its position.

A report completed for the new administrator argued that even greater use should be made of private-sector groups as intermediaries between AID and population and family planning programs overseas. These middlemen were needed because the absorptive capacity of the agency's bilateral program was insufficient to spend all the money Congress was providing. One review by AID staff recommended that "AID operate essentially as a planning, funding, and monitoring agency, with projects implemented by intermediaries to the extent feasible" (Stern, Birnbaum, and Arndt to Hannah, December 13, 1971, p. 26, gift file). The increasing use of intermediaries encouraged a program or functional orientation rather than a geographic organizational structure at AID headquarters, because most private development-assistance groups were program and not geographically specific.

Hannah continued to encourage missions overseas to develop new projects, although not with the energy that Office of Population director Ravenholt and his staff thought was needed. In a typical example of this difference in approach, Ravenholt and his deputy, Randy Backlund, drafted a cable to be signed by Hannah and sent to all missions; the draft cable concluded: "to support your efforts, I want to assure you that you are not inhibited by unnecessary policy or procedural constraints." In the version that Hannah actually sent, a more cautious final note is sounded: "I urge each Mission Director to make every effort to submit soundly conceived proposals to expand

AID efforts in support of population program objectives. You will, naturally, be guided by judgments of both political and administrative feasibility in your local environment" (AIDTO A2409, November 10, 1969, 286-73A-716).

On July 18, 1969, the White House released a Presidential Message on Population in which President Nixon formally instructed the secretaries of State, Treasury, and Health, Education, and Welfare, the AID administrator, and the directors of the Peace Corps and the U.S. Information Agency "to take steps to enlist the active support of all representatives of the United States abroad . . . to encourage and assist developing nations to recognize and take action to protect against the hazards of unchecked population growth." A confidential cable drafted by Philander Claxton, special assistant for population affairs to the secretary of state, and sent to all diplomatic posts at the same time, encouraged American ambassadors and Country Teams to give developing countries "all possible encouragement to adopt national population programs designed and administered to bring about substantial reductions in birth rates." The cable suggested that population targets—for both birth rates and population growth rates—be promoted even though "U.S. representatives . . . have encountered heavy opposition, particularly from Latin Americans, to the insertion of this kind of population target" (To All Diplomatic Posts . . . from Department of State, CA-5859, October 28, 1969, p. 3, no source).

Less than a month after the circular message from the secretary of state, AID Administrator Hannah sent another cable saying, "The scope and level of AID's population program efforts must increase. . . . We must raise our sights on the provision of staff and funds to support this broader and more vigorous programming effort. . . . Our goal is to achieve as rapid an increase in FY 1970 as is consistent with sound programming" (AIDTO A2409, November 10, 1969, 286-73A-716).

Subsequent administrations continued support for population—never at the level that partisans thought appropriate, but sufficient to make AID a very influential donor. Such dark clouds as did appear were not concerned (until the Reagan administration) with the soundness of the program's fundamental rationale that rapid population growth posed a serious, multifaceted threat to the ability of poor countries to modernize and, partly for that reason and partly simply because of the huge numbers of people added to the world each year, to the international system the United States wished to preserve. There were traumatic moments, as disputes flared within AID and among those it supported over questions of what to do, with whom, how fast, and for how much money, but the consensus that the United States should be in the international family planning business held.

In 1984, McGeorge Bundy—national security advisor to presidents John Kennedy and Lyndon Johnson, and former president of the Ford Foundation—said he found it remarkable that opposition to America's international family planning program was so slow in coming. From 1965 onward, AID's population control program gained a steadily larger appropriation of federal funds. The international population control movement gained converts. More officials in more developing countries concluded that rapid population growth hurt their countries' development prospects, and more foreign aid agencies in developed nations began to contribute to growth reduction efforts either bilaterally or through the United Nations. Progress was not always uniform, but during the fifteen years from 1965 to 1980, population and family planning activities gained widespread legitimacy as not only appropriate but essential steps to improve the health of women and children, to enhance the development prospects of poor countries, and to safeguard the world system.

Funding

The official American commitment to slowing population growth in the developing world is demonstrated by the budget allocations of the U.S. Agency for International Development, the government agency responsible for the design and implementation of America's overseas population program. Unfortunately, it is impossible to produce completely accurate figures on the amount of aid that specific countries received, because a large proportion of foreign assistance funds pass through a variety of organizations, making careful tracking of who gave what to whom and when very difficult. Moreover, there is a good deal of confusion about what constitutes assistance for population and family planning. (How much should one allow for a comprehensive primary health care program that promotes better nutrition, higher immunization rates, and greater contraceptive use?) Definitions, fiscal years, exchange rates, length of commitments, and accounting procedures vary substantially, adding to the problems of identifying allocations. Not only do estimates from different sources differ, several estimates from the same source will often conflict. The estimates by AID and by the Population Council can vary by a factor of five (Ness, Pressman, and Hutchings 1982; Office of Technology Assessment 1982, p. 184).

From a starting point of $2.1 million in 1965, funding for AID's population and family planning activities increased almost steadily to a high of $185 million in 1980—an increase of 88 times the original appropriation (see Table 3.1). Resources increased each year after that as well, reaching $249 million in the budget proposed by the Reagan administration for 1985. The budget for international population activities equals roughly what it costs to operate one of America's mid-sized cities for a year. On the other hand, one nuclear submarine costs at least six times what AID spends yearly on population control (Office of Management and Budget 1988).

Despite the central role of population in the thinking of many of the development experts at AID, the proportion of AID's budget spent on population activities has never been very large. In part, this reflects the isolation of the Office of Population and the narrow definition of "population and family planning activities" that guided the staff's thinking for most of its history. Projects not likely to have a direct and almost immediate effect on the level of contraceptive use or on the conduct of family planning programs were discouraged. One result of this may have been to keep the budget for the population account lower than it would have been if more collaborative projects had been undertaken among the various offices and bureaus of AID. Population assistance never represented more than about 4 percent of America's total official development assistance (Gille 1982, p. 377; Office of Technology Assessment 1982, p. 181). In a typical year, AID's budget contained two and a half times more money for agriculture and rural development projects than for population and family planning activities, but twice for population control what it allowed for the agency's health program. The health program cost 23 percent more than AID's education and human resources development assistance (AID 1982, p. 6). Funding for population, however, has increased slightly as a percentage of all development assistance projects since the early 1960s.

Between 1965 and 1980, the United States was the dominant donor to international population activities in terms of total dollars and, thus, in terms of the percentage of all population assistance provided by a particular country. But Sweden and Norway top the list in terms of contributions to population activities as a percentage of total development assistance. Sweden's contributions to population activities, for example, represent about 5 percent of its development assistance budget. A Norwegian development assistance statute set the level of aid to population at 10 percent of all assistance, and in some years the proportion was slightly higher than that (Gille 1982, p. 376).

Nongovernmental funds have also been extremely important in the movement to control world population growth. Before Western governments provided support for population control programs, pri-

Table 3.1. International and U.S. Aid for Population and Family Planning by Year (Figures in Millions of Dollars)

Year	Total International Aid (Including U.S.)	Total U.S. Government Aid	Percentage U.S. Government Aid
1965	13.6	2.1	15.4
1966	36.8	3.9	10.5
1967	31.4	4.4	14.0
1968	52.3	34.8	66.5
1969	78.9	45.4	57.5
1970	117.5	74.6	63.5
1971	140.8	95.9	68.2
1972	184.7	123.3	66.7
1973	199.4	125.6	63.0
1974	193.9	112.4	58.0
1975	217.4	109.9	50.5
1976	257.4	135.5	52.4
1977	275.4	143.4	52.1
1978	314.9	177.6	56.4
1979	346.9	184.9	53.3
1980	354.3	185.0	52.2

Source: Data on total aid and U.S. contributions from R. T. Ravenholt (1978), "Population Program Assistance: U.S. Agency for International Development, 1965–1978." See also Table 2, in "AID Investment of $1 Billion in Family Planning/ Population. It is Resulting in Sharp Birthrate Declines," *International Family Planning Perspectives and Digest* 4 (4) (1978): 127–28; and *Population and Development Review*, 6 (3) (1980), National Security Council Request for years 1977–79, supplemented by Office of Technology Assessment 1982, p. 182.

vate organizations represented the only source of assistance. Three American foundations—Ford, Rockefeller, and the Population Council—played a dominant, indeed almost exclusive, role in supporting population and family planning activities throughout the 1950s and early 1960s. In 1965, for example, the Ford Foundation provided $10.8 million for population and family planning, while the Population Council contributed $5.4 million and the Rockefeller Foundation added $3.2 million (there is some double counting here, because both Ford and Rockefeller supported the Population Council); in the same year, the International Planned Parenthood Federation (IPPF) and the Swedish government each provided less than a million dollars for population and family planning, and AID spent only $2.1 million. Four years later AID's budget had grown twenty times (Ruprecht and Wahren 1970, p. 4). Even in 1975, by which time its support for population had started to decline, the Ford Foundation contributed over $10 million to support population activities around the world. This amount was larger than the amount given by every country except West Germany, Norway, Sweden, and the United States; in fact, Ford's contribution in 1975 was greater than the combined total given in the same year by Australia, Belgium, and Japan (Gille 1979, pp. 391–92). This pattern of funding explains the influence that Ford Foundation staff exercised in everything having to do with the population growth of the developing world. The situation has changed because of the foundation's new program orientation, but until recently the Ford Foundation's cumulative expenditures for population activities were greater than the cumulative expenditures of every country but Sweden and the United States. Until 1980, Ford's investment in international population control was more than twice that of most industrial countries' development assistance programs, including those of Canada, Denmark, West Germany, Japan, and Great Britain (National Security Council 1980, p. 513).

Historically, only about one-third of AID's resources have been given to direct bilateral assistance. Nearly half (46 percent in 1980) go for indirect bilateral assistance—that is, funds are passed through private American organizations and then to developing-country projects. For several years, the United Nations received nearly one-fifth of America's international population assistance funds; much of the remainder went to the International Planned Parenthood Federation for redistribution to IPPF affiliates in the developing world (Office of Technology Assessment 1982, pp. 182–84). But a 1985 Reagan administration ruling curtailing assistance to organizations that support abortion, even with nongovernmental funds, has meant a withdrawal of U.S. government support to both IPPF and the United Nations' Fund for Population Activities (UNFPA). (U.S. government funds have not been used to support abortion services since 1973, following the enactment of the Helms amendment to the Foreign Assistance Act.)

Two figures demonstrate the prominence of America's international population program better than other indicators. The first is the proportion of total international assistance attributable to the United States. The second is the percentage of national family planning program budgets contributed by international sources. Most accounts conclude that the United States provided 50 percent or more of all assistance until 1973, when the U.S. share declined and the percentage provided by other countries increased. The proportion of all assistance contributed by the United States remained at about 40 percent throughout the late 1970s. Clearly, 40 to 50 percent of all international assistance is a dominant share. But my analysis suggests that this figure, based on only government contributions, greatly underestimates the impact of American foreign assistance for population and family planning. Data are limited, and double counting—that is, considering the Ford Foundation as one source and then including a Ford grant to the Population Council in the Council's allocation as another source—is likely; but the total amount given by U.S. government and private-sector institutions dwarfs the amount provided by others. Before 1968, only the U.S. and Swedish governments provided support for population activities. From 1968 to 1972, the American government and private American foundations provided over 80 percent of all international assistance for population and family planning. So it was only after almost ten years of support for the international population control movement that America's share of population assistance began to decline (Gille 1979, pp. 391–92; Corsa and Oakley 1979, p. 351). In 1973, three-quarters of all assistance came from American sources; thereafter, the proportion of population and family planning assistance coming from the United States declined to around 50 percent.

The impact of the American effort can also be seen by looking at the proportion of developing-country population and family planning budgets contributed by foreign sources. I collected data for sixty-one countries on the proportion of national population and family planning budgets (expenditures) that came from international sources during the years 1965–80. I would have preferred to include only American funds, but the data are not available for that type of precision. In fact, data for every year are available for only four countries— an indication of the limited character of the information on international transfers of population assistance.

The data available illustrate the pervasive influence of American foreign aid for population. Sixty percent of the developing countries for which data are available report having had at least one year between 1965 and 1980 in which only foreign aid funds were spent for domestic population and family planning work. The proportion of countries relying exclusively on foreign aid to support population control activities was particularly high in Latin America: 95 percent— 19 out of 20, with only Trinidad and Tobago not included. Although this high level of foreign support is not surprising given the hesitation of Latin American countries to promote contraceptive use as a matter of national policy, government funds doubtless paid for a variety of things that supported the family planning effort but were not reported. These figures should be taken to indicate the importance of foreign funds, not the fact that there was no local support. Another 8 percent of the countries—four in Africa, and one in Asia— had at least one year in which 90 percent or more of the funds used for population and family planning work came from international sources. Thus, over two-thirds of the countries for which we have data had at least one year in which they received at least 90 percent of their population and family planning funding from outside the country. Another eleven countries had at least one year during which between 50 and 90 percent of their population and family planning budget came from international sources. Thus, 87 percent of the developing countries had at least one year between 1965 and 1980 in which they received half or more of the funds used for population and family planning from foreign sources.

Also noteworthy is the large number of countries that came to rely on foreign aid for support of population and family planning projects. Thirty-three countries, over half of those for which we have data, had three years between 1965 and 1980 during which international sources provided at least 85 percent of the money spent on family planning and population. Countries in all regions are represented in the thirty-three, as are countries with strong, well-regarded government family planning programs (e.g., Thailand) and those with programs yet to demonstrate a substantial impact (e.g., Kenya).

One should not conclude either that the very high percentage of developing-country population and family planning funds provided by foreign sources was an evil, alien influence, or that it was an effective pump priming the system. Much more information (some of which is presented in Chapters 8 and 9) is needed for such judgments. The data presented here are intended to demonstrate the impact of the United States on the population programs of the developing world. At the same time, the figures point to the relative importance of reducing population growth for developing-country leaders. Until recently, few Third World governments considered population growth sufficiently important to allocate a significant amount of their own resources to lowering fertility; most funding for population control programs came from the United States and a few other industrialized nations. Because the family planning program in many countries was heavily financed by the United States, local political leaders often did not pay it very much mind, especially if it maintained a low profile. Daya Abeywickrema, executive director of the Family Planning Association of Sri Lanka, says: "Because there is a lot of funds available for family planning from foreign aid, people seem to wonder why should we contribute. . . . This . . . is certainly affecting our raising funds locally. And also the people who manage programs take the very easy view about it. 'Let's get the aid, rather than worry about raising it locally.' This availability of large funds has made us more and more dependent rather than independent" (author's interview).

If the United States felt strongly about the need to slow growth and was willing to underwrite the program, all that was needed was the support of a few local leaders to get started. Few Third World political leaders felt at home discussing health-related topics, so if doctors at a national university's medical center wanted to quietly begin a family planning program, they were unlikely to encounter strong resistance from their country's political leadership. Today, an increasing share of the costs of family planning programs is paid by developing countries themselves. International donor assistance remains important for population and family planning programs, but increasing local support is also available.

So far, I have examined the roots of America's international population policy, traced the early history of the federal government's involvement in the effort to reduce population growth in the developing world, and highlighted the importance of U.S. support for population and family planning activities in the Third World. The next chapter reviews this population control effort in finer detail: I describe the strategy favored by most Americans active in the international population movement and spell out what I regard as some of its most important implications.

4

· The Family Planning Consensus

From the very earliest days, a consensus existed among those involved in the organized American effort to lower fertility and to slow population growth in the developing world that new contraceptives were needed and that widely available, publicly subsidized family planning services were the essential first step toward lower fertility and reduced population growth. While the community of donors who funded population activities, and the interested specialists who advised them, recognized that voluntary family planning might not be sufficient to lower population growth rates to desirable levels in the long run, few were willing to argue for more aggressive programs in advance of major increases in the availability of contraceptive services.

The idea that a mass distribution of contraceptives was the key to solving the population problem was not new in the 1960s. In 1937, Clarence Gamble had attempted to lower birth rates in rural North Carolina by hiring a nurse to distribute condoms door-to-door. Christopher Tietze, a newly arrived immigrant from Austria who went on to become one of the leading figures in the family planning field, was employed by Gamble to evaluate the program (Reed 1978, pp. 247–48, 272).

The Ford Foundation began supporting population projects in 1952. Of the $101 million the foundation spent between 1952 and 1968, $72 million went to assist family planning programs or for research in reproductive biology (Harkavy, Saunders, and Southam 1968, pp. 543–45). In 1965, AID spent $2.1 million on international population assistance while the Ford Foundation spent $10.7 million, almost two-thirds of it going to family planning and reproductive biology. The Rockefeller Foundation began its support of population and family planning in 1923 with a grant to the Social Science Research Council. Like the Ford Foundation, the Rockefeller Foundation spent large amounts to support research in reproductive biology aimed at improving fertility regulation techniques; between 1959 and 1982, the Rockefeller Foundation gave the Population Council $6.7 million for biomedical research (Rockefeller Foundation 1982, p. 33). In its first fifteen years, the Population Council spent roughly two-thirds of its funds on biomedical research aimed at developing new contraceptives or providing technical assistance to developing-world family planning programs (Notestein 1968, p. 559). Likewise, the Agency for International Development, the organization with the largest budget, spent nearly all of its money directly on family planning services and most of its research budget looking for ways to improve contraceptive technology and its delivery. The AID budgets indicate that 80 percent or more of the money the agency allocates to population activities goes to support family planning (AID 1982).

Foundation officials believed that increasing family planning services and encouraging their use was—depending on the official with whom you spoke—the only, the best, or the most appropriate option available for controlling population growth in the developing world. A lot has been said by those who have examined America's international population program about the relative importance of subsidized contraceptive services versus other factors in reducing fertility. Very few family planning advocates thought that social and economic development was unimportant—but they argued that their programs could lower fertility at least as well as, and probably better than, any reasonable alternative.

Bernard Berelson once crafted what he termed "an instructive entertainment," paraphrasing and quoting experts in the field to summarize the argument. In it, debaters "FamPlan" and "DevDev" exchange views on the importance of contraceptive services:

> *DevDev*: . . . the lowering of population growth rates is . . . dependent on such things as higher living standards, more equal income distribution, higher levels of employment, education, health care—and not by pills and loops alone. . . . The results [of your family planning programs] were a dismal and expensive failure.

> *FamPlan*: . . . you can turn the point around—the relative failure of economic development programs has hampered the attainment of family planning goals. . . . From experience to date, about all I would claim is that in the more favored of the developing countries, modern family planning . . . can contribute to a decline in the birth rate of about 10 points in a decade; and in the less favored . . . to about half that. . . . [We] have been searching

for additional ways to reduce fertility . . . but without much success. . . . The measures which are generally discussed by advocates of "beyond family planning" policies are almost uniformly vague, or are politically or ethically unacceptable, or technically or administratively infeasible. (Berelson 1975, pp. 10, 12, 16, 17)

Those who saw the problem of rapid population growth as first and foremost a result of the failure of couples to have sufficient knowledge of and access to modern contraception, diagnosed the problem of population growth in a way that fit nicely with the American value structure and activist orientation. Supporters of the point of view that increasing contraceptive information and services was the most important step in controlling high fertility were not simple-minded. They attacked targets they thought they could reach, and they tried to do so in the most cost-effective fashion. One can do something about a lack of contraceptives. If the problem of fertility regulation were deeply rooted in the culture of a particular country, avenues of intervention would be harder to identify and far more difficult and expensive to manipulate. Saying that population growth is the result of women's failure to regulate their childbearing because of an absence of appropriate means also frees the women of responsibility for their actions. High fertility, in short, is no one's fault. Village couples, given full availability of family planning services, would choose not to have all the children they are now having. Defining the population problem in terms of a lack of contraceptive supplies enabled the United States to intervene quickly, cheaply, and without much attention to local circumstances. America could help slow growth without gaining an understanding of language, religion, or culture. Moreover, a technological fix to the problem of high fertility and rapid population growth must have been particularly appealing to public health practitioners and policy makers who saw the impact that technology—for example, spraying for mosquitoes—had on mortality rates in developing countries.

Conflict

Not all observers shared the enthusiasm of the country's foundation executives and public health physicians for contraceptive services as the most effective means of lowering fertility. Objections were raised by scholars who had studied developing-country societies and their population trends.

Most of what we know about population growth and its consequences comes from university professors and academic researchers.

The debate about the importance of controlling population growth for economic development and political stability and the arguments about the best way to lower fertility did not take place on the editorial pages of the nation's newspapers. No American state house or assembly ever came alive with discussions of the pros and cons of international family planning. Nobody marched in protest or support of U.S. assistance to family planning programs around the world. Congress has been the most consistent reviewer of American efforts to slow population growth, but even Congress has been heavily influenced by the academic understanding of population growth and its consequences. To a remarkable extent, the debate about how the United States should deal with the problem of population growth occurred in scholarly journals and at professional meetings.

Although almost everyone agreed on the usefulness of better and more widespread family planning services, objections were raised as to what seemed to some the preoccupation of policy makers and program implementers with contraceptive services. Paul Demeny argued that people had large families because they wanted them. Fertility was determined by people's desires, which, in turn, were shaped by the social and economic circumstances of their lives. By stressing the structural dimensions of childbearing together with the fact that women had children because they wanted them, Demeny and others ensured that they could never lose the argument about the effect of family planning programs. If family planning programs appeared successful, one need only remind the audience that it was not family planning that made the difference but people's changing desires, which had adjusted to evolving social and economic conditions. If programs failed, it was not because of lack of resources or poor implementation; it was because they were not needed. Tackling the advocates of strong government support for family planning programs head on, Demeny wrote:

> Knowledge of and access to contraceptives is only one of the many elements that condition fertility choices. It is hardly ever the dominant one. If people want to have fewer children, why do they not have fewer children? To say that they do not know how to prevent them is hardly persuasive. Don't they know where babies come from? There is ample historical evidence, including evidence from populations that were once poor, rural and illiterate, that fertility can be greatly reduced without access to modern methods of fertility control. There is no reason to assume that the same thing would not happen anywhere in the contemporary

world if that is what people really wanted. (Demeny 1975a, no pagination)

Sociologist Nicholas J. Demerath has put forward a representative version of the same argument: ". . . the promotion of family planning Anglo-American style is a poor way to reduce fertility in poor countries. Family planning emphasizes the values of health and contraception but misses the complexities of fertility behavior and human motivation. . . . Whatever the benefits of family planning programs, the control of fertility in poor countries is not one of them" (Demerath 1976, p. 118). He goes on to argue that one needs to locate "the right institutional levers" and change them in order to lower fertility effectively. Among the levers that he suggests might help to lower fertility are better education, which could change "the norms and aspirations and involvements of educated persons," work outside the home for women, and better schooling for children. Demerath goes on, "more than any other development factor, the expansion of interests and satisfactions beyond the family may create an environment conducive to smaller families" (ibid., pp. 143–44).

Some critics thought that family planning failed as a population policy because it left unresolved the conflicts between the fertility goals of individual couples and the demographic goals of the society. Kingsley Davis, for example, said his complaint was "directed not against family planning programs as such but against the assumption that they are an effective means of controlling population growth" (1967, p. 736). He noted that voluntary family planning is just that—voluntary; what slowing population growth demands is fertility *control*: "The need for societal regulation of individual behavior is readily recognized in other spheres—those of explosives, dangerous drugs, public property, natural resources. But in the sphere of reproduction, complete individual initiative is generally favored" (ibid., p. 737). Davis thought that the difference between the number of children that individual couples wanted and the number that most developing countries needed in order to prosper was likely to be, and to remain, substantial. Thus, employing family planning as the main avenue of intervention to lower population growth, while politically palatable, was very likely to be insufficient to achieve the level that many growth control advocates thought necessary.

Supporters of family planning were more optimistic in their appraisal of the future of population growth. As early as 1967, well in advance of most of his colleagues, demographer Donald Bogue announced "the end of the population explosion," predicting that "the world population crisis . . . will be largely if not entirely a matter of history when humanity moves into the 21st century" (1967, p. 11). And yet, a decade from the twenty-first century, Bogue's bright vision is still in doubt. He saw a promise in the progress of family planning programs and the reproductive behavior of couples throughout the Third World where others saw trouble. Paul Demeny, for example, worried that Bogue's optimism about the future of population growth would lead to less attention to controlling that growth: "a realistic examination both of the demographic record of the last few decades and of the world's current demographic prospects calls for increased concern with population issues . . . rather than a relaxation of interest" (1984, p. 7). Demeny also attacked Bogue for his positive judgment about the value of family planning programs, saying that such programs follow rather than lead the expansion of fertility regulation behavior (1979, p. 18). Bogue disagreed, finding "a large unmet demand for contraception in less developed countries," which family planning programs could help meet (Bogue and Tsui 1979, p. 15).

Paul Demeny's and Kingsley Davis's criticism of family planning programs might be called the critique of exaggerated individualism, in that they suggested that simply allowing individuals to make their own reproductive decisions would not enable countries to achieve a level of population growth commensurate with national development aspirations. The criticism had two sides in that Demeny and Davis judged family planning programs unlikely to be successful because such programs do not take account of the customs, beliefs, and attitudes that encourage high fertility. In addition, they argued that the provision of contraceptive services aimed at helping couples obtain a certain family size avoided the more important issue of how countries could balance individual and collective interests; that is, how a country could achieve a lower level of population growth when the level desired was below that which would result if all couples were able to have just the number of children they wanted.

Much of the recent history of the population control movement can be best understood within the framework of the debate about the merits of family planning programs. Early in the American effort to control population growth the movement's leading thinkers concluded that more widespread and more effective contraceptive practice would be the essential ingredient in any systematic attack on high fertility. Others thought that the enthusiasm for family planning encouraged people to avoid the more complex and difficult reasons (other than simply a lack of adequate contraceptives) that caused women to have a lot of children.

The Critique of Contraceptive Services

Criticism of the theory that increasing the availability and reducing the costs (both financial and other) of contraceptives was the most important element in the effort to reduce fertility was almost always offered as a carefully considered scientific analysis. However, much of the argument between those who favored family planning and those who found it at best a very partial solution to the problem of rapid population growth was rooted in the values of the protagonists. Most social scientists were conditioned by their training, their professional inclinations, and their experience to be deeply suspicious of what they saw as the technological "quick fix" of a contraceptive-based solution to the population problem. Demerath, for example, refers to "obsession with technique" as "the first reason why family planning fails in poor countries" (1976, p. 90). Social scientists understood childbearing to be controlled by well-established, deeply rooted cultural institutions. Public health professionals, on the other hand, understood the possibilities of well-planned, carefully targeted intervention. The differences in perspective are, in turn, related to the way the two groups defined those whose fertility they were trying to modify.

Most of the social scientists who studied population saw reproductive behavior as far more fixed and difficult to change than did the physicians who argued that improving family planning services could significantly reduce fertility, and who found people more malleable than did their social science colleagues. There were some social scientists, including a few of the nation's most distinguished sociologists and economists, who supported family planning programs and were ready to acknowledge their ability to contribute to significant changes in childbearing. Nevertheless, the majority were so struck by the force of society's institutions in holding behavior within certain traditional patterns that they ignored the existence of widespread deviant behavior among people resisting the established rules or wishing desperately that they could avoid the taken-for-granted ways of behaving. Moreover, social science theories were better at explaining tradition and the functions of existing social structure than they were at accounting for changes in attitude and behavior. Family planning activists, for their part, saw women as eager to accept family planning, and they could not understand the perspective that said society's institutions would restrict the number of women who would accept contraception.

The difference in perspectives was compounded by the different focal points used by the proponents of each view. Social scientists studied, discussed, and found important social aggregates. They knew that religion, social class, and educational experience exerted a strong influence on behavior. Dennis Wrong, for example, argues that "[t]he fertility of a population depends . . . on the balance between those parts of its culture and social systems that favor reproduction and those that hinder it" (1961, p. 47). Public health professionals focused on individuals and saw that people were not completely shaped by the societies in which they lived. The health professionals were less concerned about the impact of traditional culture in maintaining high fertility because they counted the many women eager for change as a more reliable indicator of the society's fertility desires and a more accurate harbinger of things to come than women held in check by traditional social structure, and thus not able or eager to practice family limitation. Malcolm Potts represents this point of view when he notes, "I am a physician and have seen too many abortions not to be convinced that a lot of people want to limit their families and yet find it bloody difficult to get at the means" (author's interview).

Some people see society as a collection of individuals and emphasize the multiplicity and diversity; others consider society *real*, in the sense of having an existence beyond that of its individual members. Both orientations have played a role in thinking about the control of population growth. The first emphasizes the problems and benefits of high fertility for individuals or families, while the second stresses the advantages and disadvantages of controlling population growth for the community or the society. The individual perspective on childbearing and population growth is expressed in arguments about the economic costs and benefits of childbearing and the health consequences of high fertility; control of reproduction, in this context, is seen as an advantage because it enables parents to take better care of a smaller number of children, or saves mothers from the suffering and poor health caused by excessive childbearing. The group perspective underlies discussions of the relationship between rapid population growth and economic development or political stability. Somsak Varakamin, former director of Thailand's national family planning program, notes that during the early days of the Thai program, the emphasis was not on the welfare of individuals but on the economic development of the country as a whole; it was only later, after the program had been accepted politically, that its impact on women and children began to be emphasized (author's interview). Many of the population movement's conflicts are rooted in differences regarding whether a high level of childbearing is a problem for individual women, for the family unit, for the society or country, or for all or none of them. At the same time, the diversity of orientations helps explain the public acceptance of the movement to control world population growth.

The individual orientation toward high fertility and population growth is most often expressed by physicians, social workers, and others engaged in the helping professions. This view is exemplified by those who promote birth control to provide autonomy, better sexual adjustment, improved health, and the like. As family planning became a topic of greater importance in medical practice (the pill, IUDs, and sterilization greatly increased the involvement of doctors), the emphasis on individual well-being became a major rationale for contraceptive programs within the United States. Better health for the world's poor was also a strong motive in the public justification of American involvement in the population affairs of other nations. Although it was never as forceful as the argument that slowing population growth would speed economic development, many people, especially health professionals, argued that contraception saved lives.

One early and well-known review of the relationship between the health of children and fertility was carried out by Joe Wray. He concluded that "the consistent trend of the consequences associated with either increasing family size or decreasing birth interval is striking and uniformly negative. When the full spectrum of these effects is seen, it is, in fact, alarming. . . . For everyone concerned about the welfare of children, everyone who believes that each child born deserves a chance to achieve his own best potential, the message is clear: we must, at the very least, make it possible for parents who do want to control their family size to do so" (Wray 1971, pp. 406, 456). Wray's argument was adopted by AID Administrator Peter McPherson to justify Reagan administration support for international family planning. McPherson said, "For a mother, the ability to space or limit pregnancies may mean the difference between illness and health, between life and death. For children to be reasonably spaced may mean the chance of adequate nutrition or even the chance to survive at all" (1985, p. 9).

Another reason for the conflict between those who thought family planning to be the best, most practical solution to the problem of rapid population growth in the Third World and those who believed that such a strategy was too narrow to be effective was the difficulty in establishing acceptable programmatic alternatives to publicly subsidized family planning. It was easy (and correct) to say that family planning was a very limited approach to changing the fertility of women in the Third World. It was much more difficult to specify alternatives that poor countries eager to slow growth could realistically consider implementing. A variety of actions could be proposed, but acceptability and affordability were a constant problem. There was a catch, too, in that some solutions—such as incentive schemes that paid couples not to have children or to accept contraceptives—were sometimes not tried because a society's elites decided that people would not accept them, or foreign donors would not participate in programs based on them because they were considered to be too heavy-handed or even coercive. Such economic incentive schemes were rarely put to the test of whether the people themselves would accept them. Some governments avoided non–family planning avenues to lower fertility and population growth because they were afraid that such programs would alarm the citizenry. The Third World is short of democracies, and in many cases political leaders feared, not the reaction to the growth reduction schemes themselves, but popular protests against government attempts to control reproductive behavior when freedoms were already greatly limited. Indira Gandhi was among those who learned this lesson first hand, when she lost power following a series of dictatorial measures that included attempts to force sterilizations.

In a dictatorship where freedom of the press does not exist, where political rights mean little or nothing, where officials are almost uniformly self-interested, the right to have the number of children one wants may seem particularly inviolable. Thus, many governments avoided pressuring couples to regulate fertility, although they might provide contraceptive services for those who wanted them or even allow a lively illegal abortion trade. Some government leaders were also slow to encourage fertility control because they worried that campaigns to change family-building practices would be seen by rural villagers as an attack on their valued traditional culture and ways of life and a tacit admission that the political leadership could not deliver promised economic improvements.

To some extent, the dispute over the usefulness and impact of family planning programs is also linked to the biographies of the advocates of each point of view. Cliques have developed based on the different perspectives. Special organizational arrangements have become a means of accommodating differing points of view. (Demographer Philip Hauser once claimed, "demography has so long been the pessimistic science that perhaps it is well to have the family planning enthusiasts balance the scale with large doses of optimism" [1967, p. 409].) Each perspective on the significance of family planning in lowering fertility tended toward an intellectual totalitarianism that at best ignored, and at worst belittled, those holding different points of view.

Those with backgrounds in the biological and health sciences stress the values of adaptation, survival, good health, and longevity. The economic version of this orientation values prosperity and welfare at the societal level and an increased standard of living for individuals. In both its health and economic manifestations, this view stresses rationality: both public health doctors and economists believe that people act in their own interest—to get or maintain health or wealth. Sociologists, on the other hand, see individual freedom of action as dependent on the larger social system. Change, in this view, disrupts accepted and patterned ways of behaving. While social scientists recognize the importance of individual voluntary action, in general the individual is considered less important than the group. Tradition is important. Identity, affiliation, and maintenance of standards are also important. Even those social scientists who are schooled in Marxism and conflict theory highlight, not the range of actions available to individuals, but how society affects different groups and limits individual choice. Justice and progress are more important than individual choice.

This complex of values has led sociologists like Demerath to sing the praises of China and "the institutional changes achieved by Maoism." Demerath was correct in claiming the Chinese believed that "fertility reduction is too important to be left to health planners or to family planners," but cruelly misguided when he judged the murderous destruction of Western-educated physicians and the use of the party, the state bureaucracy, and a host of secondary groups to pressure people into reducing fertility to be a more humane and sensible policy for American support than government-subsidized family planning:

> The basic strategy deserves particular attention inasmuch as the Chinese experience sustains a theory that is quite well-grounded in prior research and in certain established concepts of social science. . . . I conclude . . . that populationists and politicians in Third World nations may well look to China if they are serious about reducing fertility in their own nations. As an example of successful antinatalism in the Third World, it is probably unequalled. And that this success is attributable to a societal, multi-institution strategy is a fact whose implications are as extensive as they are "dangerous" for those who resist change in the present world order. (Demerath 1976, p. 189)

Contrast Demerath's view to that of Reimert Ravenholt. Ravenholt would vary the details but not the basic prescription: provide contraceptives. When he was most cautious and convoluted, he referred to the "availability of family planning information and means" as "usually a dominant determinant in the complex of forces influencing reproductive behavior." Whatever other factors were involved, the primacy of contraception meant that "no . . . final judgments of additional measures which may ultimately be needed to achieve a desired rate of growth can be made in advance of the full extension of family planning services" (Ravenholt 1968, p. 572; also 1969, p. 124).

In Ravenholt's view, the full extension of family planning services sometimes required such extreme measures as nailing contraceptives to the doorposts of homes in the rural villages of the developing world. His AID colleagues insist that he once seriously advocated such an approach. When confronted by critics saying he would never allow American women to receive contraceptives in such haphazard fashion, Ravenholt was ready to try a similar system of distribution in the United States (author's interview). Duff Gillespie remembers that as chief of the Office of Population's research division at AID, he assigned a physician on his staff to investigate the laws governing oral contraceptive distribution in response to Ravenholt's desire to distribute pills in Washington, D.C., without a doctor's prescription (author's interview). Allan Rosenfield, dean of the School of Public Health at Columbia University and former head of the Presbyterian Hospital's Department of Obstetrics and Gynecology, also remembers being pressured by Ravenholt to find a way to establish an experimental contraceptive delivery system in New York City based on the free-wheeling model that he was encouraging in developing countries (author's interview).

Ravenholt's ideas were not as outlandish as they may first seem. Although he was initially dismissed by most specialists in demographic and development-oriented research and remained cordially disliked by many people in the population and family planning movement until he left AID, many of his ideas, including his view that the availability of contraceptives was a decisive factor in determining the level of fertility control, gained wide acceptance.

In one of his more thoughtful statements, one he repeated on several occasions, Ravenholt described his view this way: ". . . bearing and rearing children is hard work, and few women have unlimited enthusiasm for the task. If given the choice, each month, of whether they wish to be pregnant that month, many considerations other than ultimate family size guide their reproductive behavior; and for many women postponement of pregnancy means reduction in completed family size" (Ravenholt 1968, p. 572). He trusted the collective wisdom of women exercising freedom of choice about child-bearing. Although he would rant about the dangers of high fertility among those who could not afford to take proper care of their children, hours of discussion would leave him arguing that there would be little problem if all contraceptive choices, including abortion, were easily available to every woman. He was not ready to accept the proposition that some women would continue to have children they could not support and that societies would have to help these children.

Individual differences and freedom of choice did not matter to Demerath, and would not in totalitarian regimes. More important was the achievement of a socially valued goal. The contrast between Ravenholt and Demerath, and between those who share their views, is striking. The effectiveness of family planning programs was never really seriously at stake; instead, what one notices is the contrast of worldviews. Ravenholt held that individuals given the right choices would have the good sense to behave in their own best interests, and that society would be served at the same time. Demerath thought that individuals' actions would not advance society's goals but would help perpetuate inequality and continue rapid population growth.

Maintaining the Consensus

Others have written about the network of American elites who provided visibility and leadership for the family planning consensus and for the movement to promote U.S. investments in family planning programs overseas (Bachrach and Bergman 1972). Most frequently discussed have been the interlocking memberships on the boards of major American population organizations. This pattern of one person holding positions on several boards remains important. Less well understood, but much more important for the day-to-day conduct of the population program, is the network of population and family planning professionals who work together to design, implement, and evaluate America's international population activities.

A failure to understand the pervasive links between the staffs of various organizations has led to mistaken conclusions about the differences among American population organizations, and about the extent to which there was an American consensus regarding the problem of rapid population growth and the appropriate ways to deal with it. Donald Warwick, for example, draws a sharp distinction between the Agency for International Development and the Ford Foundation. He finds Ford "the major donor most different from AID in its style of operations" and approvingly quotes the opinion of a

Ford official that "the Foundation staff are extremely well informed and culturally sensitive. I can't think of examples where we've pushed things down people's throats or where it was against the culture" (Warwick 1982, pp. 51, 55). Warwick also agrees with AID's critics who charge that the agency "held simplistic beliefs about the value of contraceptive technology and ignored the broader cultural and developmental context" (ibid., p. 50).

The Ford Foundation and AID were very different from some perspectives, but the differences were a matter of degree. Fitzgerald's characterization of missionaries in China nicely sums up the distinction between America's private population organizations and AID and those it supports: "The early Catholic missionaries, . . . realizing that the emperor was the font of . . . orthodoxy, saw that to convert the throne, to make a Chinese Constantine, was the swiftest and surest road to success. They concentrated on the court. They used their scientific skill to gain acceptance, they gained a foothold in official circles, they made some conversions among men of influence, and they themselves became accomplished Chinese scholars" (C. P. Fitzgerald 1964, p. 121). The Ford Foundation, Population Council, and Rockefeller Foundation were Catholic in orientation, concentrating on policy-oriented research (to convert the throne), and high-level training. On the other hand, AID was Protestant in orientation. As such, according to Fitzgerald, its representatives "paid no attention to the court, and tended to ignore the official class also. They endeavored . . . to win a wider audience and convert the people. The Protestant missionary . . . thought that what was most urgently required was to bring some knowledge of the Gospel to all Chinese. . . . He, therefore, tended to diffuse his activity over as wide an area as could be covered from the mission-station base" (ibid., p. 122). The agency supported house-to-house contraceptive distribution schemes and trained family planning workers to provide services in rural areas.

But despite these differences in orientation, American population groups shared a common set of goals. As the files of the Agency for International Development make clear, Ford and AID worked very closely together. When David Bell left AID, he joined the Ford Foundation as vice-president of its International Division. Soon after taking up his post at Ford, he wrote to his old deputy and then-Acting Administrator William Gaud, encouraging AID to provide more support for contraceptive development through grants to the National Institutes of Health (Bell to Gaud, March 19, 1968; Gaud to Bell, April 16, 1968, no source).

The contacts between AID and the Ford Foundation were not just at the uppermost level. John Nagel, a program officer at Ford, in a characteristic exchange wrote to David Frost, chief of the Health Division of AID's Latin American Bureau: "We are sending you a copy of the information paper for the Foundation's Board of Trustees. . . . This document represents a distillation of the best thinking and experience of the Foundation's population specialists. It is, of course, quite confidential" (Nagel to Frost, October 22, 1968, 286-73A-474). Exactly a month later Ford and AID were back in touch. Rutherford Poats, deputy administrator of AID, wrote to Oscar Harkavy, the officer in charge of the foundation's population program, about "organizing a consultative arrangement on population research funding. . . ." Ford and AID frequently shared interests in the same program and at times negotiated privately about how projects that both considered important could be supported. Poats, for example, told Harkavy: "You . . . asked for an indication of AID's thinking about expanding our institutional grants to include . . . [the] Center for Population Studies at the University of Michigan. It is very unlikely that AID will make any [211(d)] grants in the population field during the current fiscal year" (Poats to Harkavy, November 22, 1968, 286-73A-474). The following year, Nagel wrote again to David Frost, asking, "I wonder if I could sit down with you some day soon . . . to get up to date on the general question we mutually ponder of using IPPF, UNDP [United Nations Development Programme], and FEPATEN as conduits or channels of funds in support of population activity in Latin America" (Nagel to Frost, August 21, 1969, 286-73A-286).

Ronald Freedman, one of America's most distinguished demographers, was the long-time director of the University of Michigan's Population Studies Center, one of the nation's most important demographic research and training programs. His analysis of changing fertility in Taiwan was frequently used to support the American consensus about the role of organized family planning programs in the control of population growth (Freedman and Takeshita 1969). He and other university-based researchers were important members of the population network. Traveling overseas, he sent informal memos to AID to keep its staff posted on events of interest around the world—for example, he reported on his discussions with Thai government officials regarding Thailand's participation in the AID-funded World Fertility Survey (Freedman, February 1, 1974, 286-76-304). Freedman was by no means alone in providing information to AID staff. Charles Lininger of the Population Council was one of those who sent copies of noteworthy reports to his AID colleagues (Lininger to Frost, no date, 286-73A-474). Nor was the communication all one way. John Cool, who was later to work for the Ford Foundation, served for a while at the American Embassy in New Delhi. When he wrote his AID colleagues describing the Indian family planning program and AID's development efforts in India, he sent copies of his letter to senior professionals in the population field, including Alan Guttmacher at the Planned Parenthood Federation, Oscar Harkavy at the Ford Foundation, Notestein and Berelson at the Population Council, John Meyer at the Rockefeller Foundation, Philip Hauser at the University of Chicago, and Carl Taylor at Johns Hopkins (Cool, March 4, 1970, 286-73A-716).

The population and family planning network's connections were strengthened not only by exchanging reports and correspondence, but also by regular site visits, evaluation and needs assessment missions, conferences, workshops, study tours, exchanges, temporary and visiting appointments, consultations, meetings, and assorted junkets. The case of Indonesia is typical. In Jakarta, the AID mission reported that it was "making every effort to coordinate . . . closely with other donors. . . . Mission given access [to Indonesian Planned Parenthood Association] files. . . . Review meetings involving Ford Foundation, [Indonesian Planned Parenthood Association], Ministry of Health, etc. frequent" (Jakarta to Washington, Cable no. 6636, June 20, 1968, 286-73A-716). Meanwhile, in New York City, AID officials met with the senior staff of American population organizations to get information and the views of private groups on Indonesia's population program. Present at one such meeting were Frank Notestein and Sheldon Segal of the Population Council, Anna Southam of the Ford Foundation, Richard Lincoln of the International Planned Parenthood Federation, and Elton Kessel of the Pathfinder Fund (Memo, July 24, 1967, 286-73A-716). The AID "spring reviews" of population were attended by staff of the agency administrator's office as well as by outsiders from the academic community, the United Nations, the World Bank, the Population Council, and the Ford Foundation (Agenda, Spring Review, 1970, 286-81-082). This pattern of interagency coordination continues today. The Agency for International Development, for example, organizes regular coordination meetings to help the various groups it supports keep track of population activities in specific countries.

The links among AID, the Ford Foundation, the Population Council, and the other organizations active in the international population movement were the inevitable by-product of doing business in a small field where everyone knew everyone else. Being in the network served the individuals involved and the institutions they represented by providing them with information, opportunities to lobby for funding for projects, and other forms of support that movement members could provide each other. Sometimes, however, becoming acquainted with the way an individual or an agency did business, discouraged collaboration. One well-known demographer with close ties with AID reports: "I have never had any money from AID. . . . I just found them insufferable. . . . I've considered it a number of times, but I have always felt that they would subvert the truth" (author's interview).

Network members occasionally promoted common causes through loosely organized mail campaigns. One example came at the time of a planned AID reorganization to be carried out at the start of the Carter administration. Senior staff worried that the Office of Population would be dismantled. The network responded with a flood of letters to then-AID Administrator John Gilligan discouraging the changes (see David to Gilligan, October 28, 1977; Morgan and Wilson to Gilligan, November 17, 1977; Humphrey to Bair, December 5, 1977; Ambrou to Fawcett, August 16, 1977, gift file). Copies of the letters were sent to the Office of Population and circulated to other network members to ensure each author's good reputation. A few of those who served at AID's Office of Population believe that this type of political backing was the main value of some of the organizations that they supported (author's interview).

At times, the network reached the highest levels of government. Ravenholt's brother was a special assistant to Vice-President Hubert Humphrey. Ravenholt claims that their connection did not help the AID population program, and I have found no evidence of his brother's intervention—but it is easy to believe that ambitious politicians and worried bureaucrats would have been leery of attacking Ravenholt and his program lest they upset the vice-president's office. From time to time, for whatever reasons, Humphrey did become involved in AID's population control effort (see Humphrey to Mann, February 15, 1965, 286-73A-474). Network members even got to the White House. General Draper once wrote AID Administrator Gaud urging him to read a report from Jack Lippes, the Buffalo, New York, physician who helped popularize the intrauterine device, about population control in India. Draper also got Maryland Senator Joseph Tydings to write Gaud urging that he read Lippes's report, and Tydings wrote the president about the report. The White House reacted by writing to Gaud at AID saying, "The President would like your comments on Senator Tydings' letter and Dr. Lippes' memo" (Draper to Gaud,

November 30, 1966; Tydings to Gaud, August 2, 1966; Gaud to Tydings, August 24, 1966; Tydings to the President, August 2, 1966; Carter to Gaud, August 17, 1966, 286-73-159).

The network of population and family planning specialists was not just a result of the needs or inclinations of the individuals involved. Especially during the early days of its population program, the U.S. government channeled a great deal of its population and family planning assistance to foreign governments through U.S. universities and nonprofit groups, thereby enlarging and promoting the network for its own use. These relationships were also established and maintained in part to protect U.S. interests by camouflaging the extent of government involvement in overseas population programs. Giving funds to American organizations for them to spend overseas allowed the United States to publicly deny that it had a population policy for poor countries, and allowed those in developing countries receiving aid to deny that they were being supported by a foreign government.

John D. Rockefeller III, chairman of the Population Council's Board of Trustees, once discussed the appropriate role for the U.S. government during a meeting at AID. According to one participant, Rockefeller "said he was persuaded that it would be a mistake for the U.S. government to take too much leadership in the population field abroad, that it was better to leave the pioneering to private groups" (Hall memorandum, February 8, 1967, 286-73A-474). Rockefeller proposed "the possibility of a consortium approach in relation to family planning in countries that have passed through the pilot project stage" in which "local governments . . . contribute at least half of the cost of any population program" (Rockefeller to Gaud, March 3, 1967, 286-73A-474). He also argued that "in every case we should wait for initiative from the local government" (Hall memorandum, February 8, 1967, 286-73A-474). When Herbert J. Waters wrote Rockefeller about AID's reaction to the consortium idea, he said "he would welcome this initiative" (Waters to Rockefeller, March 22, 1967, 286-73A-474).

The Rockefeller consortium was not a force in an organized way, but the network of those interested in population control continued to exercise influence. The Agency for International Development and the Population Council, which John D. Rockefeller III had founded in 1952, continued to work together. Senior AID officials would include the Population Council on the distribution list for confidential material of the sort that the United States did not want officials of other governments to see. In 1969, for example, Rutherford Poats sent Bernard Berelson, president of the Population Council, a confidential AID report, noting that "in view of the lingering sensitivity to population planning in certain countries, I would appreciate your restricting the distribution of this message to your key professional staff" (Poats to Berelson, November 17, 1969, 286-73A-716).

Private organizations helped the government deal with the problem of how it could support family planning activities in countries without explicit policies encouraging contraceptive use, or in countries where contraceptive sales were prohibited. The Mexican case was one that concerned AID officials several different times. Thomas Favel, a counselor at the American Embassy in Mexico City, once told AID officials that "Agency for International Development support for [population and family planning], however indirect, could be counterproductive"; the same view was expressed by the executive director of the family planning association of Mexico (Memorandum from David Frost, September 29, 1969, 286-73A-474). The problem was discussed in late 1970 at the AID Population Officers' Conference in the following terms:

> Another major area of concern is in the funding of population projects by international organizations. The question arose primarily in conjunction with those countries where direct population assistance from the United States wasn't acceptable. Mexico and Brazil are examples. . . . In these countries, efforts in the area of population and family planning are moving forward but not under official government programs.
>
> The governments concerned seem inclined to let these efforts move as long as direct political confrontation does not emerge. . . . Direct U.S. assistance might surface this undesired type of political confrontation. Yet the level of present assistance from private organizations is not sufficient. . . . If we . . . are not able to respond positively to the need of population efforts within a country . . . then we have in a sense failed. (Trip Report, Bush to Ravenholt, December 7, 1970, 286-73A-474)

Participants at the 1970 Latin American Population Officers' Conference agreed that there was "need to work out a system for making private and international agency program grants with no attribution to AID as the funding source." Officials at AID were also "investigating possibility of mechanisms for use of unattributed Title X funds for training . . . and delivery systems." The AID administrator was asked to allow a grant to the International Planned Parenthood Federation "whereby AID and private IPPF funds would be co-mingled thereby freeing AID funds for wider use" (LA Population Officers' Conference, November 9–13, 1970, Panama City, Major Conclusions and Actions; Minutes, 286-73A-474).

The official worry about too visible a U.S. government involvement in international population control activities, and AID's readiness to take a back seat to private-sector groups, were at times very widespread. In a typical example, a comic book dealing with population, *El Doble Dilema* (The double dilemma), produced by the United States Information Agency and sent to all AID missions in Latin America, was not attributed to the U.S. government; instead, "space on the back cover can be used for attribution to local organization if desirable" (AID circular A2353, October 30, 1969, no source). In Africa, one group of American officials informed their colleagues in Washington, "the opportunity for misinterpreting U.S. intentions regarding the reasons for pushing family planning are high. Therefore, the U.S. Mission intends to pursue its . . . indirect approach" (Cable TOAID no. 595, November 28, 1969, no source).

In Indonesia, a country that announced a policy encouraging population control in 1968, local officials were less worried about American support for family planning than were the Americans. Despite a cabinet minister's claim that "there is no problem with direct U.S. assistance to the [Indonesian Planned Parenthood Association], USAID remains concerned . . . that AID identification at this time with a still highly contentious subject may not prove to be in U.S. interest." The American ambassador in Jakarta requested that "AID Washington explore, [and] advise [on the] possibility of channeling assistance through IPPF as first preference or the Population Council" (American Embassy/Jakarta to Secretary of State/Washington, November 9, 1967, TOAID 420, 286-73A-716). This cable is particularly interesting because it was authorized by Ambassador Marshall Green, who went on to become one of Washington's better-known spokesmen for population growth control, serving for a while as the Department of State's coordinator for population affairs and later on the staff of the Population Crisis Committee, the population lobbying group in Washington, D.C.

Predictably, during the early days of America's population program, AID officials worried about keeping some of the details of the agency's program not only from the scrutiny of citizens of other countries but from Americans as well. In 1969 the administrator noted that some of AID's assistance to "family planning agencies in particular Latin American countries . . . [was] considered too sensitive to advertise in an official publication" (Poats to Fowler and Hedges,

January 31, 1969, 286-734-474). The agency tried, for example, to delete testimony on its assistance to population programs in Latin America from the published transcripts of congressional hearings. In one instance, AID Administrator Poats wrote Congressman John E. Moss reporting that an advisory committee of

> . . . outstanding experts on population problems and fertility control programs strongly urged that . . . AID try to keep out of sight, out of print, and out of politics in Latin America on birth control assistance. They recommended that we channel our aid wherever possible through private intermediaries such as the International Planned Parenthood [Federation], Pathfinder Fund, Population Council and local private organizations and through international agencies such as the United Nations. . . . They cautioned especially against implying that the U.S. government has a population program for Latin America. . . . (Poats to Moss, December 5, 1968, 286-73A-474)

Poats suggested that the deletions in the public record could be followed by a parenthetical note such as "there followed discussion of population growth rates and the development of family planning programs."

While senior U.S. officials struggled not to be too bold or visible in the effort to control population growth, they were pushed by militant family planners—including the most militant official American of all, the director of AID's population program, Reimert Ravenholt. Ravenholt and those who supported him in and outside of the government, as well as senior members of developing-country governments and prominent citizens of countries around the world, urged the United States to increase its support of population control programs. Even those who thought it best for the United States to move slowly valued the work AID was trying to accomplish. When Administrator Poats wrote to Congressman Moss, he said that AID was cautioned to take a behind-the-scenes role by "the President of a Latin American country who is quietly encouraging family planning activity by public health units and private hospitals and other organizations but who cannot risk more open collaboration with AID" (Poats to Moss, December 5, 1968, 286-73A-474).

From the start of its effort to slow population growth, the United States lived with contradictions and ambiguities in its international population policy. American aid was hidden and urged by the same officials. But America had an international population policy that represented a consensus, if not unanimous agreement, about what should be done about population growth. Group influences were ignored, and programs promoting individual choice were supported. Welfare and development were stressed, control overlooked. Family planning services were encouraged because no one was willing or able to invest in more fundamental changes that seemed likely to lower fertility; no one was even sure what the most effective changes would be. Promotion of family planning was America's vote of confidence in demographic democracy.

5

Organization and Reorganization

Enthusiasm for population control and for family planning grew within the Agency for International Development as its leadership changed, as the influence of demography on development became clearer, and as the history of successful program implementation was documented. But the understanding of rapid population growth that prevailed at AID, and that influenced the way the agency's programs were designed and implemented, remained very narrow. Instructions to AID staff in the field illustrate the single-mindedness of those directing the population program in Washington. By the late 1960s, AID personnel overseas were no longer supposed to wait for host country requests for help in slowing rapid population growth. Instead, AID mission staff were told, "where needed country policies and programs do not now exist, Missions should take appropriate steps to encourage them." Moreover, it was made clear that family planning should be promoted as the key policy option for reducing fertility. Missions were reminded that "in explaining the concept of family planning, it is important to foster rapid official awareness of the progressive deleterious effects of too great population growth on economic and social development." Instructions also specified what constituted "realistic country action on the population growth problem": after "a thorough assessment of the country's demographic and sociological situation in relation to plans for national economic development . . . ," a country needed "an effective information and education program to explain to the people the population problem, the concept of family planning, and family planning methods and the availability of services . . . [and] creation of effective mechanisms for ensuring full availability of effective and acceptable means for family planning" (AIDTO 121, October 18, 1968, 286-76-095). Nothing but family planning programs was even mentioned in the headquarters' recommendation to the field about how best to address the problems associated with rapid population growth. The organizational consequences of this dominant AID orientation toward population control affected both the agency's Washington staff and its field programs. This chapter focuses on the conflict between those who thought the best way to implement AID's population program was through a specialized population group, and those who thought implementation by geographic bureaus would be more successful.

When AID first began to support population activities during 1965 and 1966, most of the day-to-day program planning and monitoring was carried out by a small population branch within the agency's Office of Technical Assistance and Research. In 1967, in response to the world food crisis and the definition of it as, in large measure, a problem of the balance between resources and people, AID's food, nutrition, and population activities were reorganized into the Office of the War on Hunger.

The papers of AID personnel who staffed the agency's regional bureaus and who were responsible for the overall development assistance program in a particular geographic region are filled with hostility toward the growing role of the specialized population group in planning, budgeting, and carrying out activities. According to one participant, disputes between the population group and the regional bureaus were "at bottom . . . a plain ordinary garden variety power struggle," caused in part by "Ravenholt's belief in [the War on Hunger's Population Service] primacy on all matters pertaining to population; disdain for an organizational way of life; and unfamiliarity with the way a Mission must play its role vis-á-vis a host country government to be effective as an agent of developmental change" (Jones, WOH/PS Role in Population Assistance, September 22, 1969, no source).

When the Office of the War on Hunger was dismantled in 1969 and AID's population work was transferred to the Technical Assistance Bureau, staff from AID's regional bureaus sought what one of them termed a "fruitful confrontation" with the Office of Population. The conflict had nothing to do with the regional bureaus' view of how to lower fertility. The bureaus wanted responsibility for U.S. assistance to the population and family planning programs in the countries in their regions. A centralized population group with a universally applicable program posed a serious threat. The suggestion (eventually enacted) that all grants to voluntary groups be coordinated by the Office of Population was an idea that one bureau official said

. . . we must resist with all vigor. Such an arrangement would make cohesive country programming all the more difficult; further strain relations between [the War on Hunger's Population

Service] and regional bureaus and between AID/Washington and Missions. . . . Centralizing the programming and management of such grants would be inconsistent with the . . . precepts upon which AID is founded. . . . The responsibilities [the Population Service] has tried to take unto themselves in pushing into regional programs and intervening in country activities are beyond the authority that central office staff can discharge efficiently. (Jones to Vinson, September 25, 1969, 286-73A-716)

But the independent population group prospered. Faced with growing concern among the public, members of Congress, and other development groups about the impact of rapid population growth, the regional bureaus had no fertility reduction strategy to propose as an alternative to the assistance being offered by the Office of Population. For their part, neither the director nor the staff of the Office of Population had the time or the interest to master complex and difficult-to-implement country-specific population strategies, mixing a variety of different program elements. Regional bureau people were not invited to meetings and had to shout to be heard. Ruth Fitzmaurice voiced a typical complaint: "all of the people at the meeting were exclusively population oriented and there was no attempt to put this problem in the context of our country strategies" (Fitzmaurice to Brinberg, August 7, 1969, 286-73A-716).

As the regional bureaus tried to exert influence on the Office of Population, staff of the office attempted to extend their domain. Ravenholt fought to approve all agency staff involved in any way with population activities, even those employed in regional bureaus. He made his case, he said, to save time and resources that would otherwise be squandered because "at present there is a noticeable tendency for those regional administrators with the least understanding and judgment of what needs to be done in the population field to buttress their misjudgment by appointment of sycophants with similar lack of knowledge and judgment as 'population officers' " (Ravenholt to Bernstein, February 4, 1970, 286-73A-0975).

The Office of Population had a program; the bureaus had a desire to control resources and to develop a more efficient organization. When the bureaus proposed new ways to control the flow of funds, such as having each grant that was made to a developing-country organization by an international organization receiving AID assistance reviewed and approved by the U.S. ambassador and the AID mission director in the country before it was awarded, Ravenholt claimed the idea was "superficially attractive but would subtract greatly from the potential value of such a grant. . . . The prime purpose underlining such a grant [he said] is not to extend U.S. control over planning developments in the recipient countries but to provide alternative support for incipient family planning activities and programs" (Ravenholt to Claxton, June 23, 1967, 286-70A-2036).

A report prepared early in the Nixon administration for the new AID administrator strengthened the hand of those favoring a centrally directed population program. The report concluded that by 1971 the excess capacity (countries receiving aid had declined from 82 in 1963 to 42 in 1971) of the geographically based organizational model led AID "to over-supervise and over-regulate field units and . . . creates a preoccupation with means and procedures rather than ends. Responsibility for policy, programs, budgeting and services is diffused. Lack of clear management responsibility inhibits both crisp decision-making and effective communication of policies" (Stern, Birnbaum, and Arndt to Hannah, December 13, 1971, p. 2, gift file). The agency's population program was reshaped again and more power was given to the Office of Population, but the conflict with the geographic-based bureaus was not resolved.

In 1972, John Hannah, Nixon's appointee as AID administrator, directed that the Office of Population be moved from the Technical Assistance Bureau to a newly established Bureau of Population and Humanitarian Assistance. Current and former Office of Population staff think that the organization in place at AID from 1972 to 1977, in which all population activities were coordinated by their office, was "virtually ideal" (author's interviews). Ravenholt and most of the Office of Population senior staff consistently argued that because the work of the agency was concerned with a handful of programs—population, health, food, and agriculture—it behooved AID to organize along functional lines, with adequate but much-stripped-down bureaus for geographic coordination (Ravenholt to Furman, March 23, 1976, gift file). Ravenholt once proposed that AID's health activities be organized like its population program, and he predicted that health and population activities would be better integrated if both programs were organized in the same way (Ravenholt to Levin, April 20, 1977, gift file).

But two complaints continued to characterize the relationship between the Office of Population and the rest of AID. First, the regional bureaus were unhappy because the Office of Population "had no systematic procedure to assure that the AID country Missions' evaluations of bilateral programs take place, that the evaluations address operational concerns, and that the findings are used . . . to improve project design, assure efficiency and effectiveness, and contribute to the accomplishment of U.S. objectives" (Inspector General of Foreign Assistance, Comments on original report issued August 21, 1975, 286-73A-716). Second, development experts in the regional bureaus, staff of the Bureau for Policy and Program Coordination, and others at AID and elsewhere who were eager to see population growth slowed, were worried that the Office of Population's strategy to support national efforts to reduce fertility was too limited. Many people believed that "the Office of Population has not given high priority to the acquisition of knowledge needed to structure country-specific development assistance projects to influence fertility" (Comptroller General 1978, p. 54). Instead, the office designed its entire program centered around the provision of family planning services.

The fertility reduction strategy promoted by the Office of Population made certain conflicts inevitable. The program discounted both the need to emphasize country-specific factors in providing assistance, at least until contraceptive services were widely available, and the need to incorporate development activities of a more general sort in a systematic fertility reduction plan. But criticism of the program did not have much impact on AID's strategy primarily because there were few examples of the success of other approaches: nobody could list the country-specific elements or development projects that were sure to be a more reasonable fertility reduction strategy than expansion of family planning services. So family planning prospered, while the experts complained and worried about what else to do.

Funds and worldwide interest in population and family planning increased during the 1970s, adding to the ease with which the Office of Population worked. The availability of money was particularly important. During the early days of its support for population control, AID had more money than sound projects—a trend that some people at AID thought continued into the 1970s. In 1973 one AID staffer concluded, "no reasonable, sensible project has yet been turned down for lack of funds. Our problem is less a shortage of funds than a shortage of ideas for new approaches to solving the population problem" (C. J., "Comments on Dr. Kieffer's memo," April 16, 1973, 286-79-0120). One result of the surplus of funds and the shortage of sound ideas was that AID and other international population donors sometimes fought over the best potential grantees. This is not an uncommon situation in development assistance, where there is sometimes an excess of resources available for specific projects or countries but only a small fraction of what is needed to really solve the development problems that the project is meant to address.

The 1972 formation of a Bureau of Population and Humanitarian Assistance is particularly important because it centralized all of AID's population activities and staff within a single organizational unit.

Before 1972, each of AID's four regional bureaus had had its own staff concerned with population and family planning programs. Because of the shortage of trained and experienced personnel, bureau staff varied widely in interest and ability. Two bureaus could and sometimes did fund the same institution for the same activity carried out in different countries or world regions. The Population Council, for example, had grants from different bureaus for the same activity in different regions. Because of the confusion, inefficiency, and cost of this haphazard and overlapping funding by different AID regional bureaus, the agency was encouraged by the auditor general to consolidate its population program (see FLS Audit Report 70-89, November 24, 1969, 286-73A-716). Centralizing all population activities also made the purchase of family planning commodities less cumbersome, as well as reflecting the unitary approach to population matters that was characteristic of AID—and, to a lesser extent, of the entire population field at the time. Some AID grantees, however, preferred the older organizational model, in part because no one person or office had complete control over their entire AID budget or program.

The reorganization greatly strengthened the ability of AID's population staff to implement their own programs. The Office of Population were the only people in the agency who had both line and staff responsibility. Unlike other technical staff at AID, population professionals not only provided advice at the request of regional bureaus, they also designed and implemented their own programs. This situation irritated personnel from the regional bureaus, who claimed that centrally funded and administered contracts were not meaningfully related to country programs.

Over time, the staff of the Office of Population remained confident that they knew the best way to slow rapid population growth in most developing countries. Others in the agency, however, objected vigorously to what they saw as the oversimplified policy prescription and the organizational disregard characteristic of the Office of Population. In 1975, for example, a special study was undertaken to review "alternative arrangements for carrying out the Agency's population/ family planning programs and for relating them to Agency health and nutrition activities" (Mann to Assistant Administrators, June 5, 1975, gift file). But no major changes in the organization of AID's population program were made until the early days of the administration of President Jimmy Carter.

The agency's population program was reorganized again in November 1977 when responsibility for the design, implementation, and monitoring of country-specific population activities was transferred to the regional bureaus. Technical offices within the newly established Bureau for Development Support had as their primary responsibility "to support Mission and Geographic Bureau development efforts . . ." (AID General Notice, November 16, 1977). The Office of Population continued to have significant responsibility for interregional programs, but bilateral population programs came under the jurisdiction of AID's regional bureaus, as did the staff who worked on them. The population office managed agency support to U.S. universities and population organizations, and to multinational groups such as the United Nations Fund for Population Activities and the International Planned Parenthood Federation; it also continued to control the purchase and distribution of commodities. The principal consequence of the 1977 reorganization was that the Office of Population lost veto power over the population and family planning activities supported by the regional bureaus.

Curbing the Enthusiasts

One of the most persistent adversaries of the Office of Population and its director, Dr. Ravenholt, was John H. Sullivan. Sullivan had served on the staff of Congressman Clement Zablocki, one of the legislators who worried most about American support for developing-country family planning programs. From 1977 to 1979 Sullivan was AID assistant administrator for Asia. During discussions of planned reorganization in the fall of 1977, a member of Sullivan's Asia Bureau staff drafted a memo to be sent by all four regional assistant administrators to Eugene N. Babb, the coordinator of the reorganization. The memo argued that "the approval of population projects and allotment of population funds for bilateral programs reside in regional bureaus—and not in the population office." The assistant administrators also wanted the administrator to rule that "no centrally funded, in-country activity would be approved without the positive approval of the regional bureaus" (Sullivan et al. to Babb, September 7, 1977, gift file). This was already the case in most respects because centrally funded in-country projects required mission approval. The response of the Office of Population staff was predictable. Carl J. Hemmer, chief of the office's policy division, saw it this way:

The draft memorandum that Jack Sullivan is currently circulating to the regional [assistant administrators] is a clear and simple effort to balkanize the . . . program . . . i.e., breaking the offending . . . parts into fragments which the regional bureaus can then digest. Sullivan's plan, if adopted, would eviscerate the central population unit. If its operation were confined, as proposed, to research and technical advisory services, [the Office of Population] would have little resemblance to an effective operational unit. It could think and suggest, but it couldn't do anything. (Hemmer to Ravenholt, September 14, 1977, gift file)

The Office of Population had the allegiance of a network of supporters who worried that the proposed reorganization would "weaken population programs both directly, by partially dismantling the Office of Population, and indirectly, by making conditions even less attractive for skilled professionals" (Piotrow, circular letter, November 28, 1977, gift file). Fifteen advocates of America's international population control effort—including Philander Claxton, former special assistant for population to the secretary of state; Richard Gamble, son of Clarence Gamble and an executive at the Pathfinder Fund; William McBeath, executive director of the American Public Health Association; and Jessma Blockwick, of the Population Department of the United Methodist Church—met with Sander Levin, assistant administrator of AID, and Eugene Babb, special assistant to the administrator for the reorganization, to express their concern about the impact of the changes in AID on America's international population program.

Congressman James H. Scheuer (Democrat–New York), chairman of the House Select Committee on Population and a long-time supporter of international population assistance, wrote to AID Administrator John Gilligan questioning whether the proposed reorganization reflected "a lessening of U.S. commitment to international population planning assistance" and a weakening of "the US ability to provide effective leadership and funding for international population activities" (Scheuer to Gilligan, December 6, 1977, gift file). Gilligan replied in a letter drafted by Levin and Babb saying he was "committed to broadening the scope of our population programs in order to increase demand for family planning services, improve their administrative implementation and interrelate them more effectively with other programs which affect fertility." Gilligan noted that administration support of population control would be shown "in a substantial increase in population funds. . . ." He also promised that "the Office of Population will continue to have a major role in the ultimate decisions on the country programs" (Gilligan to Scheuer, January 4, 1978, gift file).

The Population Crisis Committee (PCC) criticized the reorganization by attacking Administrator Gilligan's claim that too much of AID's program was focused on Washington or the capital cities of the developing world rather than on the rural areas. The decentralization of population activities was seen as one way to help remedy this situation by shaking up the status quo. To the extent possible, power was to be shifted away from Washington-based regional bureaus and the Office of Population to AID missions overseas. The Population Crisis Committee argued that reorganization would greatly diminish the role of AID's professional and technical staff and would result in less effective assistance being provided to the missions, and through them to country programs. Moreover, PCC complained that private organizations of the sort that had been so important in implementing population control programs would be neglected. Pure motives and a lack of self-interest became identified by PCC with functional programs. With larger missions, government agencies—not private groups—would receive most of the available U.S. government attention and support. PCC found that

> the much vaunted "collaborative style, decentralization of deci-
> sion-making, and the need for an integrated strategy in each
> recipient country" tends in practice to become a costly relation- ,
> ship between elitist officials in developing country governments
> and sympathetic staff in local AID Missions. All too often, as was
> the case in Vietnam, these officials all work together to make sure
> that no one rocks the boat or questions basic assumptions, and
> that the host country program is defended, right or wrong, effi-
> cient or costly, oriented toward the poor or not. In short, good
> relationships with the government become more important than
> good results with the people. (Population Crisis Committee, No-
> vember 23, 1977, "Comments on Task Force Report," gift file)

Some Office of Population staff took the unusual step of complaining directly to AID Administrator Gilligan about the proposed reorganization. William D. Bair, who had served as an AID population officer in Colombia before being assigned to Washington to coordinate population activities in Latin America and Africa, wrote to Gilligan saying, in part, "Some of us who have been around for quite some time and who, perhaps immodestly, believe they have been associated with successful program implementation over the years are beginning to think that experience with the Agency has become a . . . criterion for being suspect. We may indeed be 'overaged, overpaid and over here' but we are what you have." Bair went on to say he did "not believe all the reorganization proposals will be effective" ways to increase the responsibilities of AID missions overseas (Bair to Gilligan, November 25, 1977, gift file; see also Pedersen to Administrator, August 17, 1977, gift file).

The territory that was fought over in the war between the regional bureaus and the Office of Population was not just bureaucratic; it involved the power to design America's international population policy and to control the resources allocated to deal with the problem of rapid population growth. At stake was the nature and orientation of America's international population and family planning effort. Following the 1972 reorganization of AID's population program, the so-called functional statement of the Office of Population had made the office's director the chief architect of America's international population policy. According to the statement, the director "develops strategies and policies concerning the direction and content of the AID population/family planning programs" (Functional Statement for the Office of Population, 19-3, October 1, 1973, gift file). The 1978 revision of the statement drafted in conjunction with the new reorganization made the director's key function to "direct and supervise the activities of the component units of the multidisciplinary staff of [the Office of Population]" (McMakin, 1978, p. 1, gift file).

When Ravenholt reviewed the revised statement of his responsibilities, he fought to reinstate his policy-making prerogatives. In one memo to his boss, Assistant Administrator Sander Levin, Ravenholt described his view of the exchanges over the functional statements with characteristic overstatement: "To object to our voicing indignation over the grossly inappropriate way in which the functional statement has been prepared and handled rather than correcting the basic disorder is analogous to deprecating the screams of a woman being raped rather than protecting her from the assailant" (Ravenholt to Levin, March 15, 1978, gift file).

The Office of Population and the assistant administrator argued over the functional statement and over the far more important issue implicit in their skirmish—namely, who would run America's population program. The statement was revised to say that the Office of Population director would no longer develop strategies and policies but would "participate with the geographic bureaus, [the Bureau of Program and Policy Coordination,] and the Department of State in the development of strategies and policies concerning the direction and content of the AID population/family planning programs" (Thacker to Office Directors, April 26, 1978, gift file). Ravenholt tried to return to the original language, but to no avail—the version that diminished the office director's powers was put in force (Functional Statement for DS/Office of Population, May 1, 1978, gift file).

The role of the director was not the only issue that divided the Office of Population and the assistant administrator: also fought over were the personnel implications of the reorganization. Ravenholt and his colleagues were concerned that transfers of staff from the Office of Population to the regional bureaus would "seriously weaken our ability to effectively manage the population program" (Ravenholt to Levin, December 20, 1977, gift file). Of particular concern was the transfer of Randy Backlund, a long-time Ravenholt ally and a well-regarded Office of Population associate director (Ravenholt and Speidel to Levin and Joseph, August 18, 1978, gift file). The assistant administrator, for his part, claimed that Ravenholt exaggerated the likely impact of the personnel actions, saying he did not believe that "professional personnel transferred within AID/[Washington] represent a cut in technical numbers." Levin also reminded Ravenholt of the "difficult bind in which AID in general finds itself" with respect to personnel ceilings and the fact that large portions of AID's population funds were managed on a "wholesale rather than a retail basis" (Levin to Ravenholt, January 9, 1978, gift file).

Ravenholt stayed on as director of the reorganized Office of Population, but the jousting between him, Sullivan, and the other assistant administrators continued. In August 1979, John Sullivan wrote the administrator a memo entitled "The Smell of Burning Rubber," ironically using a report prepared by Steven Sinding, who would later become director of the Office of Population, as ammunition to shoot at Ravenholt. The Sullivan memo claimed that

> the *supply* mentality of the Office of Population as it has been run has resulted in huge inventories of contraceptives—pills and condoms—in recipient countries. Some of these inventories are reaching the end of their shelf life and must be destroyed. For example, the Nepal mission has just requested $50,000 to monitor the burning of condoms at various locations in the country. The Agency really has no alibi, since the [auditor general] has warned of excessive inventories for years. While we can't repeal the past, we can help prevent future such situations by maintaining the recently-completed delegation of population authorities to the regional bureaus. (Sullivan to the Administrator, August 9, 1979, gift file)

Sinding's thoughtful report (Sinding to Sullivan, August 3, 1979, gift file), which prompted Sullivan's memo, detailed the havoc wrought by Ravenholt's insistence that the aggressive promotion of contraceptives was the essential element for lowering fertility in the developing world. In Asia, where 75 percent of all AID-purchased contraceptives were sent, the problem was too many—not too few—contraceptives. In addition to the smell of burning rubber in Nepal, the AID mission in Bangladesh requested a moratorium on deliveries of oral contraceptives. The mission in the Philippines canceled a $6 million loan, in part because it had discovered at least three years' worth of contraceptives in storage. (The Philippines also wanted an outright grant, not a loan, to support population work.) Pakistan had the same problem, as unused supplies exceeded their shelf lives.

The contraceptive supply problem provides a useful illustration of how AID's family planning orientation influenced agency behavior. The Office of Population estimated the need for contraceptives based on mission requests for supplies. Each mission had responsibility for estimating country requirements, but the Washington Office of Population had the actual procurement responsibility. Sinding explains what happened in this way:

> Two factors conspired to lead to . . . a serious situation of . . . oversupply. . . . First, the Office of Population consistently pushed its "full supply analysis" throughout the decade of the seventies. . . . This form of analysis encouraged Missions to order orals and condoms under the most optimistic assumption about contraceptive usage rates. Second, because the Mission bore no budgetary responsibility for the contraceptives they ordered, there was no particular reason for them to resist the constant pressure from Washington to "program for success." (Sinding to Sullivan, August 23, 1979, gift file)

Jack Sullivan and other regional bureau staff were not the only ones who attacked the Office of Population's almost exclusive reliance on family planning as the best and most appropriate way to lower fertility. The Bureau for Program and Policy Coordination (PPC), responsible for agency-wide program planning, development, evaluation, and budgeting, was a consistent opponent of what it saw as the limited program of the Office of Population; the bureau provided leadership within AID for the view that more attention had to be paid to "the interdependent variables which influence the cost and consequences of demographic change as related to economic and social and political development and find and carry out more suitable strategies to encourage and facilitate the [less] [developed] [countries] in their efforts to program and wisely invest their scarce resources in this regard" (Schuweiller to Stern, May 8, 1970, 286-73A-716). As early as 1970, PPC staff viewed the need for their participation in program design and review as especially important because, in the words of one bureau staffer, it had become "particularly apparent several years ago when it was found that the leadership for population programs within AID was strongly of the opinion that success in this field depended primarily upon extending the availability of appropriate contraceptives and educating people in their use throughout the LDCs [less-developed countries]. A second school of thought . . . took the position that while the availability of appropriate contraceptives was essential, this factor by itself would not be sufficient to bring about a reduction in population growth to desired level" (Schuweiller to Stern, May 8, 1970, 286-73A-716).

Ravenholt was said to be strongly opposed to research on the determinants of fertility. (After all, Ravenholt knew what determined fertility.) Policy and Program Coordination Bureau staff noted that one request for funding for fertility-related research "was approved by the Administrator over the central population service director's objections after being unanimously recommended by AID's outside research advisory panel of experts." What was PPC's alternative? "[F]ind and carry out more suitable strategies. . . ." This solution demonstrates the problem of those who would diminish the commitment to family planning. There were few alternative programs. The PPC Bureau was also unhappy about the "tendencies on the part of the population program leadership within the central office to concentrate more or less exclusively on internal organizational problems and centrally funded program development potentials relating to family planning to the neglect of most if not all of the aspects of the broader problem, including and in particular country-program development" (Schuweiller to Stern, May 8, 1970, 286-73A-716).

The End of an Era

Throughout the Carter administration, Ravenholt had trouble with the leadership of the agency—especially with Assistant Administrator Sander Levin, who had been appointed after being defeated in an effort to become governor of Michigan. (At this writing, he is a congressman from the state.) Ravenholt and his friends insist that Levin came to AID with orders to get rid of him, a charge that Levin denies. Assistant Administrator Sullivan, whom Ravenholt accuses of being part of the cabal that was set up to "get" him, probably comes closest to describing both the motives and the aspirations of the agency's leadership with respect to Ravenholt: "[H]e was too strong. . . . I wanted when I went in there to take Rei and do like the Lilliputians and Gulliver. I was going to pin him down with a thousand little pieces of string . . . and keep him pinned to the earth. I didn't want, didn't think we could get rid of him. I just wanted to slap him into these bureaucratic modes until he got like a cage and not let him do what he wanted to do. . . . I had one mandate; it was a self-mandate and it was to get those population programs into the regional bureaus. . . . That would take care of Rei" (author's interview).

Sullivan's use of "mandate" to describe his position at the start of his tenure at AID suggests at a minimum that he and his colleagues had talked about how to control Ravenholt. Sullivan's mentor and supporter, Congressman Zablocki, had made known his opposition to Ravenholt several times, including once during hearings of the House International Relations Committee (1975) when he and right-to-life supporter and extremist opponent of family planning Randy Engel had the following exchange, which Ravenholt quotes as proof of the congressman's bias:

> *Mr. Zablocki*: "I am sure you will agree that Dr. Ravenholt is the wrong person to administer this particular program."
> *Mr. Engel*: "Most certainly."
> *Mr. Zablocki*: "I would hope we could find a way of removing him."

In addition to deeply rooted policy differences, part of Levin's and Sullivan's eagerness to sharply circumscribe Ravenholt and the Office of Population was their desire to exercise stronger control over the office's resources. Levin's portfolio was smaller than that of other assistant administrators, and over 60 percent of his budget supported population activities. As an ambitious manager who genuinely cared about population and was worried about the supply-side orientation of the Office of Population, he had to tame Ravenholt in order to get control of AID's population and family planning activities.

Ravenholt suggests that the trouble began almost immediately after Levin joined AID. He claims that "[w]ithin a few days of the time he commenced work as assistant administrator (March 18, 1977), it became evident Mr. Levin had a hidden agenda. . . . Almost immediately following his confirmation by the Congress (May 25, 1977) . . . Levin [on June 4, 1977] requested that I vacate my position as Director of the Office of Population and 'move on to another challenge' " (Ravenholt to Population Colleagues, June 2, 1980). He says that Levin mentioned no specific shortcomings but cited differences in policy.

Ravenholt's account fails to mention one incident that especially irritated Levin, Sullivan, and their colleagues. In late April 1977, shortly after Levin's appointment, Ravenholt attended the annual meeting of the Population Association of America, the professional association of American demographers, which was held in St. Louis. The April 22 *St. Louis Post-Dispatch* carried a page-one report of an interview with Ravenholt under the headline, "U.S. Goal: Sterilize Millions of World's Women" (Wagman 1977). Ravenholt's statement contained about equal measures of the thoughtful and the reckless. The article noted that the U.S. government was assisting developing countries to increase voluntary sterilization (including by training physicians at St. Louis's Washington University—a program that had already caused some controversy in the city). Ravenholt suggested that AID support could conceivably provide the means by which one-quarter of all fertile women in the world would become sterilized. He based his estimate on the fact that in countries such as the United States and India, where sterilization was safe and easily available, about 25 percent of all married women obtain the procedure.

Although perhaps imprudent, Ravenholt's description of his own program was reasonable enough. It was his analysis of the reasons for this policy that most irritated his superiors at AID and confirmed their impression that he was a loose cannon on the deck of the ship of state. Ravenholt cited four reasons for the American government's eagerness to promote sterilization. First, a decline in population growth in poor countries would increase their standard of living. Second, because the United States had helped to lower death rates and, thus, contributed to causing such rapid population growth in the first place, it had an obligation to help lower the birth rate. So far, so good. But Ravenholt was then quoted as saying that population control is needed to maintain "the normal operation of U.S. commercial interests around the world. . . . Without our trying to help these countries with their economic and social development, the world would rebel against strong U.S. commercial presence. . . . The self-interest thing is a compelling element" (Wagman 1977, p. 6). As a fourth reason, Ravenholt added the threat of revolutions potentially harmful to the United States being brought about because of deteriorating socioeconomic conditions caused by very rapid population growth.

Reading this account, Levin was furious. According to him, "The article brought to a new Administration a barrage of protest from members of Congress, letters from the public and coverage by the press in other parts of the world" (Levin, notes, no date, p. 23, gift file). Most people thought the article fairly represented what Ravenholt had told the reporter. The chancellor of Washington University in St. Louis wrote Secretary of State Cyrus Vance to endorse the accuracy of the *Post-Dispatch* story and to complain about what he termed the "inconceivable" policy Ravenholt was advertising. Ravenholt himself wrote the newspaper saying his views and those of AID's population control program had been distorted.

Throughout the spring and summer of 1977, Ravenholt and Levin continued sparring. Twice Levin asked for Ravenholt's resignation. In late August Ravenholt "brought Mr. Levin's demands to the attention of Administrator Gilligan . . . [who] stated that he supported Mr. Levin" (Ravenholt to Population Colleagues, June 2, 1980, p. 15). Levin tried again to get Ravenholt to leave his position in September. Having failed, he moved officially to dismiss Ravenholt with a formal letter of an adverse action dated October 25, 1977. The letter charged that Ravenholt was unsuited for the position of director of the Office of Population and had demonstrated his lack of suitability on numerous previous occasions. Among other things, the charges allegedly included an intemperate letter written by Ravenholt to Imelda Marcos, wife of Philippine President Ferdinand Marcos, regarding her failure to improve the Philippine family planning program of which she was nominally chief executive, and an episode in Ravenholt's office during which he called Egyptian demographer Saad Gadalla "a dumb shit" for his contribution to the failure of fertility control in Egypt. Also presented were the more important professional issues, such as Ravenholt's steadfast refusal to take non–family planning activities seriously as a means to lower fertility, or his support for targets for contraceptive prevalence in developing countries (the *St. Louis Post-Dispatch* had mentioned "as many as 100 million"). Ravenholt himself never circulated the letter detailing the charges against him very widely, although he has distributed commentaries on his undoing that refer to the charges as "assertions and allegations of minor misstatements and policy differences." (As part of the settlement eventually agreed to by Ravenholt and the Agency for International Development, the letter of charges and the record of hearings have been sealed.)

On February 28, 1979, after two years of trying to get him to resign voluntarily or to get rid of him by making his life uncomfortable, Levin formally moved to demote Ravenholt. Ravenholt protested to Gilligan's replacement, Acting Administrator Robert Nooter, but Nooter upheld Levin's action. On July 2, 1979, Nooter told Ravenholt: "you are demoted from the position of Director, Office of Population, GS-18, step 1, salary $47,500 per annum to Supervisory Population Advisor, Office of Population, GS-15, salary $47,500 per annum" (Nooter to Ravenholt, July 2, 1979, cited in Ravenholt to Population Colleagues, June 2, 1980, p. 10). Ravenholt became chief of the Office of Population's Training Division, and J. Joseph Speidel, deputy director of the office, became its acting director.

Sander Levin, who finally got rid of Ravenholt after others had tried and failed, says: "He had to go. We had a policy. He was bitterly opposed to it. Rei's basic view was that he made policy. . . . When I came to the agency . . . people would attack U.S. policy. Whether it was the Scandinavians, Third World countries, or Western Europeans, everybody had moved away beyond Rei, had come to the conclusion that programs had to be country-specific, that the problem wasn't simple. . . . The agency was four to five years behind implementing what it had already decreed" (author's interview).

Ravenholt appealed Nooter's decision to the Merit System Protection Board. In time, his attorney and AID's lawyers were able to work out an agreement whereby he was detailed to the Centers for Disease Control, where a former student and collaborator, William Foege, was director. Ravenholt was named director of something known as the World Health Surveys—an unfunded and, as yet, unimplemented worldwide survey of health conditions. In 1982, he transferred to the National Institute on Drug Abuse as assistant director for epidemiology, research, and analysis. In 1984, he moved to the Food and Drug Administration. For a time, he was treated as a hot potato by the federal health bureaucracy. He resigned from the civil service in 1987 and moved to Seattle.

Dr. J. Jarrett Clinton, the former Asia representative of the Population Council and onetime AID population officer in Jakarta, was appointed agency director for health and population. Clinton was at AID for less than a year before moving to the National Institute on Drug Abuse. He was replaced by former Arizona Commissioner of Health James Sarn. The Reagan administration made it clear they would never name Speidel director of the Office of Population, even though he had served since Ravenholt's departure as acting director; so after fourteen years at AID, including four as acting director of the Office of Population, Speidel, too, left the agency. He was replaced by political scientist Steven Sinding, who had served in AID missions in Pakistan and the Philippines.

The Office of Population remained strong largely because there was no broadly supported alternative program to compete with the increasingly well argued case that providing easy accessibility to a range of contraceptive services was an essential first step in any public policy aimed at reducing fertility and lowering population growth. Although the supply-side orientation of the office sometimes led to inefficient management, Office of Population staff could say they were trying to reduce fertility in the quickest, most direct, most acceptable, and least costly way possible. Certainly, there were logistic or bureaucratic problems from time to time—but there was no more appropriate overall approach for the population program of the United States government to take in its effort to slow growth in the developing world.

The International Development Cooperation Administration

The population staff at AID were busy throughout almost all of 1978 with the agency's reorganization. When Administrator Gilligan announced that AID would be reorganized in November 1977, he left most personnel decisions as well as numerous program-related details to be sorted out by his subordinates. In addition to the changes in the Office of Population, another change was taking a great deal of the population staff's time.

In an address to the Venezuelan Congress in March 1978, President Carter announced plans to create a Foundation for International Technological Cooperation (FITC). Carter appointed his science advisor, Frank Press, to work out the details of the foundation. Press's planning office reported to AID Administrator Gilligan in his role as the president's chief advisor on development policy. The first discussions of the new foundation envisioned the transfer to it of a significant share of the Office of Population's research program. Indeed, population activities represented the largest single category of projects targeted for transfer to the new organization (Press to Gilligan, June 14, 1978, gift file).

While Ravenholt and his colleagues were being threatened from within AID because they were too centralized and single-minded, they had to defend their program against the new development agency's supporters, who thought further distance from specific country and operational activities would help "attract more high-quality persons to the tasks of development" (Discussion Paper, Office of Science and Technology Policy Advisory Committee on Science, Technology, and Development, September 7–8, 1978, p. 10, gift file).

The research foundation was planned as a key unit of the newly proposed International Development Cooperation Administration (IDCA), which was to centralize all U.S. government foreign aid activity. Zbigniew Brzezinski sent a memo to senior Carter administration officials outlining the president's proposal: the administrator of IDCA would replace the AID administrator as the chief development advisor to the president and the secretary of state, and would become the executive branch's spokesman in Congress on development assistance. Although the new IDCA administrator was supposed to report to both the secretary of state and the president, Brzezinski said:

> the Secretary of State will not instruct the Administrator as to how much development and/or PL-480 aid should be given to a particular country to meet short-term foreign policy needs; he will provide the Administrator general foreign policy guidance, while respecting the development purposes of IDCA programs, and he will instruct the Administrator how to allocate security supporting assistance. The Administrator will submit his budget through the Secretary of State; any differences between the Secretary and the Administrator will be resolved by the President. (Brzezinski to the Vice President, April 28, 1978, gift file)

Brzezinski saw the purpose of the Foundation for Technological Collaboration as improving "U.S. support for private and public research, in the U.S. and LDCs, on problems of concern to developing countries." The administration also proposed establishing "an International Development Service within IDCA to support private voluntary organizations that assist less developed countries." Brzezinski told his colleagues they "should support transfer of the Peace Corps to IDCA . . . provided this can be done on terms that preserve the Peace Corps' special mission and identity." Brzezinski also said, "The Executive Branch should support the transfer of the overseas Private Investment Corporation to the IDCA."

Carter's plan was to move toward the universal fulfillment of basic human needs by providing U.S. development assistance for a relatively small number of programs considered fundamental to human welfare—food, health, population, and education being among the most important. No longer would AID concentrate primarily on infrastructure development. Dams, roads, and electrical power stations would take a back seat to schools, hospitals, and family planning clinics. Even in this new climate, however, Brzezinski still made the point that "the Executive Branch should seek to ensure that none of the aid changes interfere with on-going security assistance programs."

The executive secretary of AID drafted a memo for the administrator on how the agency was implementing the Brzezinski memo. On his copy, Ravenholt underlined the Foundation for Technical Collaboration in red and noted, "Here's where POP will probably go" (Newton to the Administrator, May 8, 1978, gift file). Ravenholt and his lieutenants then began to try to get the best deal possible for the Office of Population. In this battle they were supported by Levin and other senior staff, because AID would lose control of any resources transferred to the new agency.

From the start, population staff were concerned about the new foundation. In early January 1978, months before public announcement of the plan, Dr. Joseph Speidel, deputy director of the Office of Population, wrote to Ravenholt saying the goal of improving the application of science and technology to development problems was important, but "the currently proposed [Foundation for International Technological Cooperation] is seriously flawed." Speidel saw the foundation weakening AID, and further saw little reason to believe that it would be more successful in implementing research than AID was. Indeed, because the foundation staff would work independently from program people, he thought that "the scientific endeavors will likely wander off into academic pursuits . . . AID will be further weakened because what little scientific and technical capacity it now has will be largely siphoned off to the new [foundation]." In addition, Speidel argued that "any new organization would be beset with many of AID's current problems" (Speidel to Ravenholt, January 9, 1978, gift file).

Six months later, Ravenholt wrote AID's new administrator, George Wing: "Having not yet recovered from the reorganization of December 1977, which dispersed responsibility for bilateral population program assistance to the Geographic Bureaus, we view this latest proposal for future dispersal of population program responsibilities and resources with serious concern. . . . A plethora of historical experiences validates the fundamental principal that when moving to accomplish a chosen mission . . . one must concentrate on available resources and place them under unified command." Ravenholt reasoned that "the exceptional vigor of the population program generated a disequilibrium within AID which no doubt contributed to the decision to disperse responsibilities and authorities for this program and thereby 'normalize' programs within AID. Unfortunately, the 'normal' programs within AID operate at very low efficiency because of the lack of unified structure and therewith lack of well recognized leadership and clear strategy" (Ravenholt to Wing, July 13, 1978, gift file).

About the time that Ravenholt was complaining to Administrator Wing, those charged with planning for the new foundation were wondering just why they were needed and what exactly they were going to do. Princeton Lyman, for example, wrote to Ralph Smuckler, head of the Planning Office for the foundation, saying: "we need to address specifically why a new relatively autonomous institution is necessary. . . . what unique contribution can such a new institution make. While all the papers on FITC assume a foundation can do certain things better, the rationale for this view has never been spelled out very explicitly, particularly in terms of the advantages compared to the disadvantages, and in specific relationship to overall development policy. . . . Perhaps no other basic point . . . needs so much further clarification among ourselves" (Lyman to Smuckler, July 11, 1978, gift file).

The foundation's planning office issued a draft plan in October 1978 and a revised plan the following December. An interesting characteristic of the discussions about population in these documents is the absence of national security as a justification for the American support of efforts to control population growth. Instead, the plan notes that "sustained, rapid population growth rates adversely affect the quality of life of individuals, families, communities and nations, and they negate or impede efforts to improve well being in many areas." The plan also took a moderate, middle-of-the-road approach to the impact of family planning programs on population growth:

> In many parts of the world, family planning has helped to bring birth rates down substantially, and continued activities along these lines are amply justified. In other regions, however, in spite of intensive effort and great cost, little effect can be discerned. Indeed, . . . some people insist that family planning can only follow development, not facilitate it. The dichotomy, however, is artificial: FITC will operate with the recognition that both approaches—promoting family planning to accelerate development and accelerating development to promote family planning—are appropriate and mutually reinforcing. (FITC Plan, October 13, 1978, pp. 35–36, gift file)

Discussion of the proposed Foundation for International Technological Cooperation, renamed the Institute for Scientific and Technological Cooperation (ISTC), continued into 1979 (see Gillespie to Speidel, July 25, 1979, gift file, which reviews two position papers by Lyman [May 24, 1979, and July 2, 1979] and another by Farrar [May 15, 1979]). In October 1979 a new AID administrator, Douglas Bennet, wrote to Princeton Lyman, by now the acting director of the institute's planning office, telling him to terminate planning for the institute because legislation passed in the Senate as part of the fiscal 1980 appropriation prohibited the use of funds to plan for the institute (Bennet to Lyman, October 15, 1979, gift file).

By January 1980, staff work on proposed ISTC programs in science and technology to be used in conjunction with the president's budget request for fiscal year 1981 had to be approved by the AID general counsel (see McLean to Ehrlich, January 3, 1980; Ehrlich to Bennet, January 4, 1980; Bennet to Hawkins and Levin, January 9, 1980, gift file). The AID staff, especially those concerned about population, continued to worry about the impact of the institute on their program. In the view of AID, the 1980 ISTC congressional presentation continued to highlight research activities whose main characteristic was their overlap with things AID was already doing. One AID senior official wrote, "The vast bulk of the presentation is made up of AID transfer projects and items which are very close in kind to what AID has traditionally supported under the rubric of operational or applied research" (Babb to Sidman, February 6, 1980, gift file).

Preoccupied with the hostage crisis in Iran, the reelection campaign, high interest rates, and other problems, and without strong support in Congress or elsewhere, the Carter administration did not push IDCA. President Reagan, for his part, let it die—almost. The *Washington Post* refers to the International Development Cooperation Administration as "the ghost ship of the federal bureaucracy. . . . It has no funds nor separate staff nor even a telephone number of its own." The AID administrator serves as acting director of IDCA, which exists, according to an official quoted by the *Post*, because "to abolish IDCA would involve a lot of bureaucratic and legislative problems. So the simple thing for the administration is to leave it there on paper and just ignore it" (Goshko 1984, p. A15).

The International Development Cooperation Administration provides a useful case study of how hard it can be to accomplish something in the giant federal bureaucracy even when the president himself stands behind the idea, as Carter stood behind a reorganized development assistance program. Ravenholt understood this. He and the Office of Population benefited from the hard work and support of allies in Congress, in the universities, in nonprofit groups, among his staff, and the public at large. All AID gave Ravenholt when he first joined was "a niche to operate from—to begin to do battle with all the other territorial guardians in the agency—to get a piece of something that would be sufficient to do something" (author's interview). Ravenholt tried to make the most of the opportunities to do battle that his position at AID presented. In a sense, he was a casualty in the war against rapid population growth. But before he left AID, he won most of his battles. His point of view on what it takes to slow population growth remains dominant at AID.

6

A Report Card for Ravenholt

Of all the men and women (it was mostly men) who became involved in America's effort to slow population growth in the developing world, no one better represents the bullish American certitude that we knew how to solve the problem of rapid population growth than Reimert Thorolf Ravenholt.

Ravenholt was born in Milltown, Wisconsin, in March 1925, the grandson of Danish immigrants who came to Wisconsin in the 1880s. The senior Ravenholts had ten children, including two sets of twins. The family was and remains close. Reimert, known as Rei (pronounced "Ray," a variant Ravenholt used for several years; see Ravenholt to Corfman, June 7, 1970, 286-73A-314), remembers particularly the Great Depression and the 1930s when his family "suffered severely." His father lost the farm to foreclosure in 1935 and was able to keep only a few head of livestock. But the Ravenholts' problems were never said to be caused or compounded by the large family—"the scoundrels in Washington," yes, and the weather, and a host of other individuals, groups, events, and trends, but never the children. Too many children, in the senior Ravenholts' view, did not make one poor (author's interview).

Reimert Ravenholt did his undergraduate work at the University of Minnesota and received his medical degree there in 1952. He began a career in public health at a time when Americans worried more about infectious diseases than about cancer and heart attacks. Polio, influenza, diphtheria, and typhoid were still much feared. Mass inoculations were being used in an effort to control their spread.

Ravenholt joined the Public Health Service, serving first as an intern in the Public Health Service Hospital in San Francisco and then as an epidemic intelligence officer in Muskingum County, Ohio, where he was working when the *Saturday Evening Post* decided to do a piece on the "Disease Detectives." The magazine was unsure of how best to illustrate the work being done by the "U.S. germ sleuths" who worked under Dr. Alexander Langmuir, chief of the Epidemiology Branch of the Public Health Service's Communicable Disease Center, to save America "from the age-old horror of plague." Photographer Harry Saltzman was dispatched to Muskingum to take some pictures. In May 1953 the *Post* appeared with an article on the Epidemic Intelligence Service (EIS), featuring the young Dr. Ravenholt, a new EIS recruit on his first important field assignment. The article was an illustration of America's problem-solving ability. Ravenholt was shown giving the youngsters of Muskingum County gamma globulin to prevent infectious hepatitis (Brecher and Brecher 1953). What was not clear from the article was that Ravenholt had taken it upon himself to stage the pictures, because the *Post* photographer was unsure of how to portray the program.

In 1954, after a year with the Ohio Department of Health, Ravenholt transferred to the Seattle King County Health Department, where he became director of the Communicable Disease Division. He preferred epidemiology and public health to the more personal approach of clinical practice "because the reactions of individuals are infinitely varied and difficult to predict. That's the bane of clinical practice . . . you are dealing with individuals; you have to treat individuals. In contrast, reactions to a certain medication in populations are very predictable. When you're dealing with a population you can actually be scientific. . . . One can calculate, if you give *this* to a million people, what will happen" (author's interview). Ravenholt spent six years with the King County health department. His wife and four children enjoyed Seattle; he remembers it as "a very good time." In 1955, he spent a year at Berkeley, where he earned a master's degree in public health at the University of California. In 1961, the family moved to Paris, where Ravenholt served for two years as a consultant in epidemiology in the U.S. Public Health Service's European region.

While in Paris, Ravenholt decided not to return to the county health department but to accept an offer from the University of Washington in Seattle, where he had been a part-time faculty member before going to Europe. In 1963 he joined the medical school's Department of Preventive Medicine, where he was to focus mainly on research and teaching of the epidemiology of chronic disease. Problems began almost immediately.

Soon after his return to Seattle, Ravenholt began to study the relationship between cigarette smoking and cancer, resuming work he had begun before going to Europe, and producing a steady stream of papers. He developed a simple method for charting lifetime smoking experiences (Ravenholt and Applegate 1965); he estimated smoking-related mortality in the United States (Ravenholt 1964); he studied the relationship between smoking and school performance (Johnson et al. 1965); and he analyzed the effects of smoking on reproduction (Ravenholt et al. 1966).

As he researched the effects of smoking on health, Ravenholt reported his findings and proclaimed the dangers of smoking, not only in scientific journals, but also to the Seattle news media—much as he had done while directing communicable disease control activities at the health department. County health officials had allowed him to keep himself in the public eye because it kept health department programs before the city council and helped obtain extra funding for department activities. However, even though he remained a productive scientist, Ravenholt's superiors at the medical school were not pleased by his appearances in local newspapers or his militancy about the dangers of smoking.

In addition to his research on smoking, Ravenholt was also trying to develop his concept of malignant cellular evolution, an application of evolutionary principles to the understanding and the prevention of cancer. He had begun working on this concept while a medical student at the University of Minnesota, and had resumed work on it in a term paper he prepared while at Berkeley. Responding to an invitation from the American Cancer Society, he wrote a paper for presentation at a Cancer Society meeting in Palm Beach, Florida. But when Ravenholt showed a draft to his department chairman, the chairman refused to approve it for presentation and then left on a trip. After some maneuvering, Ravenholt made the presentation, leading to the disaffection of the chairman. He then sent a version of his paper to the prestigious journal *Science* without first clearing the submission with the chairman, a standard requirement at the time. The chairman was unhappy, especially so since several other faculty members thought the piece seriously flawed. The antismoking campaign had soured Ravenholt's colleagues, who wanted a gentlemanly approach to public health. Ravenholt's battle with the chairman left him without a planned-for raise in early 1965. In October, he went to the annual meeting of the American Public Health Association in Chicago, discouraged by the hard time he was having in Seattle.

In Chicago, Ravenholt complained to Ernie Tierkel, whom he knew from the Public Health Service and who was then deputy director of the Agency for International Development's Health Service. Tierkel told him that AID was beginning a population program and looking for a director. Malcolm Merrill, who was about to leave his position as director of the California Department of Health to go to Washington as Tierkel's boss, was also in Chicago and interested in having

Ravenholt join AID. In November, Ravenholt went to Washington to consider the job but was "very reluctant to leave Seattle." Sitting in the White House personnel office, he was "put off by the hurry scurry" and "made a firm decision, 'I didn't want it.'" His brother, Eiler, had moved to Washington with Hubert Humphrey in 1962 and was, in 1965, a special assistant to the vice-president; but that did not help. Ravenholt returned to Seattle ready to try again with the chairman (author's interview).

When he returned from his interviews in Washington Ravenholt realized that "the situation with the chairman was not going to be a happy one." Weighing heavily in the balance with respect to career choices was the fate of his paper on malignant cellular evolution. Implant experiments in mice had produced cancer just as he had predicted and wagered with a colleague; but his paper on the topic had been rejected by *Science*, and the British medical journal *Lancet* did not immediately accept the same paper. Altogether, it was a very frustrating time. Ravenholt began to feel that "if [he] stayed in Seattle, [he] would be drawing a high-water mark to [his] career." He also began to notice the population problem for the first time and to see the potential of AID's program and how he personally could play a key role in the new venture. Before then, he had "never thought about population per se." After his visit to Washington, however, he "became aware population growth was one of the great issues of our time." Throughout the Christmas holidays he wondered, "Should I or shouldn't I?" He demanded and got an appointment at the highest civil service level. In early January 1966, Ravenholt made "the hardest decision of [his] life." His oldest daughter broke into tears when he announced that the family was moving to Washington (author's interview).

The population program that Ravenholt officially joined in April 1966 had "no staff, no money, and no program." Moreover, Ravenholt had few of the bureaucratic skills the new job required. Throughout the first year at AID, he thought often about returning to Seattle: "Jesus, what in the world have I done to myself. I couldn't believe that I could have been so stupid, coming into that pressure cooker. I didn't have the tools to work with." His cancer article was finally published in the *Lancet* (Ravenholt 1966); if the article had been accepted a few months earlier, Ravenholt claims he would have stayed in Seattle and continued his research on cancer and smoking. He wanted to leave AID: "If I could have easily vacated that job, I would have done so, but my pride was at stake . . . and I didn't think that with any sort of honor I could jump ship and go back to Seattle" (author's interview).

Ravenholt did not acquire the bureaucrat's skills at AID. Indeed, both his successes and his failures while there were rooted in a style alien to bureaucracies. Curtis Farrar once accused him of making "a legitimate difference of opinion about the most effective means of pursuing population control objectives look like an apparent conspiracy to evade the will of Congress" (Farrar to Ravenholt, November 3, 1975, 286-79-024). Ravenholt could, quite literally, "turn a technical problem into a fist fight." Gerald Bowers, one of AID's best population officers and to this day one of Ravenholt's staunchest admirers, remembers such an incident. Ravenholt charged into Bowers's office furious about a report Bowers had prepared on new agency regulations governing support for female sterilization services. Ravenholt's screaming at very close range and his flailing arms made Bowers wish he were able to crawl to safety through his desk's keyhole (author's interview).

The ability to intimidate others physically accounts for a measure of Ravenholt's considerable influence. And it wasn't all threats. Oscar Harkavy, long-time head of the Ford Foundation's population program, recalls a shoving match between Ravenholt and the then–director general of the World Health Organization, Halfdan Mahler. The former head of the Office of Population's research division says Ravenholt once slugged him because a study "didn't turn out the way he thought it should" (author's interview).

Ravenholt's threats were aided by his appearance. He is 6 feet 3 inches tall and weighs 205 pounds. He has an edge of wildness or match-me-if-you-dare mischievousness. His wiry hair is usually not combed. His eyes, mouth, and teeth are small and seem out of proportion to the rest of him; he squints his eyes almost to closing, at times, when he talks. His wardrobe is tweedy, but he appears more like the novelist Thomas Wolfe early in a binge than a college professor ready to discuss one of Wolfe's novels.

The Judgment of His Peers

It may be unfair to dissect the career of a single civil servant as a means of examining American foreign policy, even if that civil servant actively courted controversy and publicity. Why should Reimert T. Ravenholt get a report card? Over the years, his performance was reviewed by his superiors at AID, by congressional committees, and by evaluation teams from several federal agencies. Their judgments are scattered throughout this book.

When asked individually what they think of Ravenholt, his professional colleagues give him high marks, although none fails to mention the Achilles heel of his argumentative and self-centered certainty. He is a person of great energy who worked long hours to improve family planning services and promote population control. He provided direction and set clear goals in a giant federal bureaucracy where too many people lack a clear strategic view and fail to stand up for what they believe is the right or best way to do things. He focused attention on the problem of rapid population growth and argued for controlling fertility in a way that more and more people have come to believe is the most humane and sensible. Single-minded to the point of blindness, his program allowed no middle ground. Contraceptive availability was all-important. When increasing the supply of contraceptives alone did not lower fertility—and it did not, say, in Pakistan—he had nothing else to offer. He could not deal with failure or shortfalls because he was always sure his way would work.

One is able to pick apart Ravenholt's program because of another of his strengths. He was a researcher who believed in evaluating what he was doing. He thought the evidence would show the correctness of his point of view, and he supported numerous research studies that produced much of the evidence on which this and many other studies of population and family planning programs are based. One of his former colleagues says, "He . . . believed that the data were always there to support his contention. . . . He knew he was right so there had to be some data there somewhere" (author's interview).

Ravenholt was not a nice person by conventional standards because he was always too certain of himself and his mission. His sexist ways offended many of his colleagues—particularly, of course, the women with whom he and AID worked (author's interviews). Moreover, he was a bully. Well-known family planning advocates Margaret Sanger and Marie Stopes had similar traits: David M. Kennedy says Sanger "loved combat" (1970, p. 271), and Richard Soloway calls Stopes "compulsively belligerent" (1982, p. 220)—an apt description of Ravenholt as well. Philander Claxton thinks that if Ravenholt had been less scornful toward those he disagreed with, he might not have been criticized so much (author's interview). But his former deputy at AID, Joe Speidel, says Ravenholt "thrived on conflict. If there wasn't something to fight about, sometimes he made up something. He'd beat people just to see the cut of their jib, to see how they react" (author's interview).

As America moved to control population growth around the world, Ravenholt exerted great personal authority because there was no preexisting office or program that could be drawn upon. For a period, he was the embodiment of the American government's population control movement. But as the U.S. effort to control growth became institutionalized, Ravenholt was no longer needed. He wanted to run things on his own, not to share power—and successful institutionalization requires the sharing of power. Speidel notes, "Rei was not a company man. . . . An agency like AID will tolerate incompetence . . . but you can't make waves" (author's interview). Duff Gillespie sums up Ravenholt's style this way: "He wanted to control the program; . . . he wanted to orchestrate the resources. If he involved other organizational units within AID or outside, at best he would have to take into consideration their approaches to the population problem. At worst he would have been eaten up. So he wanted to have solitary leadership. . . . As his basic approach became accepted, he still had that hesitancy, that distrust, that distaste of working with other organizations" (author's interview). Gillespie, who in time would himself become director of AID's population program, says he would not have wanted to have Ravenholt as a member of his staff. As Gillespie sees it, there was no advantage to Ravenholt's staying at AID.

What one does best, one also tends to do to excess. Ravenholt was a genius at promoting his programs. The Ford Foundation's Oscar Harkavy credits Ravenholt's "General Grant kind of doggedness" with "driving the ribbon clerks out of the business" of population control (author's interview). But being too aggressive in promoting a particular view of population control also brought Ravenholt his most serious problems. His friends claim, "He could insult, abuse, misuse, and yet . . . invoke a tremendous respect and loyalty" (author's interview). Others who were less close to him personally, and who did not share the siege mentality and thus the solidarity he engendered within AID's population group, found him offensive and thought that his militant promotion of his way to spread effective fertility control yielded at best mixed results and was frequently downright counterproductive.

Leona Baumgartner, who played a crucial role in encouraging AID's nascent interest in the problem of rapid population growth as agency assistant administrator between 1962 and 1965, concluded that Ravenholt and AID were frequently too aggressive: "I think if we hadn't pushed as hard, there would have been better success. . . . Take India . . . he pushed for sterilization . . . all those camps all over. . . . My God, they were horrible. I think he pushed too fast, too hard" (author's interview). David Bell, AID administrator during the program's early days, sounds a similar theme: "If we had found a strong person, but one who would have developed a much broader and a more effective program . . . the world would be better off, AID would be better off, and all these millions of dollars would have been better spent." Bell claims Ravenholt's "simple-minded overkill characteristics" made his tenure mixed. He goes on: "I was increasingly disappointed with the sort of 'Johnny one note' approach that AID increasingly seems to have in two senses. First, Rei's heavy attention to shoveling out contraceptives, and [second] his inattention to building local competence to analyze and understand. . . . It seemed to me splendid that AID moved on vigorously in the population field, but the way they did it seemed to me ham-handed and frequently counterproductive" (author's interview).

Others saw the same problems. One Population Council observer thought, "Ravenholt was a problem because of his hobby-horsing . . . he unduly influenced what was going on in the field" (author's interview). David Bell speaks for the majority of those who were active in the American effort to control the growth of the developing world. When asked if Ravenholt did more good than harm, Bell replied: "I certainly think the answer is yes . . . for Ravenholt and for Draper. But it's also true that both of them left lots and lots of scars and antipathy. Ideally it wouldn't have been necessary to leave that much breakage" (author's interview).

Like Bell, most observers credit Ravenholt with a series of extraordinary accomplishments. The program that he directed was straightforward to the point of narrowness, but its goals were clear, its budget was under control, and its progress was evaluated. All but his bitterest critics would probably agree with Ravenholt's own assessment of his achievement at AID: "Let's face it, the government sets out to do many programs and only a minority actually succeed to the extent that was desired or anticipated. I think probably the most important contribution we made [was] that we created a program . . . that actually worked . . . along the direction the president, the Congress, and the people actually wanted. We got effective assistance to a very large number of countries in a sensitive field during some difficult years" (author's interview).

A more important issue than Ravenholt's performance is America's. Ravenholt was, after all, an official of the U.S. government—for a time, the highest-ranking civil servant working at AID. His program was America's. As David Bell sees it, Ravenholt's approach "limited AID as a source of assistance for any country that wanted to move carefully by its own lights, that wanted to work in a nationalist setting. If AID had not been so prominent and so noisy it could have assisted a lot of programs it was not able to assist because AID was seen as having such an insensitive genocidal policy. That's stating it in exaggeration" (author's interview). But Ravenholt alone was not responsible for the AID population juggernaut. Reagan administration Assistant Administrator for Science and Technology Nyle Brady says of AID, "We tend to decide what needs doing and then look for somebody to do it to" (1984). The same view of AID and the groups it supports is expressed by Chilean family planner Anibal Faundes, who has worked throughout Latin America for the Population Council and the United Nations. Faundes's impression of the American organizations supported by AID is that "their common characteristic is to give money to individuals ready to receive it as a payment for saying yes to whatever proposal idealized in the States is offered to them" (Faundes to Donaldson, August 20, 1979).

Ravenholt represented the certainty at AID like no one else. One member of AID's field staff says of Ravenholt, "If he found somebody he disagreed with, he had to be damn disagreeable about it." Another says, "Most of us who worked overseas could realize that wasn't the best place for Rei. . . . Rei was never an easy guy to work with, particularly for people overseas." A third senior staffer says Ravenholt "lacked any sense of cultural sensitivity" (author's interviews). At times, when traveling, he behaved so rudely, promoting his point of view, that his own staff sought to keep him out of the countries in which they worked (author's interview). But some AID Washington staff were proud of Ravenholt's willingness to "chop off all the edges" and tell a less-than-eager program manager overseas, as one remembers him doing in north Africa, "Take it or leave it. You want any money from AID? You're going to do it!" (author's interview).

It was not just Ravenholt, or even AID, who was insensitive, however. It is the nature of America's relationship with the Third World that almost all Americans making their first landfall in the developing world are quite certain that they have the ability and the knowledge to solve problems there. The developing country's point of view is frequently ignored, and the superiority of the imported perspective is taken for granted. A measure of how much those who were helped were also demeaned is how little they were asked about what they wanted, and how much America's point of view was pushed. The beneficiaries of American population assistance were rarely involved in deciding what should be supported. The lesson that the Third World felt used, although never learned and often not even listened to, was one by-product of almost every international meeting.

The views of the "guests from less-developed countries" at one Rockefeller Foundation–sponsored population meeting were summarized as follows: "the blunt, honest, and impressively unanimous testimony they gave was that foreign assistance for population programs in the developing world is seen too often as too simple, too coercive, too narrow" (D. Bell n.d., p. 91). Sander Levin also complains about the dogmatism of the U.S. government's approach to the population problem under Ravenholt: "The guiding thrust . . . was that the problem was immense . . . [and] that its solution was obvious and relatively simple. . . . The answer was availability of contraceptives. Everything else was at best secondary. Everything else; whether it was a delivery system with competent people; whether it was motivation . . . whether it was the attitude of government" (author's interview).

Some critics of Ravenholt and AID argue that a conflict existed between Ravenholt and others in the population movement over the best way to advance effective fertility control. Ravenholt irritated his American colleagues because he was always too sure his way was the best way to do things. Staff at New York foundations did not like his loud-mouthed manner, but they had much less trouble accepting his program orientation. Ravenholt favored what Donald Warwick labels "vigorous but narrow action on birth control," and he dismissed as a waste of time the "broader, less direct, more nuanced and longer-term view of the problem" (Warwick 1982, pp. 50–51). But as we have seen, almost everyone accepted government support for the provision of contraceptive services as the most feasible public policy to control population growth.

Few people, American or foreign, were as extreme in their supply-side approach to increasing contraceptive prevalence as Ravenholt. Even a supporter of family planning such as Egypt's Fouad Hefnawi, former dean of the medical school at Cairo's Al Azhar University (called by some the Vatican of Islam) and director of the International Islamic Center for Population Studies and Research, claims that "Ravenholt was very stupid to supply pills to Egypt. They were not properly used. Millions of dollars were wasted by AID on contraceptives" (author's interview). Others took a lighthearted approach to Ravenholt's extremism. In 1976, when Lenni Kangas was an AID population officer in the Philippines, he persuaded a pilot friend from the Ministry of Agriculture to hover his helicopter above the ground while Kangas pitched pills and condoms out the door; another AID staffer photographed the episode and a picture was given to Ravenholt. It was Kangas's tongue-in-cheek way of showing Ravenholt just how gung-ho he was. In fact, Kangas pretty much accepts Ravenholt's views on the need for high stockpiles of contraceptives, pointing out that "ordering contraceptives is like ordering bullets for a war. You don't want to run out" (author's interview).

Distinctively American, the population program under Ravenholt depended on contraceptive technology. Ravenholt was a fan of technology and believed it would significantly advance family planning. Many people remember embarrassing moments as he promoted his latest favorite population control technique. He would unveil a menstrual regulation syringe from the breast pocket of his jacket and hold it above his head while proclaiming how the increased availability of early abortion was going to contribute mightily to lower fertility. At one point he was an enthusiast of prostaglandins. He once wrote to his staff, the AID administrator, and Philander Claxton about prostaglandins (which can cause contraction of the uterus and dilation of the cervix, and thus are used to induce abortion), calling them "the technical breakthrough which will turn the barrel of the family and population planning kaleidoscope and will necessitate appropriate modification of AID's family and population planning strategy and program" (Ravenholt to Population Staff, January 28, 1970, 286-73A-716).

Ravenholt could be more reasonable, but he hardly ever was. He once said of the pill, "They're not perfect but still damn useful" (Ravenholt to Frost, January 3, 1969, 286-73A-474). Favoring a particular contraceptive technology was characteristic of many population groups. The Population Council, for its part, pushed the IUD but had little to do with sterilization, and paid even less attention to abortion. This technological orientation was not all bad, of course. Both AID and the Population Council helped promote genuine technical innovations, such as simplified female sterilization procedures and the contraceptive implant.

There was another characteristically American element in Ravenholt's view of the population problem and how to solve it: he thought population growth could be slowed through individual action. Although he avoided picking apart the details of program implementation that would have showed how individuals sometimes were pressured to accept contraceptives, one suspects he was aware of the forcefulness of some so-called voluntary programs. But he thought such pressure was unnecessary. He believed, as he once put it, that "there is great demand for family planning at the very bottom of the barrel in the least developed families and societies. . . . The poorest of women in the poorest of countries are desirous of avoiding or delaying pregnancy" (author's interview). He was more extreme than most in his judgment about the extent to which women wanted contraceptive services and, thus, in what he thought contraception and abortion on demand would yield. He insisted that existing motivation is sufficient "to ordinarily bring the birth rate under 20"—that is, to 20 births annually per 1,000 total population, slightly above the level of the poorest developed countries, say Ireland or Poland. The notion that major structural changes in the economy and the society were prerequisites for control of population growth was never accepted by Ravenholt, who had a vintage-1960s argument: The problem of rapid population growth would be solved when individuals everywhere had equal access to contraception. Equal opportunity was as alive in international family planning as it was in the civil rights movement.

Ravenholt shared the American belief that individuals acting in their own self-interest would have fewer children and that life would improve if they did so. Others find his faith simplistic at best, and cruel at worst. One former AID staffer remembers being with Ravenholt in Mexico and visiting a church in the rear of which an obviously poor, and perhaps homeless, woman with an infant was sitting looking forlorn. Ravenholt gave the woman one hundred pesos, saying to his colleagues that if only she had practiced family planning she would be okay (author's interview). Such simplicity was rejected by almost everybody, but few Americans found it mean-spirited. Others, however, did.

The Chilean physician Benjamin Viel once argued that it was a cruel hoax for U.S.-supported family planning programs to promote contraceptive use with posters indicating that fewer children would bring prosperity by picturing a family with six or more children in rags, in a broken-down hut, and another family with only two children, always a boy and a girl, nicely dressed, listening to the radio, clearly healthier and happier than the large family. Viel understood that lower numbers and slower growth alone would not make poor families rich or poor societies prosperous. In fact, he once called it an absurdity to try to promote birth control in conditions of extreme poverty (Viel 1976, p. 168). Ravenholt and his population program, on the other hand, could be a case study in the sociology of the quick fix.

The Role of Family Planning

Each reorganization of AID's population and family planning program was marked by a debate over the value of government-subsidized provision of contraceptive services for lowering fertility and population growth. This conflict over the appropriateness and impact of family planning frequently masked a more deeply rooted conflict: at stake were values and differing professional orientations. Family planning programs were initially advocated not because people knew they were effective, but because they had faith that such programs would work and because there were no reasonable alternatives. Clearly, more-available, less-costly, more aggressively promoted contraceptives would not increase fertility, and at least since the 1920s evidence had been accumulating in Europe and America to suggest that greater contraceptive practice was a key factor in reducing fertility. Critics objected that those inclined to practice contraception would do so anyway and that government programs only transferred the costs of individual contraceptive decisions to the state. But with little else being recommended, policy makers accepted subsidized contraceptive distribution as the best means to lower fertility.

Making family planning the centerpiece of America's international population policy had consequences for all the organizations implementing the American effort to control population growth. When the effectiveness of family planning programs was seriously questioned, these organizations changed. The Population Council, for example, established a Technical Assistance Division to help developing countries implement and evaluate family planning programs; it was home for a while to some of America's most influential public health physicians—Jarrett Clinton, Henry Mosley, Clifford Pease, Allan Rosenfield, Adaline Satterthwaite, and Christopher Tietze. When the value of family planning was being disputed during the 1970s, the Council sought additional roles for its Technical Assistance Division and eventually fired the director and established a new division with a nominally broader scope. When the Council made this move, AID staff claimed they "did not perceive the Population Council as an organization interested in family planning" (Minutes, Officers' Meeting, December 16, 1976, PC/K). The evidence regarding AID's population control program suggests that, like the Population Council, the way agency officials defined both the problem of rapid population growth and the solution to it shaped the organizational model employed to implement the program.

Although David Bell, AID administrator during the first days of the agency's population program, was an economist, he did not build a program on whatever economic dimensions of rapid population growth he saw. The key roles were held by medical doctors (Baumgartner, Lee, Ravenholt) who, although they recognized the economic importance of population, were not well suited to design a program that would bring a society's economic and financial institutions to bear on the population problem. From the start, AID worked more with ministries of health and social welfare than with economic planning boards, ministries of finance, or national budget bureaus. The principal Senate supporter for increasing American assistance for international family planning, Ernest Gruening, was a medical doctor with a strong public health background. Turning over AID's population program to health professionals reinforced the dominance of the individual perspective in human fertility. The unit to which American foreign assistance was directed was not the society, or a particular subgroup, it was the individual woman who was supposedly voluntarily deciding the number of children she wished to have and then practicing whatever fertility regulation she thought appropriate to achieve that goal. The problem of how to manipulate a society's institutions to achieve lower fertility was not much discussed.

As a congressional Office of Technology Assessment summarized recently, "AID's strategy [was] based on the established public health principle of availability—making information, supplies, and services readily available so that individuals who choose to plan their fertility can do so conveniently" (1982, p. 181). In spite of working for a development agency—and, indeed, of justifying the population program in terms of its economic benefits—Ravenholt and his colleagues expected development to take place but never saw it as their responsibility. Part of their reasoning was bureaucratic: development was seen as the business of other divisions within AID. The Office of Population was charged with dealing with high fertility and population growth. Ravenholt himself would sometimes argue that the use of development projects to influence childbearing practices was not something his group should be concerned with (Comptroller General 1978, p. 79). He and his staff were first and foremost in the family planning business: if you did not want help with your family planning program, if you were not committed to the idea of making contraceptives more available as the first and overwhelmingly most important step to lowering fertility, you should look elsewhere for assistance.

Another aspect of the early AID view of rapid population growth was that it was relatively undifferentiated. People thought of rapid growth as basically the same problem throughout the developing world. Bangladesh and Thailand suffered in the same way as Nigeria, Tunisia, or Colombia. The prevailing view was that women in each place were simply having too many children. Not understood at the time was the influence of such factors as the timing of births, women's age at marriage, the proportion of married women in the population, the prevalence of abortion, the proportion of contraceptive users employing highly effective methods, and the fertility impact of contraceptive continuation rates, breast-feeding, and postpartum abstinence. Few people examined national variations in the ages at which women first married as a source of observed differences in population growth rates. Efforts to raise the age at marriage as a means of lowering fertility were infrequent and not encouraged by the United States.

Because the problem of population growth was not seen as a country-specific problem but as a global one, AID made little serious effort to take account of unique national circumstances that may have contributed to population growth. Agency officials were aware that because Nepal and Niger were particularly poor they had more serious development problems than Tunisia or Mexico. But beyond this sort of commonsense development theory, few people paid much attention to the circumstances of individual countries—certainly not enough to vary the basic formula for controlling population growth: provide contraceptives. One senior AID official, a supporter of Ravenholt and the Office of Population, once argued that "the commonalities of designing and implementing successful family planning far outnumber the original or country differences. They should be designed with the broadest experience not by those with parochial bias" (MacManus to Levin, September 29, 1977, gift file).

The agency's undifferentiated approach to the problem of population growth resulted in part from the fact that the population program did not have its roots in the requests of particular developing countries. Only a few countries delivered messages to the State Department in a forceful enough way to alert AID officials that population growth was a problem that demanded their attention. Instead, the stimulus came almost entirely from outside the agency and mainly from developed countries. A handful of politicians, a band of population control zealots, a few demographers, and a small number of foundation executives made the difference. Only a few AID bureaucrats cared very much about population when the program officially began in 1965. The program was mandated by Congress and the administration and laid over existing agency programs. Senior AID staff were given little opportunity to offer suggestions or comments.

Because AID staff were not asked to design a program themselves but rather were told they were going to have a population program, there was little opportunity for consensus building within the agency during the program's early years. Ravenholt's strong convictions about what needed to be done, coupled with his congressional support and personal style, reinforced the tendency of the population program to be self-contained and organizationally inner-directed. Even those who offered Ravenholt support, but some criticism as well, were often dismissed as an annoyance. Since senior AID officials did not push for a larger population program but had it pushed on them, it is not surprising that they chose to implement the congressional mandate by establishing an independent population group within a non-geographic-area bureau. Nor is it surprising that as the importance of population became clearer, the organizational model became less attractive.

America's international population program is an important manifestation of the nation's vision, values, and place in the world. Americans, having been trained to see family planning as a private matter, were slow to awake to the likely impact of rapid population growth on economic development or of high fertility on the health of women and children. But when people in the United States—and those with ties to America via education, employment, or foreign assistance funding—first defined the rates of population growth that prevailed in the late 1950s and early 1960s as dangerously excessive, and thus as demanding attention and intervention, they pushed their point of view with missionary zeal.

Given the revolution that has taken place in the control of childbearing around the world, and the efforts of the American government to promote massive social change, it is easy to forget that almost everyone in the population set was middle-class and conventional. Ravenholt may have had an easier time than people expected, because so many of those with whom he fought used contraception themselves. Family planning was legitimate and accepted. Ravenholt and his troops were not guerrillas, but more like the green berets—a somewhat special but nevertheless integrated battalion of soldiers who played a known and understood role in the promotion of health and development.

The World's Reaction

So far, I have been concerned mainly with the way America's foreign assistance program responded to the rapid growth of developing-country populations. Concentrating on what happened in Washington, however, may lead one to underestimate the importance of policy changes that were taking place in many developing countries. This chapter provides an overview of the evolution of population policy in the developing world and examines the differing views on the importance of population growth presented at the United Nations' decennial population conferences. The following chapter analyzes the history of the Population Council in Korea in an effort to evaluate how population policies and programs have been influenced by private American organizations.

Other international groups—particularly the International Planned Parenthood Federation (IPPF), the affiliation of national planned parenthood organizations—have played important roles in supporting family planning and encouraging the control of population growth, but none of them was as significant to the American effort in these fields as the United Nations' own population trust fund. The World Bank was a source of money for population and family planning, but the United States has had relatively little to do with the bank's program, especially during Ravenholt's years as director of the Office of Population. The officials at AID thought the World Bank was slow and cumbersome and disliked its reliance on loans to support population activities overseas, a strategy that Ravenholt and his colleagues thought was inappropriate (Crane and Finkle 1981, pp. 544–45).

Given the seriousness with which the United States viewed the rapid population growth of the developing world, the question of why a larger number of major Third World political leaders were not more interested in the problem is an important one. History will probably judge the response of many of the developing world's leaders to the problem of rapid population growth to have been quite swift, especially given the importance of children in the economy, culture, religion, and family life of many poor countries. But the view that Third World leaders had of population growth was shaped by factors unfamiliar to American politicians. In the United States, population growth and family planning were too obscure, a bit too personal, and likely to be too controversial to attract the interest of more than a handful of important politicians. Overseas, the situation was very different.

It was not a disregard for their people that caused developing-country leaders to give population a lower priority than most foreigners involved in the field on a day-to-day basis would have wished. The threat of assassination and the odds of getting pushed aside are so serious that leaders in most Third World countries worry first about how to stay alive and in power. I have lived in two developing countries, Korea and Thailand, that now appear on their way to democracy, but whose histories demonstrate this problem clearly. Since 1932, there have been thirteen coups to change national leadership in Thailand. In Korea, Park Chung Hee was shot at three times— including once when his wife, who was standing close to him on the stage, was killed—before an assassin's bullet finally killed him.

Staying alive and in power in the relatively tame and moderate countries of Asia is a lot easier than doing so in Africa. When Idi Amin overthrew Milton Obote and took over Uganda in 1971, he started on a rampage almost at once. The army chief of staff, the chief justice, and the vice-chancellor of Makerere University all disappeared. Even Amin's personal physician was beaten to death and dumped along a road. By 1979, when Amin was ousted, an estimated 300,000 Ugandans had been murdered (Lamb 1984, p. 78). When the Organization of African Unity was formed in 1963, thirty heads of state signed the charter. By 1980, "only seven were still in office. Of the others, two were murdered by their own soldiers, seventeen were overthrown in military coups but survived, two died natural deaths" (Lamb 1984, pp. 97–98). Third World leaders worry first about staying alive and in command and then, as time allows, about development.

Idi Amin aside, few developing-country leaders are mean-spirited villains. Most of them are taking what they regard as necessary steps to assist their people in obtaining basic needs. The first domestic issues that attract the attention of leaders in the developing world are national security, food, and jobs. Finding work for people is a principal concern for many developing countries. Food is another major issue; getting and distributing sufficient food in a somewhat equitable way represents a challenge for many poor countries and those who lead them. National security is almost always a very high priority. The army and the national police are typically a national leader's main source of power and legitimacy. In many circumstances, genuine national security reasons are also important. Internal groups threaten local campaigns of armed disruption and terror, and countries are often ready to take advantage of weak neighbors. When leaders have extra time or money to invest, strengthening defense forces almost always commands attention. Because the defense establishment is a source of harmony with one's neighbors and of control of the citizenry, such forces frequently benefit from resources that are desperately needed elsewhere.

In 1977, South Korea's minister of health and social affairs, Shin Hyon Hwack—who went on to become minister of economic planning, deputy prime minister, and, for a short time, prime minister of Korea—worried that the success of his country's population control program might lessen South Korea's chances for victory in a war with the North (author's interview). He made this point even though South Korea's population is 20 million more than that of the North. The leaders of other countries have similar worries. The countries of Southeast Asia moved in family planning because they moved together. I am certain that there are now people in the Thai government who worry that the larger population of Vietnam gives the Vietnamese an important advantage should the two countries become involved in a conflict. Such concerns are not a characteristic only of Asia nor are they limited to the modern age. The historical demography of the Middle East helps explain many of the region's current difficulties (Chamie 1981). In Brazil, elite ambivalence about population control is based, in part, on concerns about the fate of Portuguese-speaking people in a world where the Spanish-speaking population is growing rapidly (Merrick and Graham 1979). According to some observers, a similar concern slowed population activities in Indonesia: one analysis refers to the "longstanding Indonesian policy to increase the population of the outer islands, primarily as a defense measure to avoid infiltration of Chinese" (Cowles to Shafer, August 24, 1967, 286-73A-716).

Other programs also attract the attention of Third World leaders before health and population. For example, development depends to a very important extent on improvements in education. A literate labor force is a tremendous asset for increasing productivity and developing new industries, and the successful import and adaptation of technology requires trained people. Moreover, almost everyone values education as a means of upward mobility. Thus, national leaders throughout the Third World care about increasing the coverage and quality of their countries' educational institutions. Problems of the city are also perceived as more important than population control. The capital city is the environment for the daily lives of most developing-country elites, and the problems of the capital—reflected in the local press, in conversations at receptions, and at meetings—frequently take on more importance than they merit. The capital receives attention while other programs remain on the back burner. Improved bus routes, a new national airport, and hotel modernization schemes use up scarce resources.

Countries do not need the regular intervention of national political leaders to develop a sound family planning program, just their blessing from time to time and a statement that population control is an important national priority. Krannich and Krannich describe how the Thai cabinet, prime minister, and king all worried out loud about the consequences of rapid population growth, but only after the successful implementation of a family planning demonstration project and an alarming report on the topic from the World Bank (Krannich and Krannich 1980, p. 17). Frequently, such support from senior political figures has not been forthcoming for the same reasons that one finds slowing the involvement of American politicians in this area—namely, an anxiety about a conservative backlash and a feeling that fertility is a private affair that does not make a tremendous difference in the community's welfare.

Despite the effects of such factors that lessen the interest of developing-country governments in population, there was a steady increase in the number of people and programs available internationally for the United States to look to for encouragement of its effort to spread a concern about population growth and support for family planning. Opposition to providing contraceptives and to making the effort to change the pattern of childbearing became less influential. Nevertheless, Americans frequently found that their developing-country counterparts were less eager to express public support for increasing family planning services than they were to quietly provide contraceptives, and even to allow illegal abortion to flourish. Many countries failed to formally endorse American assistance in a way that would encourage AID's leadership to expand the program or AID's opponents to quiet their criticism. Since its founding, AID has faced the difficulty of dealing with its clients' ambiguous attitude toward foreign assistance. Developing-world leaders wanted U.S. money and resources, but they did not endorse the American diagnosis of their development problems and they resented the conditions of much American aid. However, America did not stand alone in the campaign to control growth; some important developing-world figures provided leadership for national and international population control and family planning programs.

Regional Differences

At the time of the first U.N.-sponsored Asian Population Conference in 1963, national governments in that region were ready to recommend unanimously that "participants take account of the urgency of adopting positive population policies" ("1963—Beginning of the Road" 1982, p. 28). They also agreed that slowing rapid population growth alone would not cause a poor country to develop, but the conference supported the proposition that slower growth would enhance development prospects. Since the 1960s, support for family planning and population growth control has become a more prominent feature of government development plans and health programs throughout Asia.

By the late 1960s, most Asian countries had decided that rapid population growth was a threat to prosperity. In 1952 India led the way with policies aimed at slowing population growth. Pakistan (and later Bangladesh after its war of liberation) and Nepal followed. Korea announced its policy in 1961, Singapore in 1965, Malaysia in 1966, Indonesia and Taiwan in 1968, and Thailand and the Philippines in 1970. Opinion in Asia was clear—rapid population growth was not an advantage for poor countries; growth should be slowed.

While Asian countries were establishing government family planning programs, only a few major Latin countries were doing the same. But in time, the idea of government support for contraceptive services also took root in much of Latin America. Nelson Rockefeller returned from a 1969 presidential mission to Latin America with a message about the importance of population growth: "In country after country, the problem of population growth and the need for family planning to slow that growth was voluntarily brought before the mission advisors—not only by physicians and public health officials, but also by educators, scientists, leaders of women's groups, economic ministers and planning directors. Many stated plainly that they could not take a public position in favor of family planning because the issue of birth control in some hemisphere countries is too emotional and controversial" (N. Rockefeller, "Quality of Life in the Americas," 1969, p. 123, 286-74-1216).

Cuba led the way in the early 1960s with government support for contraceptive services, and in the process took the sting from leftist charges that family planning was Western imperialism in disguise.

Indeed, Cuba and the United States have been on friendlier terms with respect to family planning than with respect to most other things. In 1966, Alan Guttmacher had a cordial visit with Cuban family planners (Kaiser 1975). Not only did Cuba represent an important model of effective public health and family planning services, but Cuban officials also encouraged other Latin nations to incorporate family planning into their national health services. At a 1975 meeting of the Economic Commission for Latin America, Cuba played what one American participant termed a "surprisingly moderate and helpful role": "In working groups Cuban delegates consistently supported proposals for more regional and multinational involvement in population programs. Minister [José Agutiérrez Múñiz] was outgoing and friendly with U.S. delegation and he and Ravenholt had two useful exchanges of views on problems of mutual interest in family planning field" (State Telegram, no. 2107, March 9, 1975, 286-81-002).

Chile incorporated family planning into its maternal and child health program in 1966, and Costa Rica did so in 1968. Also in 1968, the Dominican Republic organized its National Council on Population and Family Planning, and Ecuador began supporting family planning activities. In 1969, Panama added family planning as a specific activity of the Ministry of Health program. Colombia had an active private-sector family planning program and by 1970 announced an official policy to reduce population growth. By the early 1970s, the governments of the largest Latin American countries—Mexico and Brazil—were yet to show their willingness to subsidize contraceptive services, but private practitioners and private groups within each country were promoting family planning services on their own in advance of government support (Nortman and Hofstatter 1978, pp. 27–30).

It was only in Africa that the idea of fertility control had yet to gain credibility by 1970. As of 1968, Egypt, Morocco, and Tunisia each had an official policy to reduce population growth, but in the rest of Africa only Kenya had a growth reduction policy. The records of AID and of the State Department are full of reports and memos on the lack of interest in population among African countries and their leaders. The U.S. mission in Nigeria, Africa's most populous country, once cabled Washington that critics of family planning "range from the Catholic Church . . . to the commissioner of economic development. They discount the danger of continued population growth . . . question the motives of externally supported family planning programs, and dismiss birth control as alien to Nigerian values" (AMEMBASSY/Lagos to State, March 30, 1972, 286-76-286; see also Richards to AID/Washington, December 11, 1968, 286-72A-750S, which adds "a considerable amount of unused land . . . and a growing feeling that population growth should be encouraged to offset the effects of war" as reasons for not supporting family planning).

There are many reasons for this lack of interest, which continues throughout the African region (although Nigerian leaders seem to be growing more concerned). One crucial factor is the overall low level of social and economic modernization, which means that the development problems of security, food, employment, education, and urban infrastructure are overwhelming and thwart both policy making and program implementation in other sectors. Population control efforts have also been made more difficult by tribal rivalry and distrust, as well as by a history of colonial rule that left Africa with few strong national leaders who were schooled in the traditions and values of their own societies but able to understand the consequences of rapid population growth and what might be done about it. Journalist David Lamb concludes that few sensible politicians dare speak firmly in favor of population control: "To do so would be to challenge the growth of an individual's tribe, to deprive parents of the hands needed to till the fields today and care for the elderly tomorrow, to denounce religious and traditional beliefs that have belonged to Africa for generations" (Lamb 1984, p. 17).

The United Nations

In the years since World War II the United Nations, and particularly its various international population conferences, have provided focal points for the expression of differing national perspectives on population growth. Even earlier, in the decades between the two world wars, proponents of birth control used League of Nations gatherings to increase awareness of the problem of uncontrolled fertility and to promote international collaboration on population matters. After World War II, international meetings became occasions for those concerned about the consequences of rapid population growth in the developing world to try to orient thinking about population away from questions of eugenics and toward issues of national development. Documents presented at these meetings provide an insight into the changing views on population and its impact on national development.

The United States and other governments have recognized that the United Nations and its specialized agencies—particularly the World Health Organization (WHO), the United Nations Children's Fund (UNICEF), and the U.N. Fund for Population Activities (UNFPA), and the various international meetings that these groups sponsor—are crucial sources for legitimation of a type that eases the potential negative consequences of developed-country involvement in developing-country population activities. The endorsement of the United Nations can be used to justify countries' becoming involved in their own and others' population problems. When the United Nations takes a stand, as it did in 1968 by declaring the ability to determine the number and spacing of one's children to be a basic human right, most developing-world political leaders have a difficult time campaigning against the idea. The U.N. list of human rights can be ignored, but not opposed. This is the case in large part because the U.N. position on such issues reflects an already existing consensus among nations.

Very early in its efforts to slow population growth, the United States recognized the utility of U.N. involvement in population control activities. In 1962, the State Department's population advisor urged greater support to the United Nations for population activities (Barnett to the Secretary, May 8, 1962, no source). In November 1966, the president's General Advisory Committee on Foreign Assistance Programs noted:

> There are advantages to the United States in channeling much of its assistance on population problems through international bodies. . . . [T]he underdeveloped nations, with populations of all races, are represented on multilateral bodies. Therefore, these agencies are free from the vulnerability of the developed countries' binational programs to the charge that they seek to limit the growth only of nonwhite populations.
>
> Also, in a field of such personal sensitivity as birth control, advice and aid will be accepted much more readily from an impersonal international body than from a great power such as the United States which already faces resentment from people undergoing rapid change who perceive the United States as a source of the pressures they feel during modernization. (Perkins to Johnson, November 21, 1966, p. 5, no source)

The committee went on to note that there was no U.N. agency with sufficient size, power, and political will to undertake mass family planning programs. They recommended that the United States support the formation of a group at the United Nations to support population control programs. The advisory committee also suggested that the United States encourage the developing countries themselves to take a lead in proposing measures to expand U.N. multinational programs in the population field. The committee worried that without the strong endorsement of developing countries, "direct U.S. sponsorship would simply involve the birth control issue in cold war politics and alleged conflicts of interest between developed and underdeveloped countries."

Throughout the late 1960s and early 1970s, the United States worked hard behind the scenes to move the United Nations to greater support for population control activities. In 1967, for example, Robert Barnett, at the time deputy assistant secretary of state for East Asian and Pacific affairs, wrote the American ambassador in Thailand about his encouraging economist Puey Ungphakorn, one of Thailand's most respected educators, "to stimulate some additional [multinational] activity in the field of population control" (Martin to Barnett, August 2, 1967; Barnett to Martin, July 12, 1967, 286-76-286). American officials serving in Europe were encouraged to contact local government personnel and urge greater allied support for population control programs (See Marx to Claxton, October 25, 1967, and Claxton to Saxe, July 31, 1967, 286-72-7553).

Philander Claxton, the State Department's population specialist, described the "vigorous efforts" being made by the United States to bring U.N. agencies "to the stage of developing and pursuing effective population programs." He complained that "for cultural, religious and bureaucratic reasons, this has been a slow process," but he was optimistic about the prospects of the various U.N. agencies working together and about the extent to which involvement would help to advance population control efforts. He overrated what WHO and the World Bank would accomplish, imagining (in the case of the Bank) a significant but fuzzy return—to wit, "the Bank . . . because of the weight which its position as an important funding agency gives it, should be able to make an important contribution to the effort to reduce excessive fertility rates, although the nature of it remains unclear at present" (Claxton to Inter-Agency Working Group on Population Matters, December 10, 1969, 286-76-286).

Claxton's views about the United Nations were widely shared in Washington. Moreover, Claxton, who had a key coordinating role during a crucial stage in the development of America's population program, was expert at creating a cloth of consensus and agreed-upon policy from the threads of a dozen different, and at times contentious, meetings. He would gain new support by proclaiming the extent of his existing alliances. In a typical memo, he once wrote to Assistant Secretary of State Joseph Sisco telling him, "The Senate Committee on Foreign Relations has stressed the need to make maximum use of the U.N. organizations in the population field [and] Secretary Rusk has instructed me that he wishes to see a major effort to get the U.N. to play a leading role in this field" (Claxton to Sisco,

February 15, 1968, 286-76-286). Not many people would be ready to fight for less U.N. involvement under these circumstances, regardless of what they really thought about the appropriateness of the multinational strategy.

When the United States provided the first $1 million in funding to the United Nations to help it establish a specialized population agency, Americans sought a measure of control over the way the program was to be implemented. The first grant "was made contingent on United Nations Development Program administration . . . future U.S. contributions to the Population Fund would be similarly conditioned" (Claxton to Inter-Agency Working Group, December 10, 1969, p. 10, 286-76-286). Proper administration was a concern because the United States thought centralized planning and coordination were essential for program development, and wanted to avoid allowing individual countries to exercise too much influence. Many people thought that the U.N. Population Division, a department of the U.N. Secretariat, should play a major role in the design and implementation of any U.N.-sponsored population activities. However, U.S. officials and activist leaders like General Draper disagreed: they believed that giving the Population Division a strong role would lead to an overly academic program, and they fought to get and maintain the population trust under the United Nations Development Programme (UNDP). The UNDP officials themselves were eager to administer the trust fund and, encouraged by U.S. backing, worked to maintain control of the new population program. Paul Hoffman, the head of the UNDP, informed General Draper that Hoffman and his colleagues "were determined to gain complete control of total resources in the fund, coordination and evaluation functions, population program offices, and strongly opposed any collegiate organizational arrangement as proposed by [Milos] Macura [the head of the U.N. Population Division]"; at the same time, "Draper offered UNDP his assistance in fund raising activities and outlined his $15 million goal for 1970" (quoted in Yost to Secretary of State, December 1, 1969, 286-75-153). Draper's reputation as a successful fund-raiser and lobbyist doubtless encouraged Hoffman and other UNDP senior staff to think that a special trust fund could be made to work.

The U.S. government used its influence to gain support for UNFPA. Then–U.S. Ambassador to the United Nations George Bush and the U.S. mission to the United Nations backed a strong population program and believed the United Nations had a crucial, perhaps essential, role to play. At the time, Bush noted: "Major world problems like population and environmental protection will have to be handled by large and complex organizations representing many nations and many different points of view. How well we and the rest of the world can make the policies and programs of the United Nations responsive to the needs of the people will be the test of success in the population field. Success in the population field, under United Nations leadership, may, in turn, determine whether we can resolve successfully the other great questions of peace, prosperity, and individual rights that face the world" (Bush 1973, p. ix). But Bush also cautioned Draper that the U.N. involvement could slow things down. The future president "emphasized the urgent need to make things happen instead of consuming resources in debates and studies" (U.S. Mission/New York to Secretary of State, March 4, 1972, 286-75-153). Draper continued to argue his case for a strong U.N. population program. He appealed to the AID administrator to provide what Draper regarded as adequate funding for UNFPA. After visiting Bush to encourage his continued support, Draper would see Secretary General Kurt Waldheim to urge greater U.N. support for UNFPA.

Predictably, some people at the United Nations were displeased at General Draper's promotional efforts. U.N. Under–Secretary General Philippe De Seynes complained to the U.S. mission of the involvement of "powerful groups" who were "assuming a role in decision-making within the United Nations (i.e., General Draper and, in particular, his call on the Secretary General . . .)" (U.S. Mission/New York to Secretary of State, April 1972, 286-75-153). The U.N. bureaucrats were particularly upset at Draper's pushing Secretary General Waldheim to proclaim 1974 "Population Year" and to name U Thant to oversee the year's special activities. Draper also had a favored slate of nominees to serve as director of the U.N. Population Division, and his promoting them irritated U.N. staffers.

Not all members of the U.N. family of organizations were eager to see a new UNDP-administered trust fund established to promote population control. At about the same time that the UNDP, pushed by the United States, was moving toward a targeted, focused program to lower fertility and promote population control as a valuable health and development intervention, WHO was increasingly advocating a comprehensive model of health planning and provision of care. In addition, WHO was arguing for the need to respect expressed national priorities—which in practice, especially before 1970, often meant limiting WHO involvement in family planning to countries that already had national family planning programs. Efforts were made by WHO to claim a share of the American contribution to the newly established U.N. population fund, but its staff could not produce a plan of activities that was aggressive enough to satisfy AID (see, for example, Rogers to U.S. Mission, Geneva, P111849Z, April 14, 1969; and Mace to Claxton, March 25, 1969, 286-72A-7553).

Neither were American officials uniformly enthusiastic about the advantages of implementing the U.S. population control program through multinational organizations. Everyone agreed that U.N. agencies moved slowly and were overly political, but most people thought their credibility made up for the inevitable delays. A few observers, however, disagreed, and thought that U.N. programs were not relevant to the family planning needs of the developing world. The official U.S. belief that the United Nations was a particularly valuable element in its worldwide attack on rapid population growth probably created unrealistic expectations regarding what the United Nations and its member nations could accomplish and how easily they could work together.

The U.N. Fund for Population Activities became a major recipient of AID Office of Population support and provided a useful way of allowing AID to undertake programs that would otherwise have been more difficult, if not impossible. Ravenholt used UNFPA when other more straightforward channels of assistance were not appropriate. For example, Ravenholt describes how UNFPA became involved with the World Fertility Survey (WFS), a massive, multi-million-dollar effort to measure fertility in the developing world through a series of national surveys, as follows: "Because of the sensitivities inherent in national surveys of fertility and the fact that the United States was then embroiled in the Vietnam war, we realized that the WFS must be created in partnership with the United Nations in a suitable international organization and with headquarters preferably *not* [emphasis in original] located in the United States." He goes on to explain that influencing UNFPA was not difficult: "because USAID provided $14 million (50 percent) of the UNFPA's 1972 budget and $29 million (90 + percent) of its 1973 budget, we had considerable powers of persuasion with the UNFPA at that time" (Ravenholt 1984, p. 3). (UNFPA is no longer an instrument of U.S. policy and, in fact, it gets no direct U.S. government support.)

The 1974 World Population Conference

The population movement's more militant leaders, including General Draper and Office of Population Director Ravenholt, began to see the 1974 World Population Conference to be held in Bucharest, Rumania, as an opportunity for the expression of near-complete consensus regarding the dangers of rapid population growth and the advantages of population growth reduction targets. At U.N.-sponsored regional meetings held in preparation for the Bucharest conference, the United States pushed its point of view, saying that while recognizing that "population policies are matters for each sovereign country to decide," the United States thought that "agreement on additional goals for reducing world growth [would be] highly desirable." The American targets called for reducing population growth in developing countries to 2 percent per year by 1985, and to .6 percent per year in developed countries over the same period (Secretary of State to American Ambassador, Mexico, no. 65938, April 2, 1974, 286-81-002).

Lack of agreement on the part of most other conferees on the appropriateness of targets was just one of the problems the Americans faced at the 1974 World Population Conference. The conference was a particular disappointment for many American members of the population movement because of a split between the family planners—between those who identified the government-subsidized provision of contraceptive services as the most important means to slow population growth, and those who believed that broadly based social and economic change was the essential ingredient in fertility reduction. Before the Bucharest meeting, it had seemed to many people that there was growing agreement about the importance of population growth and ways to control it. But not only did the meeting reject growth reduction targets, it also showed how few poor countries accepted the U.S. analysis of the population problem or preferred the U.S. solution to slowing growth by promoting family planning.

Most often, the 1974 World Population Conference is described as a confrontation between population control enthusiasts of the United States and the other industrialized nations, and more development-oriented representatives from the Third World who held population to be an important but not singular influence on economic development. This view is best elaborated in a thoughtful article by Jason Finkle and Barbara Crane (1975). Finkle and Crane capture the ideological element, but they miss something of the backstage interaction.

Draper and Claxton wanted the conference to recommend specific population growth reduction targets. General Draper's persistence in this regard is generally regarded by key figures in America and overseas as a negative force at the conference. Frank Notestein found him a "damn nuisance"; another American involved remembers Draper as a "menace" (author's interview). Most countries were not ready to endorse targets for their own or others' population growth. (Many were not even ready to endorse government support for family planning.) In part, this was the case because in 1974 most other countries saw rapid population growth as decidedly less important than did the United States. Draper and Claxton probably saw the targets as something of a culmination of the more than twenty years of work aimed at bringing the dangers of rapid population growth to the attention of the world's leaders. But for the leaders of most developing countries, regardless of what they thought about the consequences of rapid population growth, there was little to be gained by endorsing a set of world growth reduction targets. Such targets could easily be misperceived as intervention into the sovereign affairs of independent nations and as exaggerating the importance of population in the development process.

Economic planners, especially those from the Third World, found population to be a less important variable in the development equation than did the population movement enthusiasts who had engineered the 1974 World Population Conference. All but a small number of such people put jobs, trade, and general development assistance ahead of population control. A principal theme of the conference debates was that a solution to the population problem required economic progress, which, in turn, required a more equitable international economic order. The World Population Conference was the first U.N.-sponsored international conference following the General Assembly's adoption of the "New International Economic Order" resolution, and thus it was a natural setting in which to trumpet the resolution's virtues. High fertility and rapid population growth would not be slowed merely through the provision of family planning services ("What Happened at Bucharest?" 1974, p. 3). Even when the need to slow population growth became apparent, it was first seen in large, increasingly unlivable cities. Problems of migration and population distribution were more important for many people than the simple growth in numbers.

In a report on the World Population Conference prepared for internal circulation, the State Department's Bureau of Intelligence and Research accurately caught the sentiments of many developing countries. The report concluded: "There may have been serious apprehension among LDCs that if the conference gave too enthusiastic an endorsement to population problems, Western countries would prefer to donate millions to population programs rather than billions to economic development. There was evident concern among LDCs that collective endorsement of demographic policies or goals would inevitably enfringe on their sovereign right to determine their own population policies and programs" (INR R-38, November 22, 1974, 286-81-002).

After the conference, Americans tried to mask their disappoint-ment at the rebuff their ideas had received at Bucharest. The State Department cable to American embassies around the world summa-rizing the conference claimed that ". . . despite opposition from many LDCs and Communist countries to certain provisions, we be-lieve all basic U.S. objectives were achieved and there were many accomplishments" (Department of State Airgram A-8199, 286-81-002). In a more accurate expression of prevailing sentiment, former Population Council President Frank Notestein found the population conference's World Plan of Action "a weak document in many re-spects," but he valued its support for family planning as a basic human right (1982, p. 669). Philander Claxton says the 1974 confer-ence fulfilled all his hopes, save for its failure to endorse specific growth reduction targets (author's interview). But the title of the State Department's report showed that the Bureau of Intelligence and Re-search was less certain of the outcome: it was called "World Popula-tion Conference in Bucharest: Some Positive Results." The report itself is one of the less optimistic analyses of the conference. It notes that the Plan of Action that was issued by conference participants "[did not] admonish LDCs to strive for more manageable rates of population growth." The report found that "the conference failed to inspire a common sense of urgency and a commitment to population policies as indispensable components of national development strate-gies" (p. 5). It concluded without a ringing endorsement for the conference Plan of Action, noting only that "the Plan provides a serviceable strategy for countries desiring to get on with their popula-tion programs" (INR RS-38, November 22, 1974, 281-81-002).

Finkle and Crane sum up the conference best:

> The confrontation at Bucharest might have been less acute if the developed countries had fulfilled their commitments to the developing countries. . . . Instead of meeting their pledge of greatly increased aid, the industrialized nations decreased the percentage of their GNP that they were allocating to develop-ment assistance, thereby giving the poor countries a feeling that the West had lost interest in their plight. Population might have been somewhat spared from the spillover of international ten-sions if the United States had not in the span of a few years transformed its concern over rapid population growth in the Third World into an American cause. At a time when the United States was reducing its development assistance efforts—and was experiencing severe strains in its relations with the Third

World—it boldly assumed world leadership in the population
movement and gave it a distinctive American identification.
(Finkle and Crane 1975, p. 108)

They go on to point out that the 1974 World Population Conference
was a product of radical changes in the way developing nations regarded industrialized countries. Many political leaders and a large
share of the Third World's university professors, newspaper editors,
religious figures, and other professionals began to accept the notion
that the underdevelopment of their countries was at least partly a
result of the economic status and policies of the industrialized countries. Countries, like individuals, came to be viewed as elements in an
often rigid stratification system that put the developing countries at a
particular disadvantage. By the time of the World Population Conference, developing countries thought that their economic and trade
relationships with the already industrialized countries were more
important in determining their well-being than the problem of rapid
population growth. They sought a "new economic order" and were
leery of endorsing population policies proposed and backed by the
United States without protest or modification. However, Finkle and
Crane correctly predicted that "The developing nations will not turn
away from their demographic dilemmas merely to spite the West.
They are more likely to follow the example of China, India, Mexico,
and Egypt in pursuing the cause of a new economic order in the
international system—while simultaneously carrying out population
policies as part of their development plans at home" (Finkle and
Crane 1975, p. 109).

In spite of the sentiments that developing countries expressed at
Bucharest, support for family planning grew considerably in the ten
years between the Bucharest conference and the next U.N. world
population conference, which was held in Mexico City in 1984. In
many countries, the right of women to select the number and spacing
of their children became accepted in law and practice (Isaacs 1983). A
new social order was born. Agreement that women were entitled to
contraceptive advice and services, and that planning families was
proper, became almost universal. Family planning suffered an occasional attack of extremist opposition from intellectuals who saw an
imperialist plot, from leaders of minority groups concerned about
central government domination, or from human rights activists worried about coercion. Moreover, agreement on principles did not diminish the controversy surrounding who should deliver services,
what services should be delivered, and how much investment governments should make in family planning. But the debate over the

reasonableness of government support of fertility control had lost its passion and its most ardent participants.

Following Bucharest, even those countries whose formal opposition to family planning was most pronounced at the conference demonstrated support for government provision of contraceptive services. At the U.N.'s 1974 conference, the delegate from the People's Republic of China declared, "Population is not a problem under socialism. . . . The primary way of solving the population problem lies in combating the aggression and plunder of the imperialists, colonialists, and neocolonialists, and particularly the super powers." And a delegate from India, much quoted by other delegates and the press, said, "Development is the best contraceptive" (INR R-38, November 22, 1974, 286-81-002). But less than two years after Bucharest the government of India proclaimed in a formal statement, "If the future of the nation is to be secured . . . the population problem will have to be treated as a top national priority. . . . To wait for education and economic development to bring about a drop in fertility is not a practical solution" (quoted in Demeny 1984, pp. 1–2). The Chinese also instituted a national population growth policy that depended on restrictions on family size and the aggressive, sometimes coercive, provision of contraception and abortion. The Chinese program has had a substantial impact on that country's birth rate.

Family planning was probably attacked at Bucharest more because of the narrowness of the perspective it represented than because of a lack of concern about population growth, or a commitment to alternative fertility reduction strategies. Development bureaucrats and politicians represented most governments at the Sali Palatului Republicii conference hall at Bucharest, not the family planning enthusiasts who overwhelmed the American delegation—causing American delegate-demographer Ansley Coale to return home thinking the United States had exaggerated the negative impact of rapid population growth (Coale 1978, p. 419). Given the passion of the members of the American delegation who wanted to target the amount of fertility reduction required in order to achieve what they saw as desirable demographic goals, but who were not eager to talk about the issues of relative economic wealth and assistance that so troubled the Third World, it is not surprising that conflict arose.

The 1984 International Conference on Population

The 1984 U.N.-sponsored population conference in Mexico City should have been much more congenial for the United States. The developing world by then had accepted the American analysis of the population problem—that rapid growth was a serious threat to economic development—as well as the U.S. solution to the problem: provide contraceptive services. But the growth of the conservative political and the right-to-life movements in the United States, as well as the increased political activity of Protestant fundamentalists and some Catholics, forced a change in the American position, which again put the United States in opposition to most developing-world representatives, ironically by taking a stand close to what developing countries themselves had argued ten years earlier—namely, that economics was a more important force in the prosperity of developing countries than was the growth rate of their populations. Strong and outspoken leaders, solid organization, and support from the White House produced America's position at the 1984 conference, much as organization and political leverage had shaped the 1974 statement. The intellectual framework and demography were supplied by pro-natalist economist Julian Simon, but the final draft lacked the nuance of which Simon was capable (Rasky 1984). A draft version of the U.S. statement said that population growth "is, of itself, a neutral phenomenon." The U.S. position paper found population growth in the developing world "a challenge," which "provoked an over-reaction by some, largely because it coincided with two negative factors . . . government control of economies, a pathology which spread throughout the developing world . . . [and] an outbreak of an anti-intellectualism, which attacked science, technology, and every concept of material progress. . . . The combination of these two factors—counterproductive economic policies in poor and struggling nations and a pseudo-scientific pessimism among the advanced—provoked the demographic overreaction of the 1960's and 1970's" (Kimmitt to Hill, May 30, 1984, pp. 3–5, gift file).

In Mexico City, the United States produced a reappraisal, or at least a formal redefinition, of the importance of population in the world's development agenda. The official American statement presented by conservative James Buckley—former senator from New York, former undersecretary of state, and, at the time of the conference, director of Radio Free Europe—was reminiscent of the Chinese and Indian approaches to the population problem ten years earlier. The Chinese had declared that overpopulation was no problem under socialism. In 1984, the Americans declared that overpopulation could be solved by capitalist development.

Some people believe that the U.S. attitude made the Mexico City conference a success. According to this view, people throughout the developing world enjoy criticizing the United States. The U.S. policy in Mexico invited everyone else to favor family planning, and the conflict brought the conference worldwide publicity. Following the conference, the Agency for International Development continued to support family planning, and America's demographers continued to argue that rapid population growth had a negative impact on the development prospects of poor countries (National Research Council 1986). But the American position in Mexico City was at odds with AID's long-standing policies in the population field, and before long there were, in fact, signs that the consensus was unraveling.

By 1984, the population problem had lost its prominence on the agenda of America's senior development officials. Paradoxically, this decline in interest in population growth and ways to slow it came at a time when family planning programs had been demonstrated to have an important impact on fertility. Moreover, the need for continued attention to all the demographic processes—fertility, mortality, and migration—was very clear, particularly in the world's poorest countries. A few months after the population conference in Mexico City, the world was shocked and troubled by reports of the African famine, worst in Ethiopia but widespread across the sub-Saharan region. Few people thought that family planning alone would solve Africa's problems, but just as in the 1960s, it was widely regarded as a humane and practical step to take in the presence of great need.

The Reagan administration's attempts to reduce family planning assistance as part of international aid met with limited success. In 1981, the Office of Management and Budget suggested zeroing population assistance out of the federal foreign aid budget; the attempted cuts were restored, reportedly by Secretary of State Alexander Haig. Because of congressional intervention, total U.S. funding for international population assistance has remained at about the same level, but the Reagan administration withdrew funding from arguably the two most important international population organizations—the United Nations Fund for Population Activities (UNFPA), defunded in 1986, and the International Planned Parenthood Federation (IPPF), defunded in late 1984. Action was taken against UNFPA because it provided support to China's family planning program (against which charges of coercion had been raised), and against the IPPF because of the issue of abortion.

At the Mexico City conference, the Reagan administration announced that it intended to stop funding nongovernmental organizations that were associated in any way with abortion services in developing countries, even if they used non-U.S. monies for the purpose. The IPPF, by refusing to terminate support for its national affiliates that provided abortion services, became the first organization to lose U.S. funds. The administration also attempted to stop AID funding for Family Planning International Assistance (FPIA), a division of the

Planned Parenthood Federation of America, because FPIA refused to agree to be bound by the new abortion policy; however, FPIA brought suit against the government, and funding of its programs continued, pending the outcome of litigation.

As a result of the administration's position on the consequences of population growth, the Agency for International Development and much of the population community has had to search for additional justifications for continued U.S. foreign assistance to family planning programs. The negative health consequences of high fertility have been adopted as one such justification. Improved health has always been an important rationale for family planning, and from a humanitarian standpoint, health is clearly compelling. Nevertheless, in a period of tight budgets, this rationale may not be enthusiastically embraced if the health of people overseas is seen as taking precedence over domestic health problems. The compelling economic and foreign policy reasons for population assistance still need articulation in the contemporary context.

Thus, the international population and family planning community finds itself at a crossroads. Support from the United States for population-related foreign assistance has weakened. Cynics continue to dispute whether family planning programs have contributed significantly to the creation of a demand for fertility control, or whether they have just satisfied an already-existing demand. But no one has yet offered sound, feasible alternatives to family planning programs. The giants among the leaders of the family planning movement have passed from the scene, and so the field lacks a sense of direction and a set of agreed-upon goals. The momentum seems to have gone out of the international family planning movement.

8

The Population Council in Korea

Korea and the Population Council represent important landmarks in the evolution of thinking about population and development. Before Korea, there were no successful government-supported national family planning efforts in the Third World; and before the Population Council, there were no developed-world organizations dedicated to lowering birth rates in the Third World.

The effort to control fertility and to slow rapid population growth in Korea merits review because the work that was done there and in other developing countries provided legitimacy for America's international population program and helped establish the limits of American intervention into the reproductive lives of developing-world families. Some initiatives—such as assistance to increase abortion services—were consistently rejected by officials in most countries, while others—grants for training, for example—were almost always welcomed. The give-and-take of project negotiation, implementation, and evaluation contributed to the body of scientific, bureaucratic, and popular wisdom regarding what was acceptable and what worked. Concentrating on a particular country provides the best vantage point from which to examine many of the issues surrounding the relationship between foreign aid for population and family planning activities and the modernization of reproductive behavior in the Third World.

Korea is a good place for such an examination because it is among the best known and most widely cited examples of the modern decline of fertility. In the late 1950s, Korea's population grew slightly less than 3 percent per year; the rate of natural increase was 2.6 percent per year between 1960 and 1966, reflecting a decline in fertility associated with the end of the post–Korean War baby boom. By 1980, the growth rate had dropped to 2.0, making the decline in population growth in Korea one of the fastest in history. Because mortality was also declining throughout the period, the decline in population growth was caused entirely by reductions in fertility. From 1960 to 1980, the average number of children borne by Korean women declined by 60 percent. A woman married at the end of the Korean War (1953) was likely to have more than five children, whereas her daughter will probably not have more than two children. In the early 1960s, fewer than 10 percent of all married women practiced contraception; by 1984, 70 percent said they used family planning (Gendell 1986, p. 15).

Although Korea provides an important case study, it is not necessarily representative of other developing countries. So many unique historical, cultural, social, and economic factors determine the character and pace of the social changes that take place within a country that it is easy to make too much of the extent to which the lessons of one country's experience apply to another. Nevertheless, the process of economic development has many common elements across a wide variety of countries—and in this sense, the Korean experience is typical. In 1953, Korea was a desperately poor country whose development had been slowed by the harsh colonial rule of the Japanese and by a bitterly fought civil war. In 1960 Korea had the same per capita income as Ghana. By 1980, per capita income in Korea had increased at least five times, while Ghana's had declined by one-fourth (Repetto 1985, p. 758).

Korea is worth studying not only because it shares a common background of dependency and poverty with the rest of the developing world, but also because it represents the success story that poor countries everywhere seek to emulate. By every widely used measure—per capita income, educational attainment, life expectancy—life in Korea has improved spectacularly in the more than thirty-five years since the end of the Korean War.

The experience of the Population Council in Korea merits attention because it was the Population Council that first institutionalized international technical and financial assistance in population and family planning. Before its founding by John D. Rockefeller III, in 1952, there were no organizations primarily concerned about the causes or consequences of rapid population growth in the developing world. The International Planned Parenthood Federation, which represented private voluntary family planning groups, was also founded in 1952, but it lacked the clout and the flexible resources of the Population Council. The Council broadened the context in which population issues were discussed to include the impact of rapid growth on economic development and the health consequences of high fertility. The work of the Population Council demonstrates the important role that private organizations played in the design and implementation of

America's international population policies. The Council's experience also provides a valuable illustration of changing donor perspectives toward assistance programs, and of the interaction among local and foreign institutions and how their differing needs and goals influence program implementation.

The Population Council's Role

The experience of the Population Council and its efforts in two very different areas—the manufacture of intrauterine devices and economic planning—illustrate the range of issues that foreigners sought to influence. In the case of the Population Council in Korea, it was largely the enthusiasm of key staff that prompted Council involvement in these issues. There is no indication in the files of the Population Council that anyone in its New York headquarters would have continued to promote support for the manufacture of IUDs in Korea in the mid-1970s if George Worth, the Council's representative in Seoul, had not pushed the idea. Likewise, nobody in New York would have encouraged the Council's support for work at the Korea Development Institute on the relationships between population and development policy had not the representative in Seoul kept the idea alive.

The importance of the population officers stationed at AID's missions in developing countries parallels that of the Population Council's field staff. The AID staff had less flexibility in program development than did Council personnel, but because they had veto power over all in-country activities, at times had their own budget, or could request support from Washington for specific projects, AID population officers had considerable influence over the implementation of AID's program in the field. The experience of the Council staff reflects many of the same issues that AID staff overseas confronted.

Council staff arrived early in the evolution of Korea's population program and stayed until the program was well established. The Population Council's first representative in Seoul began work only four months after the prime minister's office issued Instruction no. 18, "Family Planning Encouragement Plan," in September 1963.

The prime minister's statement was the result of several years of evaluation of the importance of population growth for Korea's economic development. The review began between the fall of the government of Syngman Rhee in April 1960 and the start of the regime of Park Chung Hee in May 1961, during which time much freer discussion of family planning was possible than ever before. Results of the 1960 census showed an average annual rate of population growth of 2.9 percent between 1955 and 1960, higher than most experts had expected. As a result, there was considerable discussion of the implications of this rapid population growth for Korea's development and an eagerness in many quarters to promote family planning. A good deal of publicity about family planning was to be found in local newspapers and magazines. Interested Koreans established the Planned Parenthood Federation of Korea (PPFK) in April 1961 (Donaldson 1981).

The Supreme Council for National Reconstruction, which took over the government in May 1961, was composed of a group of relatively young military officers who sought advice on important issues from Korean experts who served on special advisory committees. The Sociology Committee was composed of three members, all of whom had a strong interest in population. In addition, according to one participant who served in a key administrative post at the time, "there were many professional civil servants . . . who were aware of the population problem and used their influence in their work of general policy advice and planning through the successive administrations of those years" (Lee to Caldwell, May 20, 1969, PC/K). A proposal to begin a national family planning program was drafted by the Sociology Committee and, after review and revision, was brought to the Supreme Council. The Ministry of Health and Social Affairs had also developed a plan that included government support for contraceptive services. Meanwhile, the Supreme Council itself instructed the Committee on Health to prepare a report on family planning and population trends. In November 1961, after considering the various reports, the Supreme Council announced its approval of a national family planning program as an official government policy. The announcement was made by President Park Chung Hee himself, acting as chairman of the Supreme Council.

The family planning program was officially placed under the jurisdiction of the Ministry of Health and Social Affairs. From the outset, however, the private Planned Parenthood Federation worked closely with the ministry to develop a national program. Although the program remained funded through the health account, family planning was always promoted as an economic development measure. The program received a boost when Lee Byung Moo (1967) translated a summary of the Coale-Hoover (1958) analysis of population growth. The translation provided easy access to this important work; less than a year after it appeared, the Economic Planning Board approved an increase in funding for family planning (Caldwell 1969, pp. 24–26).

As it generally did before becoming actively involved in other countries, the Population Council dispatched a team of Council staff and outside consultants to evaluate Korea's demographic situation, to judge the need to slow population growth, and to suggest ways to design and implement policies to achieve demographic targets that would serve the country's development goals. Donald Warwick (1982), among others, has criticized this strategy on the grounds that the team members had made up their minds well in advance of their arrival in Korea about the dangers of rapid population growth, and about the potential effectiveness of a government-supported family planning program in lowering fertility and slowing growth. This was doubtless the case, but the dissemblance was double-edged in that the Korean officials at the Ministry of Health and Social Affairs, who formally invited the Population Council team, did so precisely because they wanted an international, particularly an American, endorsement of their judgment that the government and the private sector together should work to slow population growth.

The Population Council team reported that slower population growth would indeed benefit Korea. The team's visit also provided the occasion for the Koreans to present their first request for assistance to the Council. When the Council mission left, Minister of Health and Social Affairs Chung Hi Sup wrote to then–Population Council President Frank Notestein about the team's visit:

> I am with a great pleasure to inform you that during their stay in Korea we had many topics to discuss with them, which are most important and urgent in solving serious questions for achieving family planning activities satisfactorily, and those were the assignment of consultant in Korea, demonstration survey program of family planning in rural and urban areas, strengthening of the information and education services, application of plastic intra-uterine devices, which are foreseen to be solved in the prospective future. It is my confidence that these problems . . . could be solved in close cooperation with your Council. (Chung to Notestein, November 21, 1963, PC/K)

Projects to promote the delivery of family planning were established by Seoul National University's School of Public Health and by Yonsei University's Department of Preventive Medicine. A nationwide advertising campaign to encourage contraceptive use was designed by the PPFK. The Population Council also agreed to provide scholarships for Korean students to study in America, and to provide plastic and molds to enable a Korean firm to manufacture intrauterine devices. The basic Council program thus combined a focus on the immediate—the provision of contraceptive devices and the support of promotional activities—and on the long-range through support for training and research. This mix of practical projects with a hoped-for immediate payoff in terms of greater program impact, and of more academic undertakings aimed at strengthening the population sciences and family planning infrastructure, was characteristic of the more successful Population Council country programs.

The Council sent Paul Hartman, a Navy veteran who had served as a health educator at the AID office in Seoul, to Korea to administer its program. Hartman worked for the Council in Korea until his death in August 1968. Eight other expatriates served on the Council staff in Seoul between the opening of the Seoul office in 1964 and its closing thirteen years later; at its busiest, the office also employed ten Koreans. Work in Korea also benefited from frequent visits by Sam Keeny, the Population Council's East Asian representative based in Taiwan. Keeny, who joined the council in 1963 at the age of seventy, was an old Asian hand whose career in development assistance had begun after World War I. He was the hand in the glove for much of the Council's early program development work in Korea.

Day-to-Day Work: June 1968

The best way to get a sense of how the Population Council worked is to concentrate on what happened during a single month at the height of the Council's involvement in Korea. Such an analysis also provides a concrete illustration of how the policies formulated in the United States were interpreted in the field. We can add flesh to the dry bones of bureaucratic and scholarly disputes by examining how arguments over the most effective fertility control strategy influenced day-to-day program operations of one American international population control organization.

June 1968 was a typical month for the Council staff in Seoul. Most attention was paid to research and training activities—especially applied university-based research to evaluate the family planning program and to establish ways to improve its performance. Despite its being the underlying rationale for the program, little was done or said about the economic impact of rapid population growth or the prospects for manipulating elements of the economic and social structure to help lower fertility.

Hartman's monthly reports to the Council's New York headquarters detail the extent of his involvement. In August 1967, for example, he wrote New York: "A highly successful start was made . . . on the mammoth but vital task of meeting on a discussion basis with every possible practicing physician in Korea to inform them about the family planning program and the loop and oral pill methods of contraception. The occasion was the first of 455 local level medical society meetings scheduled in 1967" (Korea Office Monthly Report, August 1967, PC/K).

The importance of the Korean emphasis on, and the Council's support for, training and information dissemination is noteworthy. Few of those who proclaim the benefits of national family planning programs explain the time, resources, and managerial leadership needed for successful program implementation. The steady stream of seminars, workshops, study tours, conferences, and courses was one important way in which the Koreans increased their skills, interest in, and commitment to family planning.

In June 1968, Council-supported training activities included three 12-day-long refresher training courses for family planning fieldworkers and six separate radio programs on family planning aired by the Korean Broadcasting Service. Earlier in the year, the Council had helped with a different type of effort to increase knowledge of the family planning program when ". . . in cooperation with the ROK Army Air Force some 300,000 leaflets were dropped in remote areas by airplane" (Monthly Report, April 1968, p. 3, PC/K).

The best known and most highly regarded element in the Population Council's training effort was a fellowship program that supported graduate study in the United States. This program provided Korea (and over seventy-five other countries) with a cadre of population professionals trained to the highest international standards, and it also provides an important indication of the Council's approach to the population problem. Unlike AID, which preferred short-term, highly specialized training, the Population Council concentrated its support of training on graduate education at the highest level. This approach was rooted in the belief that the sensitivity of the population issue and the huge variety of important local differences in the determinants and consequences of population change required that local experts, and not foreigners, analyze problems and propose solutions (author's interviews).

One thing the Council training program does not indicate is an eagerness to rethink the nature and importance of population in the development process or the role of family planning services in lowering growth rates. In fact, most of the time of the Council staff in Korea was taken up with relatively short-term projects that were the building blocks of the national family planning program. No one engaged in heady reviews of the importance of ongoing demographic changes for Korea's development. Having accepted the proposition that rapid population growth was detrimental, Population Council staff concentrated on aiding those who wished to study ways to increase contraceptive use and lower fertility.

In the June 1968 monthly report, one of the last reports he wrote before he died, Paul Hartman described the progress being made by the Korean family planning program and discussed the status of the activities the Population Council was supporting. The report provides a glimpse of the range of things the Council tried to do. As had become his standard practice, Hartman began his report with a review of the monthly number of accepters of the various contraceptives offered by the government, noting that there were 18,690 IUD insertions and 716 vasectomies. He promised to investigate what he termed the "low figure for condom acceptance," recipients of which totaled 109,387 against a goal of 150,000. He noted that "June is the busiest month in rural Korea" and that extra work might have kept demand lower than usual (Korea Office Monthly Report, June 1968, PC/K).

In June 1968, Hartman began discussions with the Swedish International Development Agency (SIDA) and the Korean government about a building to house family planning program evaluation and training activities. The Swedish government was particularly important in the first decade of Korea's family planning programs. Not only did SIDA provide support for the construction of new quarters for the training and evaluation divisions of the national program, but the agency also gave the government its first large supply of oral contraceptives. The Population Council had provided oral contraceptives to Korean medical researchers several years earlier; their studies of the acceptability and use of the pill helped pave the way for the SIDA donation. Council field staff frequently acted as go-betweens among officials of the Korean government and other foreign aid agencies, illustrating the importance of the interlocking system of agency relationships for shaping foreign aid programs in population.

Research and evaluation of the Korean effort to lower fertility, another special concern of the Council, experienced what Hartman described as "a minor explosion of activity" during June 1968 when new IBM equipment was installed. Korean evaluators also visited Taiwan to work with their counterparts in East Asia's other important experiment in fertility control.

The Council had made grants to several Korean universities to support demonstration projects aimed at showing that family planning services could be made easily available and were acceptable in both rural and urban areas. A study in Kyunggi Province conducted by Yonsei University evaluated the effectiveness of what were known as mothers' classes—regular gatherings of the married women in a community—in promoting contraceptive use. Over 320,000 families were involved in the study, in over 2,000 villages.

Among other research projects mentioned by Hartman were a study of a "two-brand" pill program compared to the existing "one-brand" program, and a study of the advantages and disadvantages of the 28-day pill pack compared with the 21-day pill pack. Results of these product-oriented research projects, of a type that commercial firms in the United States would undertake to evaluate consumer attitudes and improve sales, enabled the Korean family planning program to adjust to its market as successfully as any Western retailer.

In June 1968, the family planning programs in Korea and Taiwan were the most frequently cited developing-world government efforts to control population growth. What happened in those countries was well publicized through Population Council reports and other international publications and conferences. Sixteen of the thirty-four articles in the Council's *Studies in Family Planning* during 1968 dealt with Korea or Taiwan. Because relatively little is known about how developing-world leaders made decisions about which program innovation to endorse, the effect of all this publicity is impossible to prove. However, the programs in Korea and Taiwan probably had a major influence because they encouraged the belief that government-supported family planning programs could be culturally acceptable and could have an important effect on the extent to which contraception was used and, thus, on the level of childbearing and population growth. Frank Notestein engineered Population Council involvement in Korea and Taiwan because, as he put it, "family planning desperately needed a success" (author's interview). As the success of Korea's family planning program became more apparent, there was a steady stream of visitors from the rest of Asia who came to see what was happening in Korea. Leaders of the family planning programs in Indonesia, Thailand, and the Philippines can be seen as young bureaucrats or students on their way to or from American graduate schools in fading photos in albums saved by the Population Council.

The Loop Program

The initial success of Korean family planning programs was built on the availability of the plastic intrauterine device. Between the opening of the Population Council office in 1964 and its closing thirteen years later, IUD accepters outnumbered pill accepters 2-to-1 and exceeded sterilization accepters by almost 6-to-1 (Donaldson 1981, p. 241). The IUD revolutionized family planning in Korea and elsewhere because it dramatically increased the ease and effectiveness with which couples could regulate childbearing and greatly lowered the cost of government support for fertility control. The Council staff favored the loop (as the IUD was called in Korea) as a means of fertility control. The enthusiasm was rooted less in demography or medicine than in economics: the device was inexpensive to manufacture and did not require a sophisticated infrastructure for delivery.

The IUD was in fact better suited to Korea than it might have been elsewhere because the country had a large number of private practitioners to insert the devices, and a population density that put all but the most remote villagers less than a day's trip away from a qualified physician. The willingness of doctors to provide a relatively cheap, safe abortion in the case of IUD failure was also of clear importance soon apparent to most women in Korea (Hong and Watson 1976).

When the Korean government first began its family planning program, oral contraceptives were still too expensive to be considered for a countrywide program. The Swedish International Development Agency provided 1.3 million cycles of pills and the Koreans, with Population Council help, drew up a plan for their use. The Council proposed offering the pill to unsatisfied or unsuccessful IUD users. At one stage Hartman wrote New York: "the pill has vast potential for use by those who are contraindicated for wearing the loop or cannot retain or tolerate this device, and for recruitment among new and/or dissatisfied practitioners of other methods. . . . Likewise it appears clear, the pill method is far from perfect as measured in terms of early drop-outs for minor side-effects. . . . Obviously, it is much simpler for users to quit the pill than the loop" (Hartman to Anderson, January 1967, PC/K).

Until 1975, the Population Council supplied plastic for the manufacture of IUDs in Korea by a small firm operating under a license from the Council. Early in 1975, however, because of a changing orientation toward how it could best help solve the problem of rapid population growth and an organizational budget crisis, the Council suddenly refused to give the Koreans the raw materials needed for making IUDs. The Council's representative in Seoul, George Worth, claimed that this unexpected cold shoulder "gave the Government no time to adjust to this sudden shift in Council policy" (Worth to Donaldson, June 19, 1975, PC/K).

According to Worth, with more notice the Koreans could have arranged to get the needed raw materials themselves. In fact, the government sent an official letter to the Council promising to pay for all future raw materials, but claiming that funds for 1975 were unavailable. The amount required was very small, less than $5,000—suggesting how precarious family planning program operations can be, even in countries known for strong programs.

Worth resigned from the Population Council and returned to the United States in June 1975 with the IUD issue still not resolved. The

Council's New York staff insisted that funds for IUDs were not available. Worth wrote his replacement about how to obtain funds for the IUDs and make it look like the Council was not being charged: "This can be done by showing an income item on our office report. If you want to, I am willing for some of my personal money to be used to show this income now. The materials can be ordered right away. I can then be repaid over a period of time as you sell off surplus furniture, typewriters, and the Toyota car. I can defer being paid back. It seems to me *very* important to do something soon . . . to keep up the momentum of the IUD program and . . . to help maintain the integrity of the Council in Korea" (emphasis in original; Worth to Donaldson, June 29, 1975, PC/K). The car would probably yield only $1,000. Other unneeded office items might produce another $500. The estimated bill for the raw material was $2,580. Thus, help was still needed from New York (Donaldson to Montague, July 25, 1975, PC/K).

Following unsuccessful attempts to generate the money from the sale of Council property in Seoul and additional requests to New York, including a telephone plea by George Worth to his former colleagues, the Population Council eventually supplied 1,500 pounds of Alathone-20 Barium Sulfate Blend, together with 12 pounds of azure blue thread and 6 pounds of canary yellow thread. The material was shipped to the Ministry of Health and Social Affairs on November 20, 1975. The plastic and thread cost $1,386; shipping was $2,200. When the Council's Acting President Parker Mauldin wrote Dr. Han Che Ik, director of the Ministry of Health and Social Affairs Maternal and Child Bureau, to inform him that the Council would supply the materials needed to manufacture IUDs, he closed the door on future aid: "We are sorry to inform you that this will be the last donation the Council can make to the Korean Government for the manufacture of IUDs, . . . if continued support is needed, we trust you will be able to receive it from alternative sources" (Mauldin to Che, November 6, 1975, PC/K).

The IUD request from Korea came at a bad time for the Council. A few months earlier a Council vice-president had told his colleagues that "an element of hesitancy [has] crept into our activities" (Demeny 1975b, p. 2). Within the Council, morale had been lowered by a prolonged search for a new president, and by a rivalry between those who thought the Council should concentrate on family planning programs as the best means to lower fertility and those who favored more research on the consequences of population growth and its relationship to development as a means of increasing attention to the population problem. The acting president lacked authority to set bold new directions. The Council's family planners were losing influence, and an effort to help with something as mundane as manufacturing IUDs was a good distance from the Council's emerging image of itself as a shaper of public policy.

As AID began to supply pills and IUDs to developing-world family planning programs, and as pill use increased dramatically in both rich and poor countries, the Population Council became less eager to support the manufacture of IUDs. Financial problems also befell the Council in the mid-1970s, and interacted with the lack of clear, agreed-upon, long-range plans to make cost-cutting a priority. The reaction of the Council's leadership to the continued need to supply Korea with raw materials to manufacture IUDs also illustrates the movement from a heavy reliance on technology for program expansion—the Council's position on IUDs in the 1960s—to a disinterest and even hostility among some staff toward technology and a high regard for the potential demographic impact of thoughtfully implemented social and economic policies.

Changing Economic and Social Policy

As the appeal of activities aimed directly at providing or improving family planning services declined at the Population Council, the attraction of projects related to national economic policy increased. The changing Council priorities reflected the changing concerns of the world in which the Council operated. As the previous chapter showed, throughout the 1960s and 1970s the control of population growth and the provision of family planning services became accepted goals of public policy, both in the United States and in the developing world. One consequence of this was an increasing eagerness to experiment with broader economic and social measures as a means of influencing couples' childbearing practices. A typical proposal was to charge third children more for medical care and school than first or second children (PPFK 1982). Asian countries led the way in proposing and implementing these new interventions, just as they had led the way with family planning.

Until the mid-1970s, discussion of family planning versus non–family planning approaches to regulating population growth was far more cordial at the Population Council than it was at AID, but the Council faced the same dilemma AID did. The argument that economic development and social change were more important for reducing fertility than the promotion of family planning services did not typically lead to proposals to do away with family planning programs or even to reduce appropriations for contraceptive services. But people criticized developing-country governments' reliance on family planning as the only strategy to slow population growth, and the enthusiasm of the international family planning donors, which seemed to encourage this single-minded approach by exaggerating the impact of family planning (Demerath 1976; Davis 1967). The most thoughtful people, and there were many on both sides, argued for a multifaceted approach instead of one that relied on economic rewards or family planning alone.

The discussion of the pros and cons of family planning took place everywhere population policy was talked about (Finkle and Crane 1975). The issue for both public and private population organizations was how to use scarce resources to slow growth, not what was theoretically the best approach. The Population Council and its field staff had far less success in encouraging specific projects dealing with noncontraceptive influences on fertility than they did in promoting family planning projects. Like AID (discussed above), the Council was unable to develop a set of programs dealing with economic incentives that could be funded, that held the promise of working, and that could be sold to Third World economic planners and policy makers.

Early in their stay in Korea, the Population Council field staff recognized the importance of justifying their efforts to reduce population growth in economic terms. They also saw the importance of documenting the cost-effectiveness of government-subsidized contraceptive services. The basis of their analyses is not always clear, but a reference to the economic impact of population control and the cost-effectiveness of family planning was a standard feature of the monthly reports of the Council's Korea field staff during the 1960s. In July 1968, for example, Paul Hartman wrote to New York: "Careful analysis by eminent economists indicates that one birth prevented will save the economy one to two times the amount represented by the per capita income. . . . In the long run, there is a net economic loss for each new addition to the population" (Korea Office Monthly Report, July 1968, p. 9, PC/K).

George Worth, who joined the Council as its representative in Korea after Paul Hartman died, was well connected, thoughtful, and worked easily with his Korean and American colleagues. Both groups held him in high regard—in part because they were overwhelmed by his fluency in Korean, which he had learned when he first arrived in Korea in the mid-1950s. From the beginning of his tenure, Worth lobbied New York to provide more support for research on the costs and benefits of Korea's family planning program. As a knowledgeable observer of Seoul's political and bureaucratic ways, he recognized the power of the Economic Planning Board and the Budget Bureau and their ability to decide which programs prospered.

Worth tried to increase the awareness of population issues among Korea's economic planners. He believed that "the Council had not done enough in Korea to help the economists and planners to understand and handle the population facet of their responsibilities" (Worth to Demeny, May 24, 1974, PC/K). To promote research on population he met with staff from the Bureau of Statistics (BOS), the Economic Planning Board (EPB), and the Korea Development Institute (KDI), a think tank known locally as "the brains of the Economic Planning Board."

While Worth was talking with the economic planners in Korea, Council staff in New York were discussing how best to encourage developing countries to incorporate a consideration of population in the economic planning process. Council-supported economists were already stationed at planning boards in Thailand and Indonesia, and several New York staff argued for expansion of the program. One Council document concluded, "given the central importance of development planning in most of the countries where we work, and certainly throughout Asia, it is difficult to imagine a more critically important locus for inputs of advice than planning agencies" (Baldwin to Mauldin, December 18, 1972, p. 2, PC/K).

The Population Council staff in Korea agreed that Council population specialists should work at planning agencies, but they knew that Korea's Economic Planning Board would not accept foreign advisors. The Korea Development Institute might be willing to provide a home for foreign experts, but relations with KDI were not well established. The Council's Korea staff proposed hiring an expatriate to "work with economists at Yonsei [University], [Seoul National University], and Korea University who play important advisory roles with the Economic Planning Board" (Watson to Baldwin, April 18, 1973, PC/K). But no one was hired.

Early in February 1975, Dr. Clifford Pease, director of the Council's Technical Assistance Division, visited Seoul and KDI. On his return to New York he wrote to Paul Demeny, director of the Council's Demographic Division, regarding the opportunities at KDI: "We have been heavily involved in the family planning field and have been trying for years to influence population policy beyond family planning institutions. Here is a unique opportunity and an important institute that we cannot afford to let slip by" (Pease to Demeny, February 20, 1975, PC/K).

I replaced George Worth as the Population Council's representative in Korea in the summer of 1975. My appointment centered primarily around the traditional family planning research and evaluation program. Less than a year later, I recommended closing the Council office because of New York's unwillingness to provide any grants to institutions in Korea. Support for me and the Council's local staff cost far more than the Council was providing in direct assistance to Korean institutions.

Shortly after arriving in Korea, I had started to work part-time at KDI, collaborating with a Korean sociologist who had recently been appointed as the staff population specialist. I proposed placing a foreign expert at KDI on a full-time basis to encourage more careful thinking about the interrelationships between population and economic development. Under ordinary circumstances, the Council would have been more responsive to my proposal, but they were slowed by the difficult financial circumstances that international population organizations found themselves in during the mid-1970s. Indeed, Demeny wrote to Worth describing meetings that he and his deputy had with KDI's executive vice-president ". . . encouraging him to initiate activities in the population and development planning area at the Institute and suggesting, on more than one occasion, that if the Institute signaled to us a need for help from the Council in such matters, we would do our best to be responsive. . . . For the time being, I am afraid it is not easy for us to take a more aggressive stance. Prosaic financial considerations dictate caution, in this as in other matters" (Demeny to Worth, March 31, 1975, PC/K). Providing assistance to projects in Korea was particularly difficult because Korea's rapid development and declining fertility meant that it was considered a low-priority country by most international donors and a so-called graduate country by AID, meaning that it was not an eligible recipient of normal U.S. government development assistance funds.

Negotiations to appoint an expatriate population specialist at KDI funded jointly by the Population Council, the United Nations, and the Canadian government wound through a tortuous route. The initial proposal was first made in early 1976. Negotiations continued through the summer, with recommendations made by all the donors to proceed—but shortages of money, a lack of interest in Korea, and a lack of suitable candidates for the position at KDI slowed progress.

One element in the Council's indecision over what to do in Korea, and at KDI in particular, was the declining reputation of family planners at the Council and elsewhere in the mid-1970s. At the World Population Conference in Bucharest, John D. Rockefeller III, who was chairman of the Council's Board of Trustees, had decried the limited gains made by fertility control programs. He argued for a broader development and a woman-based initiative to reduce fertility (J. D. Rockefeller 1974). The Korea lobby at the Population Council's headquarters was composed mainly of family planners—demographers who had worked as researchers in Korea or had participated in one way or another in the analysis and dissemination of information on the Korean family planning program. They were keen to keep working in Korea, but much more eager to see the work center on abortion and family planning than on questions of the relationship between fertility and development policy. Council President George Zeidenstein once told me that the Council could not make up its mind about what to do in Korea "because of a fight between the family planners and the nonfamily planners" (Donaldson to Fawcett, May 24, 1976, PC/K).

Criticisms of the Council's plans for work at KDI and arguments for continued support of family planning were put forward by some Council grantees in Korea. But most Korean family planners recognized the need to incorporate economic planners into the population movement. The appointment of a Population Council advisor at KDI was viewed as an opportunity to accomplish this. But others, particularly the head of the Planned Parenthood Federation, wished for a continuation of direct Population Council support to the family planning program (author's interviews).

In the late fall of 1976, the Council agreed to provide approximately $60,000 to support a person working at KDI. A request was made to the Canadian International Development Research Centre (IDRC) for an additional $60,000 (see Koo to Simmons, September 5, 1976, PC/K). The IDRC insisted on obtaining assurances that no appropriate Korean could be found for the position; at the time, it was said "IDRC believes that KDI no longer needs such an advisor and . . . would like to help wean the Koreans accordingly" (Baron to Demeny, November 9, 1976, PC/K). After further negotiations with a senior IDRC staff member during a visit to Korea persuaded him that a foreign advisor was needed, the Canadian government also agreed to provide support.

When attention turned to recruiting an appropriate person, the search dragged on because of the high, almost unreasonable standards the search committee imposed. Only a few able individuals met the criteria that KDI and the donors laid down, and thus the search took longer than most people had anticipated. In time, a population specialist who had considerable experience in Korea, including an earlier appointment at KDI, and who was fluent in Korean, was named a visiting fellow at the Korea Development Institute under a complex funding arrangement supported by KDI, the Population Council, IDRC, and the United Nations Fund for Population Activities.

The advisor at KDI was supposed to help KDI's Population Policy and Planning Secretariat conduct policy research and evaluation studies for the government's Population Policy Coordinating Committee, chaired by the deputy prime minister and minister of economic planning. In practice, the Population Secretariat has carried out research at the request of the Economic Planning Board and the Population Policy Working Level Committee (the only active subcommittee of the otherwise inactive Population Policy Coordinating Committee). It has played a role in the discussion of the population components of Korea's national development plans. Secretariat staff also completed a population status report (Hong 1978). Outside observers have applauded the secretariat's work, but have also complained that "the Secretariat must be more than simply another research group. Its 'outreach,' coordination, and leadership roles are crucial if it is to elicit new programme applications of the existing policies. It is not clear that as currently constituted and located in KDI, the Secretariat can do this. It is essential that it devote more of its time to policy-programme initiatives" (UNFPA 1982, p. 15). The minister of economic planning during the period of Population Council support to KDI complained that "So far . . . it is difficult to discern a substantial increase in the use of demographic parameters in development planning attributable to the contributions of the [secretariat]. In fact, the [secretariat] has not been overly active in recent years" (Nam and Ro 1981, p. 665).

The Council's office, which had been occupied for over a dozen years, was closed during the summer of 1977. Some years later, the head of KDI's Population Secretariat moved to a university professorship. The president of KDI became minister of finance, and later deputy prime minister and minister of economic planning; the director of research became vice-president of a private university; and the KDI statistician who began the negotiations with the Council took a position at the Bureau of Statistics.

Foreign Promotion or Sui Generis

Population control and family planning are now well established in Korea with several large and active public and private organizations, a share of the national budget, more than two decades of experience in implementing programs, and a pool of clients numbering in the millions. Evolution along the same lines has taken place in other countries—mainly in Asia, but also in Latin America. Over the same period, the interest, experience, and competence of various international organizations have also increased substantially. When Paul Hartman opened the Population Council in Korea, there was no United Nations Fund for Population Activities. The World Bank showed no interest in population. The World Health Organization's interest was only a glimmer. And neither AID, nor the development agencies of other Western governments, had yet begun to support population activities.

Over the years, Population Council staff involved themselves in almost everything related to population and family planning in Korea. What was the impact of the Council's aid? Were the foreigners essential, or would Korea's program have developed pretty much the same way without them? Foreigners played an important role, but it may have been more symbolic than practical. Few Koreans told me foreign funds were essential to the program's development, even though everyone was eager to accept them. Fewer still cite research ideas provided by foreign advisors as being important. More important than money was the demonstration of international concern about the problem of rapid population growth: foreign experts gave the population program a legitimacy in the eyes of the government that it would not otherwise have had (author's interviews). It is ironic that the members of the Council's field staff, whose successes and self-images most would probably link to their identification with Korean interests, would apparently be perceived as most valuable in the eyes of Korean family planners because of their identity with the United States.

The Koreans regarded the Population Council very highly. When Marshall Balfour, who had led the first Council mission to Korea, died in the summer of 1976, a memorial service was organized by Korean family planners who remembered the crucial role he had played during the early days of the program (Yang to Balfour, June 4, 1976, PC/K). In June 1977, when the Council's last representative was ready to leave Seoul, the minister of health and social affairs wrote to Council President George Zeidenstein describing the Council's departure as a "serious loss to Korea" and expressing appreciation "for the kind cooperation and assistance the Population Council has rendered to Korea" (Shin to Zeidenstein, June 7, 1977, PC/K). The links that bound the Council to family planners and other demographic enthusiasts in Korea survived even the worst onslaughts of the assistance process.

One AID-funded report written in the late 1960s concluded that Korea's national family planning program was "not a government operation but . . . [was] dependent largely on two non-government organizations, the Population Council and the Planned Parenthood Federation" (Poffenberger 1969, p. 2). The foreign flavor of family planning in Korea was more apparent during the 1960s than thereafter. But even in the 1960s, Korea's population program was not a result of foreign technical advice: it was a product of Koreans' perception of their need to become economically independent and the fact that population growth was seen as a barrier to that effort. Indeed, while Korea was taking money from the United States to promote population control, the purpose of the program was precisely to avoid a continued reliance on America. In population, as in other things, American advisory services underestimated Korea's possibilities and vacillated on the type and amount of support to be provided (Kim, Ross, and Worth 1972, pp. 35–41; for an analysis of foreign aid in other sectors, see Suh 1977).

There is little doubt the Koreans could have achieved their population successes without the aid of the Population Council. They would have moved at a slower rate and would have documented their story less fully—but beyond the initial period, there is little evidence that Korea genuinely required what the United States had to offer. George Worth, the most distinguished of the Council's field staff in Korea, summarized the impact of foreign aid for Korea's family planning program this way:

> The thing would have happened without any foreigners around but . . . they reinforced [it]. In a few cases, they were the front-line innovators. . . . The foreign money that went in to help train field workers and print the original little pamphlets and that sort of stuff was not doing anything the Koreans wouldn't have done or accomplished somehow or other, but it was encouraging them and helping them do what they wanted to do. During the first ten years, we encouraged some of the right people in the right way. It was a fluke but it happened. I really don't think that all the money that was spent say post-1970 in Korea was very significant. It . . . did interesting kinds of things, but if none of it had been spent, it would have been all right. (author's interview)

Korea's entrepreneurial resources, which helped sustain its economic development, also benefited its social programs. Well-managed government institutions, such as the Korean Institute for Family Planning (KIFP), were able to select useful foreign ideas and put them to good use. Program officials at KIFP, at the Planned Parenthood Federation, and elsewhere quickly mastered new approaches and turned them to the advantage of the family planning program. One dramatic illustration of this adaptability is the speed with which laparoscopic female sterilization techniques spread throughout Korea in the late 1970s: new, simpler techniques, and a government subsidy that dramatically reduced the cost patients had to pay, caused the annual number of sterilization procedures to jump from 35,000 to 180,000 between 1976 and 1979 (Koh, Hahm, and Byun 1980, p. 96). A combination of individual interest, organizational structure, and development status allowed Korea to take much greater advantage of this new sterilization technology than other countries.

The use of research institutes and independent policy boards demonstrates the Korean ability to adapt to Western styles of management and provides another example of Western influence modified to suit local needs. Target setting and the centralization of economic planning, on the other hand, are more traditional forms of organizational behavior and management. Korea relied on foreigners for contraceptive technology and many of its ideas about advertising. But these foreign imports, like other elements of Korea's population and family planning program, underwent considerable adaptation before they were used locally.

Why Fertility Declined

The key factor in Korea's fertility decline was the growing desire on the part of men and women to avoid the physical and financial burdens of too many children. Changing Korean sentiments about the value of children coincided with an expanding network of contraceptive information and services and a rapidly changing social and economic environment that made contraceptive use and controlled fertility not only acceptable but also appropriate, and even praiseworthy.

Education was particularly important in this transition. The better-educated couples of the 1980s have a different worldview from that of earlier generations. During the American occupation of South Korea after World War II, land reform further lessened the power of the traditional elites already weakened by the Japanese. It became clear that education was no longer a window of opportunity for the rich only: if one could afford the tuition, one could educate one's children. Thus, it was also clear that too many children might be a costly disadvantage when it came to paying school fees. The Korean War helped confirm this emerging view of the costs of children. Koreans recall that the more children you had, the more you suffered during the war.

High fertility also made more sense for rural than for urban families. During the 1960s and 1970s, as Korea urbanized rapidly and the nuclear family pattern became increasingly widespread, children became more burdensome. A farmer with two sons and one daughter is in principle much better off if one son must enter Korea's mandatory military service, or if one son or the father himself is not able to work because there will still be a son at home. But Korea is a country of notoriously small farms, so a division of the land among sons is nearly impossible. Thus, the advantage the extra son conveys is short-lived—a fact not missed by the rural population. The second son must be educated to work in town or in one of the big cities, if he is to contribute to the family's long-term prosperity.

Koreans' drive for education and their willingness to sacrifice for their children's educations have resulted in universal literacy and a high level of educational attainment, which have provided the human resources crucial for the nation's development. The educational system also performs important socialization and social-control functions by helping to promote identity, discipline, and a common value orientation (Moskowitz 1982, p. 67).

The growth of individualism is also important for understanding the changing pattern of childbearing in Korea. In traditional societies, such as pre–World War II Korea, individuals have assigned positions that tightly circumscribe the possibilities of individual choice. When there are choices to be made, they are made in consultation with one's key reference groups, of which the family network is typically the most important. The criterion for choice is not the welfare of the individual decision maker, but the welfare of the group to which he belongs. Economic development and modernization radically alter the context of decision making and the traditional patterns of exchange.

Modern societies are characterized by a greater measure of self-interest than is found in traditional communities. People try to maximize individual welfare in modern societies in a way that is unthought-of in traditional cultures (Dore 1982, pp. 22–25). Some Koreans and foreigners (Brandt 1971, pp. 76–77) would disagree with this analysis, but I believe they misjudge the importance of notions about human rights, privacy, and self-determination in contemporary Korea. These have been especially significant in the decision to use contraception or to obtain an abortion. Children are costly, and paying for an extra child diminishes the resources available for parents and for other children. People's desire for a certain standard of living for themselves and their children probably did as much as anything else to lower fertility.

The need to limit fertility is also based in part on the recognition that in modern-day Korea no one else is ready to raise one's children; there are no groups one can turn to for sure and able assistance in times of need. Sociologist Cho Hyoung notes that "the prominence of the nuclear type families and the popularization of conjugal family ideology . . . indicate the process of individuation" (Cho 1975, p. 31;

for a discussion of similar trends in Taiwan, see Thornton, Chang, and Sun 1984). So when asked, Koreans will tell you (much like Americans) that they want to raise children who are able to take care of themselves (Chung et al. 1972, p. 472). Family members and close friends will do what they can, but often that is not enough. There is a shortage of safety nets. The cost of child rearing must be borne by the immediate family. As a consequence, few envy the large family; it is a sign of potential heartache in contemporary Korea, not a sign of good fortune or prosperity (Chung et al. 1972, p. 451). It is these changes in value and worldview that are the basis for the far-reaching changes in family building that took place in Korea and that the Population Council tried to encourage.

9

The Movement and the Modernization of Reproduction

Until the 1960s, Korean women had an average of more than six children during their reproductive lives. Only a small minority of them practiced family planning. Han Dae Woo (1970) and Park Chai Bin (1978) argue that until the 1960s, Korea was a "natural fertility" population—that is, women did not attempt to terminate childbearing before the biological end of their reproductive spans, nor did they aim for a certain family size, or make an effort not to exceed a certain number of children.

Women in many developing countries had similar patterns of fertility. Colombia, for example, had a total fertility rate of 6.3 in 1968. Mexico's rate was equally high. In Africa, also, women had a large number of children, although traditional patterns of prolonged breast-feeding and abstinence from sexual intercourse following childbirth—as well, perhaps, as low fecundity because of poor health and marginal nutrition—caused fertility to stay somewhat lower than in the better-off developing countries. For example, Nigeria was estimated to have a total fertility rate of 5.8 in 1965, while in Ghana, the rate was slightly above 6.

But a revolution in reproductive behavior has taken place across much of the developing world. More aggressive family planning programs and greater contraceptive use are at the heart of these changes, but they are not the only reasons for them. Increasing age at marriage has been a significant determinant of lower fertility in several places. The proportion of teenagers aged 15–19 who were married declined in Bangladesh, for example, from 92 percent in 1961 to 76 percent in 1974. Other countries experienced similar changes (Coale 1983, p. 830). Marrying at older ages is sometimes due to the increasing education of women, sometimes to greater female employment, and sometimes to a lack of marriage opportunities because of economic or political conditions. Such changes are not directly related to government efforts to promote family planning.

The transformation of reproductive behavior, although evident among women in every region, has not occurred in every developing country. The decline in fertility in developing countries as a whole is due to very large declines in fertility in a small number of countries, together with more modest decreases in other countries, or indeed, no changes at all—or, in some African countries, increases in childbearing. Except for South Africa and a few north African nations such as Tunisia and Egypt, the countries of Africa have yet to experience any sustained reduction in fertility. In fact, fertility in Africa has probably increased slightly in recent years because many women have given up the traditional restraints on childbearing—long periods of abstinence from intercourse following childbirth, and prolonged breast-feeding—but have not begun to use modern birth control.

Fertility declines have been more widespread in Asia. The five biggest reductions took place in Singapore, Taiwan, China, Hong Kong, and South Korea. Other Asian countries had less prominent, but still important, declines in fertility. Nevertheless, in Asian countries with a total population of approximately 340 million—including Burma, Laos, Vietnam, Nepal, Bangladesh, and Pakistan—fertility has not declined at all and, in some, may even have increased recently. Fertility has also stayed high in many Arab countries. In Latin America, the fertility of women in Cuba, Costa Rica, Chile, Colombia, Brazil, and Peru has declined, but in Bolivia, Honduras, and Nicaragua childbearing remains high.

Declining fertility in the developing world is part of a demographic evolution that will probably be with us far into the future. Many women seem ready to reproduce at a much lower level than at any time in the past. The extent of the current experience is noteworthy. One aspect of the modern age that sharply distinguishes our time from that of our ancestors is that people living far apart from each other are much more likely to share common experiences today than ever before. Designer sportswear, microcomputers, and political ideologies spread quickly. The notion that fertility can and should be controlled is part of the world system of modern ideas. Not everyone, of course, shares the same view. In rural areas of the developing world, the most visible elements of a society's modernization as found in its capital are often missing, and so too are many of the ways of thinking and behaving that have become routine in the cities. Even in the metropolitan areas of fairly prosperous developing countries, modernization is not complete. But new ideas, including those based on a knowledge of birth control and an appreciation of low fertility, are clearly taking root in societies that many of us may wrongly consider completely traditional.

The changes in demographic behavior and in the regulation of fertility within marriage have been particularly rapid. Over the past twenty-five years, those countries that have achieved significant declines in fertility have moved from a situation in which couples made little or no effort to regulate the number of children they had, to a situation where fertility is well managed. The pattern of human reproduction found throughout most of the developing world in the 1960s resembled that of nineteenth-century Europe, although Europeans married later, more often remained unmarried, and had nuclear families. The first fertility decline in Europe occurred among the French upper classes in the late eighteenth century. Fertility limitation spread slowly. Etienne van de Walle and John Knodel note: "The progress of fertility decline from its early French onset can be likened to a slow burning fuse that eventually leads to an explosion: more than half of Europe's provinces initiated their fertility decline in the 30 years between 1880 and 1910" (Van de Walle and Knodel 1980, p. 30). A similar process took place in Asia and in Latin America as well. But the pace of contemporary fertility declines has been much more rapid than the historical experience of Europe. Crude birth rates declined dramatically between 1960 and 1980, going down by as much as 46 percent in Korea, 25 percent in Mexico, more than half in Singapore, a third in Jamaica, and 20 percent in Morocco. Fertility in Thailand declined as much in fifteen years as it did in parts of Europe in seventy-five or one hundred years.

This chapter addresses three aspects of the remarkable changes in childbearing that have taken place in the developing world. First, the question of why fertility declines is examined. Second, what we know about the impact of organized family planning programs on the level and pattern of childbearing is reviewed. Third, the effect of foreign assistance on developing-country family planning efforts is assessed.

Why Fertility Declines

Most adults have an intuitive sense of why fertility changes: times change. When my mother-in-law learned that one of her sons and his wife were soon to have a third child, her ninth grandchild, this sixty-five-year-old Irish Catholic mother of six responded, "It's too many children." She understood that changing economic circumstances make a large family less attractive today than when she was first married during World War II.

The less-than-eager reaction of my mother-in-law to the birth of her ninth grandchild illustrates a point made recently by Germaine Greer: ". . . the modern Western infant is wanted by fewer people than any infants in our long history—not only by fewer parents, but by smaller groups of people. Historically, babies have been welcome additions to society. . . . Parents . . . had no need to cudgel their brains to decide if they were ready for the experience, for they were surrounded by people who watched their reproductive career with passionate interest, who would guide them through the fears and anguish of childbirth and take on a measure of responsibility for child-rearing. Historically, human societies have been pro-child" (Greer 1984, p. 2).

Greer's harsh judgment about our view of children was echoed by Samuel Preston in his 1984 Presidential Address to the Population Association of America. Preston pointed out that during the 1970s, conditions deteriorated badly for America's children. The proportion of children under fourteen living in poverty increased substantially, and emotional health—judged by the suicide rate, for example— declined as well. Children's problems are caused, in part, by what Preston refers to as the "earthquake that shuddered through the American family in the past 20 years" (Preston 1984, p. 451). This earthquake included dramatic increases in the number of divorces and thus in single-parent households, as well as a growing proportion of childless couples—adults presumably with less concern than parents about children and their welfare.

It is easy to oversimplify the society that Greer and Preston describe. Individual contemporary American children are not loved less than their turn-of-the-century counterparts, or than children in traditional societies. What has changed is the social context of childbearing and the extent to which societies, not just parents, value children. In 1945, Frank Notestein argued that a crucial prerequisite of low fertility was "a shift in social goals from those directed toward the survival of the group to those directed toward the welfare and development of the individual" (p. 41). A growing sense of the significance of individuals and an increasing differentiation of social roles are essential ingredients in the modernization process. As countries develop, individuals become more important than the group to which they belong. More and more decisions are based on one's own interests and priorities. Historian James Reed concludes that "the essential cultural prerequisite for the success of the American birth control movement was the secularization of society or the celebration of material well being and pleasure" (1978, p. 62). A focus on the individual and a concern for well-being shift the criteria involved in deciding whether or not to have children. John Knodel sounds the same theme with respect to the European demographic transition: "The decline of fertility associated with the demographic transition was not simply a matter of moving from a situation of totally uncontrolled fertility to one in which rational restraint is finally exercised. Rather, the change can be characterized as largely one from a system of control through social institutions and customs to a system where the private choice of the individual couples plays the major role" (Knodel 1979, p. 501). When the pretransition generation of couples made decisions about childbearing, they were certainly concerned about their children's welfare—but they were also worried about their standing in their church, in their community, and with their own and their spouses' families. Today, when advising their daughters, this generation appears primarily interested in the daughters' welfare and that of their children.

Given the importance of changing values for changing patterns of childbearing, it follows that fertility will not simply decline sharply when contraceptive services are made available unless, of course, people have already come to recognize the possibilities of improving their own or their children's lives by means of smaller families. The social and economic changes brought about by economic development, of which education for women and children is perhaps the most significant influence, help create a context in which self-centered decision making becomes routine. Indeed, the idea of educating girl children itself represents a shift from evaluating women on the basis of group membership, based on sex either alone or primarily, to a judgment based more on individual characteristics—in particular, on accomplishments in school. Family planning programs can make a difference in such environments because organized government and private efforts increase access to contraceptive supplies and add legitimacy to the practice of contraception.

There is little doubt about the importance of government-supported family planning services in that couples, especially older ones, frequently first hear about modern birth control techniques through public family planning clinics. These clinics fill a demand for family planning services that would otherwise not be satisfied. People might have been able to lower their fertility using the same methods used by Europeans in the nineteenth century, but almost certainly they would have done so at a much slower pace than that experienced by many contemporary developing-country populations.

Today, younger Thai couples, for example, understand early in life what their parents first learned at a much later stage at a health center. Those having children today frequently learned about birth control through talking with friends or relatives, or through observing others within the community receive services at a local clinic or health post. The change in fertility and in contraceptive use in a country like Thailand illustrates how family planning can be transformed rapidly from innovative behavior to an institutionalized pattern. The national family planning program helped increase awareness of how family size could be controlled. Likewise, contraceptive methods were available at a lower cost than they would have been without the program. But as Knodel and his colleagues note (1983), it is a mistake to assess the consequences of the national family planning program without taking into account the impact of changing social and economic forces. It is the interaction of the program with these social and economic forces that has resulted in significant increases in contraceptive use and declines in fertility.

According to Knodel and his Thai collaborators (1983, p. 8), there was a substantial latent demand for contraceptive services well before modern methods of fertility control were widely available. Rapid and fundamental changes in the Thai economy and society increasingly led couples to perceive a large number of children as an economic burden. Moreover, Thai culture was particularly conducive to changing childbearing practices in response to new economic circumstances.

The economic changes that have taken place in Thailand over the past fifteen years have added to the costs of children both directly and indirectly. Increased needs for schooling, less opportunity for work at home, and more costly life-styles have all made children more expensive. Furthermore, a growth in nuclear families and a more mobile population mean that fewer and fewer people are available or eager to help with children. Each child becomes the sole responsibility of the parents—who, if they are to educate their children, must do it on their own. The nucleation of fertility decision making, the growing concern with individual well-being, the rising costs of education, and its increasing importance for social and economic position have all contributed to the fertility decline in Thailand and in other developing countries. Decisions about family size have become primarily the responsibility of the potential parents themselves and, in contrast to more traditional, less individualistic societies, are sometimes not even discussed with others.

There is a danger in exaggerating the extent to which the economy and social structure of a society have to be transformed before fertility declines. Some aspects of life in East Asian societies that have experienced remarkable fertility declines remain traditional. Korea, for example, retains a strong sense of son preference. Demographers once thought that fertility would change only following substantial change across a wide spectrum of social and economic activities. Today, most specialists believe that far less change than once thought necessary is required before fertility begins to decline.

Measuring Family Planning's Effect

Questions about the relative importance of family planning programs as a determinant of the level and pattern of contraceptive use and fertility in developing countries have led demographers to try to measure exactly what difference such programs make. One way of asking about the impact of family planning programs in terms relevant to this research is to inquire, "Has the American confidence and investment in large-scale family planning programs been justified?" Unfortunately, answering that question beyond what has already been said is not a straightforward matter. Indeed, to begin, the influence of the values and worldviews of the protagonists in the current debate (already discussed in Chapter 4) needs to be mentioned again.

Many discussions, even some scientific ones, of developing-country efforts to change the pattern of childbearing employ stereotypes. "Family planners" are made to appear as only a tiny minority of them really are: ignorant of local culture; convinced that more pills and condoms, more aggressively marketed, are alone sufficient to cause fertility to fall; and without interest or insight regarding the influence of economic factors on decisions about how many children to have. Likewise, those whose research tells them that organized efforts to regulate the birth rate are less important than the impact of changing social structure in lowering fertility are typically presented as cynical determinists who believe that public policy and conscious human effort could not possibly affect reproductive behavior. Positions have become so well established and are so related to the values and identity of the debaters that it is difficult to get a fair hearing for new evidence that supports either position.

One side is hopeful that change is possible; that intervention can make things better quickly; that the long process of demographic change that took place in Europe and North America can be short-circuited; that mass contraceptive distribution can work to control population growth, improve health, enhance development, and maintain a stable, manageable world. Free choice will be rational for all. The other side is less optimistic: change is a slow process; new attitudes and values must evolve, and that means reshaping the economy and society; the worth of children must be made to reflect their true cost to the society; people must be made to pay for their childbearing decisions, the costs of high fertility must be allocated.

Twenty-five years ago, few social programs that aimed at changing behavior as fundamental as family building had been tried in the developing world. Those who knew the developing world best were profoundly doubtful that such programs could have significant impact. Within a short time in a developing country, it is easy to become overwhelmed by the extent to which tradition and local culture channel behavior. So much of the history and culture of poor countries pushed in the direction of high fertility that it was difficult, at times almost impossible, for thoughtful analysts to credit the idea that supplying contraceptives directly to women would cause them to change their reproductive behavior. Moreover, by the mid-1960s, the earliest family planning programs had little to show for their effort.

There were other reasons why those familiar with efforts at social change in the developing world thought it unlikely that family planning programs would be successful. Especially during their initial stages, family planning programs seem characterized by a clash of power and perspective between peasants and the poor, on the one hand, and metropolitan culture and foreign influence, on the other. Throughout the developing world, medicine is marked by a tremendous difference between its concepts and practitioners and the daily lives of the majority of people it treats. Family planning programs and the premise on which they rested—that controlling fertility benefited individuals, families, and the country—seemed one more case where foreign ideas did not fit well with the culture of the local population.

At the heart of the debate about the impact of family planning is a conflict more deeply rooted in professional concerns than in any testable propositions about the state of the world. The most consistent and strongly voiced criticisms regarding the implementation of family planning programs have come from America's academic social scientists. During the mid-1960s, when the social sciences had gained their greatest prestige in the United States and for the first time were recruiting graduate students who were not at the bottom of the academic ladder, some family planning specialists were trying to demonstrate that effective intervention into such fundamental areas of life as human reproduction required no special understanding of language, religion, family structure, or other aspects of culture and social life. Social scientists knew that culture was important, and to see it so easily ignored after they had worked so arduously to establish its importance was hard to take.

The public health profession, on the other hand, had considerable experience with the successful control of a variety of infectious diseases through massive programs of public education and intervention. Significant declines in infant mortality had occurred when many of those in charge of America's population program were young physicians. Thus, they had first-hand experience of the impact on health of a whole variety of new drugs. The rediscovery of the IUD in the 1960s and the development of oral contraceptives must have seemed to such practitioners to have the same potential as sulfa drugs and penicillin had had a generation earlier.

Measuring the impact of family planning programs on fertility is also difficult because such research inevitably runs into technical difficulties. These center on the inability to measure the variety of factors that influence reproductive behavior and to isolate the influence of a family planning program from all the other factors. Wherever there is a family planning program apparently contributing to major declines in fertility, there is almost always some economic development or social change that also influences behavior. For all the apparently successful programs, there are a number of obviously unsuccessful ones, where government commitment and international resources are unable to reach more than a few of a country's married population (Davis 1982).

As critics of the research so far completed note, it is probably impossible to factor out the "independent" effect of family planning programs because the social and statistical sciences lack a way of measuring what might be called the "pure program effect": family planning's impact, minus the contribution that social change or development makes to greater contraceptive use. To compare countries on the basis of the availability of family planning services in the rural areas is to some extent to compare national road networks (no roads—no availability), not the coverage of the family planning program. Likewise, a high staff-client ratio in a program may reflect a country's educational institutions, not necessarily the quality of its family planning program. Other elements of family planning program implementation may also be rooted in cultural, political, or social factors.

The best framework may be the simplest. Several studies have found that countries with both a strong family planning program and economic development are most likely to experience the largest fertility declines. The joint effect of economic change for the better and government support for contraceptive services adds to the impact that each factor alone has on fertility.

W. Parker Mauldin and Robert J. Lapham (Mauldin and Lapham 1984) use two summary measures—a score for social setting that measures the level of national development, and a second score for program effort that measures the relative strengths of thirty aspects of a country's family planning program. Their research highlights the unevenness of the world's effort to regulate fertility. They found that "a great deal of family planning program effort exists in a small number of countries; moderate effort occurs in a large number of countries; and weak or very little effort is found in an even greater number of countries" (Mauldin and Lapham 1984, p. 32). Strong programs were found in Asia. Moderate-quality programs were found in Latin countries—Cuba, Colombia, Chile, Costa Rica, and the Dominican Republic—and Asia. African family planning programs were uniformly weak; but weak programs were also found in Asia (Nepal and Pakistan) and Latin America (Honduras and Guatemala).

The results of the Mauldin and Lapham research confirm earlier findings on the impact of family planning programs and the importance of both a strong family planning program and a growing economy. Mauldin and Lapham conclude that socioeconomic factors are important and strongly associated with declines in the birth rate and total fertility; more prosperous countries experience greater fertility decline, and family planning program effort strengthens this association. They report: "Probably the key conclusion to be drawn from our analysis is that it is the combination of improved socioeconomic conditions and more program effort that leads to the highest associations with fertility declines" (Lapham and Mauldin 1984, p. 34).

Mauldin and Lapham do not address the question of how this joint influence works, why it is so important, or what combination of factors is most effective. Neither do most others. Gayl Ness and his colleagues note, "Promoting social and economic development promotes fertility-limitation. Promoting family planning programs has a slightly greater impact. But the greatest impact on fertility-limiting behavior comes from a combination of promoting both programs and social development" (Ness, Johnson, and Bernstein, 1983, p. 20). They further note that "in the demand vs. supply debate many seasoned observers of the development scene reject the simple dichotomy and argue for promoting both supply [i.e., family planning activities] and demand [i.e., development measures] simultaneously. . . . Our results provide much support for this argument" (ibid.). Exactly how this synergistic effect works is not specified. Moreover, other research cautions that these highly aggregated analyses may camouflage important and very different country-specific relationships between individual economic well-being and family planning effort (Entwisle and Mason 1985).

Mauldin and Berelson (1978, p. 109) have argued that more prosperous countries can afford better-quality family planning programs, and that this explains the high correlation between good programs and development. But Paul Demeny disagrees, claiming that the fertility decline associated with the more highly regarded family planning programs in the economically better-off countries may only reflect the impact of economic and social conditions; in short, that "many of the successful programs were . . . more a symptom of fertility change than the cause" (1979, p. 151).

Mauldin and Lapham's analysis is based on aggregate data, information on countries and national programs, not data on the characteristics or behavior of individuals. A good deal of information, however, is available on the fertility and family planning–related behavior of individuals—in particular, on people's reactions to increases in contraceptive services made possible by family planning programs. This information has been collected during sample surveys that have been carried out in numerous developing countries since the early 1960s.

No amount of manipulation of the available survey data can put to rest the question of the precise contribution of organized family planning programs to changes in the birth rate. This said, a careful reading of the existing evidence on individual behavior indicates that the availability of family planning services does make a difference in fertility behavior. In general, research to date concludes that increased access to sources of contraceptive services results in increased contraceptive use and lower fertility. Recent analysis of the multi-country World Fertility Survey and Contraceptive Prevalence Survey, for example, indicates that contraceptive use is more likely where availability is high (Tsui 1982).

Although there are some population specialists who do not credit family planning programs with making a significant difference in fertility patterns (Hernandez 1984), the prevailing wisdom accepts the fact that the complete modernization of traditional social structures is not required in order for fertility to decline. There is now strong evidence both from the historical experience of European societies and from the contemporary developing world that declines in fertility can take place in poor, rural communities, and that family planning programs can and do speed this process. One recent review of the evidence concluded, "there is overwhelming evidence that greater access to contraceptive supplies results in increased use of contraception and fertility decline"; but there is only "rather weak evidence on the precise magnitudes of these effects and the ways in which differentials in socioeconomic characteristics . . . make these effects large or small" (Boulier 1985, p. 102).

When the modern fertility transition is better understood, national family planning programs will still be considered important—but quite possibly less because of the contraceptive services they provide than because of the legitimation they give for the idea of fertility control. Family planning programs provide the contraceptives that make it easier to control fertility successfully, and they do so in a way that makes contraceptive practice and fertility control seem more appropriate. Motivation must change before large declines in childbearing take place. Contraceptives alone, available where they once were not, can and do affect the demand for effective fertility control; but fundamental changes in childbearing practices of the sort that have taken place throughout Asia and Latin America require both a new understanding of everyday life and the psychological freedom to put it into effect.

America's contribution to lowering fertility via the support of national family planning efforts may turn out to be less important than the overall influence of American culture and society, particularly the high value given the individual and individual achievement. American influence has been important in the evolution of new worldviews throughout the developing world in part because the images of modern society that the peoples of developing countries aim for come increasingly from movies, television shows, and the attitudes of their own citizens trained in the United States. The image and role of women in the United States and other advanced industrial nations may be particularly important in this respect.

Widespread government promotion of contraception represents a crucial modernizing effort that doubtless exerts an independent effect, causing people who would otherwise not do so to begin to plan their families. In a country where women are unfamiliar with roles other than those of mother and farmer, where sex is discussed in terms of marital obligation rather than pleasure, where medicine is only thirty years removed from folk remedies, where central government bureaucrats care little for the welfare of the citizens, and where advertising is oriented toward the prohibitively expensive, a family planning fieldworker clad in a newly starched uniform who arrives at the end of a dusty road on a small motorbike clutching a health kit packed with pills and condoms and perhaps a few IUDs, and supplied with calendars, fans, and other trinkets all promoting something that appears to offer women choices in an area that is not much discussed, is a radical departure from tradition. The fieldworker's visit represents the infusion of the capital city, and indeed of the world outside one's own country, into village life. The visit personalizes the radio message promoting family planning that the government may be using to encourage greater contraceptive practice. In a word, it is modernizing. A visit from a family planning fieldworker in rural Bangladesh or Senegal is not equivalent to a proper education—however, a stranger coming into a village and offering services can have an impact. Governments know this, and that is one reason why they promote family planning. It is a mistake to separate family planning from modernization; family planning is modernization and a part of development.

It is impossible to establish once and for all, in a manner that will satisfy people of every perspective, exactly what the impact of national family planning programs is. Moreover, conflict over the impact of publicly supported family planning programs is not without benefit. A strong, vocal, thoughtful, and experienced opposition forces a more careful presentation of one's point of view and a more measured program-development process. Conflicts establish and maintain a balance of power. Social programs and government budgets benefit from being sharply questioned and ably defended.

The conflict is also valuable because it forces advocates to be careful in making their case, and policy makers and those who provide the funds to be more cautious in deciding on and paying for new public programs. There are problems, of course, when the advocates themselves or the public at large start to believe in the rightness of certain positions to the extent that analysis and advocacy can no longer be distinguished. Conflict, especially among true believers, establishes and maintains group cohesion, but at the cost of relations with those outside the groups who become scapegoats for the failure of program implementation. Few advocates of programs of any kind—alcohol rehabilitation, a manned space station, or improving the diet of school children—believe that their programs would not have been more successful if they had not been opposed.

But the need to draw together to defend family planning programs against outsiders has been an important element in maintaining and reinforcing the cohesion of population networks around the world. Such conflict has also sharpened the intellectual debate and contributed to better-designed, better-implemented, and more carefully evaluated programs.

Measuring AID's Impact

While the scientific literature is full of reports on the effect of family planning programs, very little, almost nothing in fact, has been written about the impact of foreign aid on population programs. Unfortunately, data on foreign aid expenditures, contraceptive use, and fertility rates of the type required to produce reasonable statistical estimates of the impact of foreign assistance on family planning practice and fertility are not available. Estimates of the trend in population assistance transfers over the past twenty-five years are impossible to find for more than a handful of developing countries. Trends in vital rates and patterns of contraceptive use are widely estimated but are not precisely known for many countries. (Gayl Ness and his colleagues [Ness, Pressman, and Hutchings 1982] have made the most thorough survey to date of the data that are available and the problems that one encounters in trying to use them.)

I have tried to illustrate the extent to which foreign aid may have influenced the childbearing of women in the developing world by constructing a very simple statistical model incorporating a measure of the amount of aid provided to each country, and variables indicating the level of socioeconomic development and the quality of a country's family planning program. My aim was to describe the relative importance of each of the three factors for the level of childbearing measured by changes in the crude birth rate. The resulting analysis is by no means definitive. I want only to picture what the available data suggest may be taking place.

My measure of foreign aid covers all international assistance or foreign bilateral aid provided to ninety-three developing countries during the years 1965 through 1980 and designated for "population activities." Some of this foreign aid (the exact proportion is unknown and varies by country and year) was spent in developed, donor countries and not actually transferred to developing countries. This is typically the case, for example, with funds for fellowships and training. Information on population-related aid transfers came mainly from a series of annual inventories published by the United Nations Fund for Population Activities. I also used the reports of donors and several collections of data on foreign funding for population.

I have tried to base my analysis on expenditures and not on funds programmed, budgeted, allocated, or allowed. Sometimes it was not clear if the amount reported had, in fact, been expended. Since the most comprehensive and available sources of data are those of the donor agencies and not of the individual countries receiving aid, it is often impossible to determine how much was spent on specific program activities in a given year.

Vastly different results can be obtained depending on the countries analyzed. The availability of adequate data is frequently the main barrier to better samples. Because my focus was on the impact of foreign aid in a specific sector, my analysis concentrated on countries for which I was able to obtain some data on the level of foreign aid provided in support of population and family planning activities and, of course, measures of the other variables in the analysis. Naturally, there is a problem of selectivity in that countries for which data on foreign aid are available may be more likely to have family planning activities.

During the period 1965–80, roughly $2.5 billion was provided by rich countries and international organizations for developing-country family planning programs. My analysis included only $1.3 billion, or about 52 percent of the total. The remainder of the money was not taken into account because (1) it went to countries excluded from the analysis; (2) it was for global projects—funds that were not assigned to specific countries; (3) it paid for donor agency staff to monitor a particular country's activities and, thus, was assigned to a headquarters account; or (4) it was not reported to the United Nations.

A particularly troublesome problem was that of obtaining data on all the variables for the full range of developing countries. I began with a list of 113 countries, but could obtain all the necessary data for only 69. I excluded all developed countries from the analysis, as well as 19 developing countries, each with less than 500,000 total population. Also omitted were some OPEC countries (Kuwait, Libya, Saudi Arabia), some countries that were properly considered developed for most of the period under consideration (Hong Kong, Uruguay, Cyprus), some countries for which no data could be obtained (North Korea), and countries missing information on one of the variables in the analysis. The countries that remain represent the majority of the developing world outside of China, which was also excluded from the analysis.

My measure of social setting is taken from Mauldin and Berelson (1978) and is based on the same procedures as the Mauldin and Lapham research (Mauldin and Lapham 1984). The index is based on seven variables: adult literacy, primary school enrollment, life expectancy, infant mortality rate, nonagricultural labor force participation, GNP per capita, and population in cities of 100,000 or more. The measure of the quality of national family planning programs was introduced by Lapham and Mauldin (1972) and used by them in their analysis; it is an index of program strength based on fifteen factors ranging from degree of support from key political leaders to the availability of different contraceptive methods. Data for this variable were obtained from the Mauldin and Berelson (1978) analysis.

The dependent variable was the percent change in the crude birth rate between 1965 and 1975. Change in the crude birth rate is the key goal of many developing-world family planning programs. However, the crude birth rate and changes in it are influenced by the proportion of women who are married in a population and the mean age at marriage. Indeed, an important element in the fertility changes taking place in many developing countries has been an increase in the age at marriage. Other dependent variables were considered but rejected. No comparable information was available for a large number of countries. Moreover, work by Barbara Entwisle has shown that "the comparability of cross-national fertility studies is not unduly affected by the choice of fertility measure" (1981, p. 642).

This and other analyses (Ness, Johnson, and Bernstein 1983) indicate that countries that are already fairly well-off are more likely to receive foreign assistance than the poorest countries. This difference is especially marked among countries receiving large amounts of aid—better-off countries are more likely to receive large amounts of support than poorer countries—and, among other things, is doubtless a by-product of donors' perception of local absorptive capacity.

The level of family planning program effort is also important in determining what countries get aid. Among the countries with moderate to strong programs, over three-quarters received substantial support (more than $3 million yearly). Still, half of the countries with weak programs also received large grants.

Like other studies based on the same data, my analysis indicates that both the level of development or social setting and the quality of the family planning program have a strong positive association with changes in the crude birth rate. Program effort and social setting are also related, indicating that the best programs are found in the better-off countries, a not-surprising result given the greater resources that a more prosperous developing country can devote to promoting fertility control and the greater demand for quality services that exists in such countries. None of the aid variables have the same strong relationship with crude birth rate changes that social setting and program effort do.

In the statistical models that I calculated, foreign aid is seen as influencing the quality of a country's family planning program, and through the program, influencing fertility. This model is similar to that of others in that foreign assistance is seen as having only indirect effects on fertility and contraceptive use (Ness, Johnson, and Bernstein 1983). Even in countries where foreign assistance accounts for the largest share of expenditures on fertility control, national family planning programs still depend on resources, policy makers, politicians, media, and suppliers of services very much under the control of local culture and administrative and medical practices. Both the raising of money internationally and the implementation of a service delivery program require a skilled, typically professional cadre of knowledgeable people, the relative size of which increases with development. These country-specific circumstances are very important.

The results show that foreign aid (measured in both per capita and absolute terms) has a consistent positive effect on the quality of family planning programs. Programs that get more support from sources outside the country score higher on the program-effort scale than programs that do not get much support. Both the level of development and the quality of the family planning program influence the crude birth rate. Regardless of the measure of aid (total, per capita, and their log transformations), the amount of foreign aid has no direct effect on the change in the crude birth rate, but it does have a significant effect on program quality; program quality, in turn, has a large and significant effect on crude birth rate changes. This finding is in general agreement with Ness, who concludes that "a general judgment of positive impact is warranted" (1983, p. 8-1).

Other data also suggest that aid makes a difference. Countries with higher per capita aid transfers are more likely than countries with low aid transfers to have at least a moderate level of contraceptive use. The level of development and the availability of contraceptive services remain important. Indeed, in a regression analysis both have a significant direct effect on contraceptive prevalence, but the indirect effect of foreign aid remains significant when the dependent variable is contraceptive prevalence rather than changes in the crude birth rate. In part, these results may reflect not only the contribution of foreign funds to improving program quality, but also the fact that foreign support is both attracted to and solicited by the more effective family planning programs.

I also examined the impact of international assistance in twenty-six developing countries without national family planning programs. Almost three-quarters (73 percent) received little or no aid. Among the countries with low aid receipts and no family planning program, 68 percent also scored low on the measure of development. The results of this combination are predictable: none of the countries without a program, with low aid transfers, and with low social setting experienced a significant fertility decline. The situation is somewhat different in countries that had higher social settings or received a substantial amount of aid. However, the small number of countries involved (seven) makes any final judgment impossible. Only one of four countries with no program, low social setting, but high aid transfers experienced a significant crude birth reduction; two out of the three countries without programs, but with higher social setting and a large aid transfer, experienced crude birth rate declines.

Foreign assistance does not have the same effect in all countries, nor is it more important than other factors that influence the level and pattern of childbearing in developing countries. But foreign aid appears capable of making an important difference in the level of fertility in countries receiving aid. Through its impact on program quality and coverage, population-related foreign assistance can influence the rate of demographic change.

The population movement has contributed to the modernization of reproductive behavior. In the decades since William Draper, Clarence Gamble, and John D. Rockefeller III first drew attention to the impact of high fertility in the Third World, millions have come to understand the advantages of slower growth. The women of the developing world have transformed their childbearing in response to changing social and economic conditions and the availability of contraceptive services. Organized family planning programs made fertility regulation easier, cheaper, and more convenient. American foreign aid helped to improve family planning programs and increase their impact.

Epilogue

I started working internationally in the population field in the early 1970s when America was at war in Southeast Asia. Thailand, where I was living, was flooded with American troops, those at air bases in the northeast and soldiers in Bangkok on leave from Vietnam. The AID offices were bloated with police, public safety, and security advisors who soiled the agency's reputation as a development organization. At the university population institute where I worked, foreigners were more numerous and more influential than local scholars.

Ten years later, American forces had left Thailand. The Thai government had begun an amnesty program for Communist guerrillas. The AID staff and program had shrunk and the Ford Foundation, the Population Council, and Pepsi-Cola had moved into one of the buildings AID once occupied in downtown Bangkok. Thais who had been studying in the United States had returned to the university population center where I worked and were directing it. No foreigners remained on the staff.

The American foreign aid that appeared suspect to me in the Thailand of the 1960s and early 1970s, now seems to have contributed to the country's modernization. While living in Thailand, I was particularly discouraged about the way American foreign assistance was used because I saw more opportunity than I do now for the creative use of foreign aid to stimulate development and to improve poorly designed or poorly implemented social programs. However, after seeing the shortcomings of even well-administered assistance programs and after being schooled for two years by the economists from the Korea Development Institute, I concluded that the creation of nonagricultural employment was far more important for modernization than was the effective use of foreign assistance for social development projects. Countries become modern when the structure of the economy shifts from traditional occupations to modern ones. The greatest need in most places is not for more humane social policies but for more and different types of work. The modernization of Korea, which took place with considerable speed and with relatively little inequality, depended on the ability to create employment. Foreign aid played a useful but by no means a decisive role. Population policy and a national family planning program made little difference to Korean development. All of those who participated in the key years of Korea's economic growth development had been born by 1960, when official policy started to shift toward population control. Moreover, Korea's large population and densely populated metropolitan areas may have helped modernization because the competition for jobs kept wages low and thus increased the attractiveness of Korean exports on the world market.

Another lesson to be gleaned from the experience of Korea is that development does not come cheaply. Someone must pay for modernization. One can complain about the inequalities in income and quality of life found in developing countries, but someone must be rewarded for work that promotes development and others must be punished by not being given a fair return in order that the surplus can be used for new investment.

Foreign investment and aid frequently do nothing to lessen the inequality within developing countries and may even add to it. The impact of foreign aid and investment is mixed because its effectiveness is determined by the complex social and economic relations and historical circumstances that influence the lives of people working in a particular sector of the economy in a particular country. In the case of population-related foreign assistance, it is clear that senior government policy makers in the United States and other guardians of American culture and interests held a worldview that was threatened by the rapid growth of the Third World, in part because of the perceived destabilizing influence of the growth in population and in part because of what was thought to be the negative impact of rapid population growth on the development prospects of poor countries. Continued development and participation in the world trade network were linked as key goals in the effort to maintain and promote prosperity and stability.

This understanding of the development-population-stability interrelationship led to heavy investments in efforts to slow growth. In numerous countries, although by no means in all those receiving foreign aid, contraceptive use increased dramatically even among the poorly educated, rural population. This suggests a widespread consensus regarding the value of fertility control. Governments too came to accept the view first proposed in the early 1950s by India, Sri Lanka, and Nepal, and then backed by Sweden and the United States, that rapid population growth slows development. The evidence for this is beyond dispute and suggests that American foreign assistance helped developing countries to modernize in a way that their governments and their people wanted.

There is another perspective from which to judge population assistance. Working on this project, I began to understand more clearly than I had in the past that the United States cannot be counted on to share the costs of development, nor will America give money to Mexico because a rich nation should help its neighbors. No such notion is in our Constitution, our history, or our value structure. Moreover, many Americans would view the institutionalization of such assistance as demeaning to the Mexicans. To help by providing work may be acceptable, but to give someone a handout is always a last resort. We fear being labeled "bleeding hearts."

In many of the interviews I conducted during my research for this book, people told me how important it was for aid to be provided on a businesslike basis with a clear understanding that foreign assistance is ultimately in America's own interest. There were exceptions, of course. Oscar Harkavy notes of the Ford Foundation, "We were liberal do-gooders. . . . There was a general . . . bleeding heart liberal motivation . . ." (author's interview). The typical motive, however, is the one Duff Gillespie attributes to Dr. Ravenholt: "Rei was not a bleeding heart. He believed in self-sufficiency" (author's interview). For most Americans, almost any show of concern or pity is ostentatious. To be openly compassionate is to be weak.

The effect of the routine elements of everyday life is another crucial element in understanding American foreign assistance in population and family planning. The limited impact of foreign aid is often attributable to the force that routine activities exert. As we have seen, the staff of foreign aid programs become preoccupied with considerations of bureaucratic territory, career, and the like. It is these that often make a difference in how effectively a program is implemented.

The importance of routines can also help explain the diffusion of contraceptive use. The key to the contraceptive revolution was that controlling fertility through certain means became a routine, taken-for-granted aspect of everyday life. At some point, women needed little further encouragement to practice family planning because contraceptive use had become expected behavior. This explains why fertility declined and why the existence of an organized national family planning program no longer exerts much influence on childbearing in a country like Korea.

The importance of the routine also means that history and our society have made us. But although we are heirs of our past, we are not its prisoners. I do not want to leave only the bitter taste of my own disappointment at lost myths about the role of Americans around the world. I share AID's own judgment of the contribution of foreign assistance to international development: "there is ample evidence of major progress in developing countries and . . . foreign assistance has played a small, but vital role in these achievements" (Stern,

Birnbaum, and Arndt to Hannah, December 13, 1971, p. 8, gift file).
America's international population program mixes self-interest and
concern. It is far from perfect, but compared to most programs it
seems remarkably humane, well designed, effectively implemented,
and useful.

Perhaps Frank Notestein, the most influential American demographer of the twentieth century, summed up America's international
population control effort best. On a bright spring afternoon nine
months before he died, I asked Notestein what he thought the impact
of America's population program had been. He did not rave about the
achievements or regret the shortcomings. He said simply: "I don't
think we did so damn bad."

Appendix

Sources of Data

Several aspects of the material used for this investigation of America's international population policy merit more attention than they could properly be given in the preceding chapters. This appendix covers those details of the data collection and analysis which are not discussed elsewhere.

I interviewed people I thought were important for understanding America's international population program. To capture the diversity of thinking on this topic, at times I bypassed the opportunity to interview a well-known figure in order to talk to a person who worked behind the scenes and could add something about life backstage. In addition to following my own hunches, I sent a questionnaire to twenty prominent experts in the population field asking them to name the ten most important Americans in international population and family planning. Some of the people mentioned most frequently—John D. Rockefeller III, Alan Guttmacher, William Draper—had died, but many of the others—Reimert Ravenholt, Frank Notestein, and Bernard Berelson—were alive and active. I tried to interview all of those who were mentioned most often by my respondents. (The five most frequently mentioned were: Ravenholt, Rockefeller, Notestein, Draper, and Berelson.)

Of all the data I collected, the material from archives presented the greatest amount of work and the largest number of unanswered questions regarding quality and coverage. I reviewed material from several archives, of which the most important was the Washington National Record Center where the records of the Agency for International Development are stored. Other sources used included the Eisenhower Presidential Library, the files of the Central Intelligence Agency, and the Federal Bureau of Investigation.

I also used government documents obtained from individuals, not from official archives. One source of material was a large package of memos, reports, letters, and other material from the Agency for International Development and the executive branch of the government. Many of the documents related to the Carter administration's efforts to begin the Foundation for International Technical Cooperation. The package, which was sent to my office, had no note or return address. No one has ever mentioned sending it, and I have never asked anyone about it. Another source of government documents was a former AID employee who had kept material he regarded as particularly interesting. I met this person by accident following a conference and, to my surprise, he informed me that he had been waiting to meet me because he had some things he thought I would be interested in. I reviewed his files during several trips to his office; one condition of being able to use his collection was that I not remove anything from his office.

The CIA and FBI files produced no useful information. I filed a Freedom of Information Act request for material related to the Population Council and the Agency for International Development's population program; nothing of value was discovered during the searches. The FBI files contained a tiny bit of material on Population Council grants to Africa. The CIA had, but would not release, a few pieces of personal correspondence collected during the agency's mail surveillance program. There was such a long wait between the time a request was made to the CIA and when it was finally answered—twenty-six months in one case—that it became unrealistic to ask for further searches.

There are several problems with the material obtained from the AID archives. All agencies of the government produce a huge mass of paper and I examined only a small (and unknown) fraction of the output of one group. Moreover, many of the themes discussed transcend the work of the Office of Population. By and large the AID files were concerned with operations—not policy. Much of interest and impact was not put in writing. In a typical example, one AID official wrote of a committee report on America's foreign assistance: "All concerned should realize that this report was prepared for the President, and therefore there are certain things in it that one must read between the lines" (General Advisory Committee, 9.2, World Food Situation, 286-73-159).

I began my work by asking for AID files concerned with population and family planning. By the time a topic has become a label on a file folder in a Washington bureaucrat's drawer, it has already been deemed relevant by the agency's leadership. One could measure a topic's institutionalization by the file space it receives. I should have spent more time in examining the records of AID's administrators and assistant administrators and their changing views in population and family planning. Much of what they thought and did comes through in the Office of Population documents and in other ways, but a direct investigation of more of their papers would have been useful. I tried to obtain the files of the several special assistants for population matters to the secretary of state; unfortunately, most of these files, which dated from the earliest days of America's international population program, were destroyed during reviews in 1975 and 1980.

Another sampling problem is a shortage of material from AID officials on assignment in developing countries. A decisive stage in the implementation of AID programs occurs when population officers meet local officials. In my experience, the skills of AID's population officers were extremely uneven. It would have been valuable to see how more of these men and women implemented country programs. Some of what different officers in the field were thinking and doing is apparent in their cables and reports; however, more material would have been useful. It was, in part, to make up for this shortcoming that I decided to concentrate on the experience of the Population Council in Korea. Because I served on the Population Council staff in Seoul, I had access to material that never found its way to the Council's headquarters in New York. I also consider the Korean experience in some detail because the country is such a very important example of rapid demographic change and economic development. In addition, about half the people I interviewed had spent significant portions of their careers, in a few cases their entire careers, working in the developing world. Several played key roles in the implementation of U.S. population assistance programs overseas.

The usefulness of the material from the archives varies widely. It is occasionally difficult to judge the significance or authenticity of a report. Since the analytical task requires building a pattern of evidence, the case never turns on a single piece of paper. One of the archives yielded a sharply worded letter from a Filipino physician protesting a funding agency's apparent insistence that one of its staff investigate the reliability of the doctor's data by matching his reports with official hospital records. In the letter the doctor displayed hurt feelings at not being trusted, offered to resign as principal investigator of the project, and complained that he had not asked for research support in the first place. Attached to the protest letter was a handwritten note the physician had sent to the same person as the protest: "Enclosed is the formal letter you wished me to write. I hope it helps."

In this case the protest letter was not authentic in that the doctor sent it only after it had been requested for use as ammunition to get someone to relax procedures for checking data reliability. But, based on the report of the person who had been sent to engineer the protest note, the letter appears to be an accurate, albeit overly dramatically expressed, reflection of the doctor's feelings about the reliability check.

Although not discussed in detail in the text, I also used published data on the flow of foreign aid for work related to population and family planning to construct a statistical model of the impact of foreign assistance. There are only a few sources of relatively complete data on international assistance in population and family planning. The United Nations Fund for Population Activities, through its publication, *An Inventory of Population Projects in Developing Countries Around the World*, gives the most detailed information available for the period 1973–80. Various editions of the *Inventory* provided most of the estimates of assistance.

Citations

Although it is difficult for me to imagine anyone retracing my steps through the various archives, I have provided full citations so that someone interested in locating a document should be able to do so. All the material from the Agency for International Development archives is cited following the conventions used by AID and the Washington National Record Center. The key item is the location number, which describes the record group (286) and accession number (76-084). I have added a date and the name of the document's author and, in the case of letters and memos, the person to whom it was primarily directed, omitting the numerous people to whom copies were sent. Because of the haphazard way in which some AID documents were stored and shipped, it was at times impossible to tell exactly where an item had come from. In addition, all the documents that had to be declassified before I could use them were provided without complete location information. I have used the designation "no source" to refer to documents from the AID archives that do not have location information.

Material from the files of the Population Council in Korea is cited as "PC/K" and also includes the date and the author's name. Since the Population Council's office in Korea has closed, the material cited is available through the Council's New York office or the Rockefeller Archive Center in North Tarrytown, New York. Copies of some letters and memos were not routinely sent to New York from the field, so a few items may be impossible to obtain.

Material from individuals' files that either was sent to me or I was allowed to use is cited as "gift file." Quotes without citations are from interviews I conducted for this project and are so noted in the text. Most other material is cited following the guidelines of the *American Journal of Sociology*. To limit what could otherwise become an extreme case of "citenitis" and a mass of parentheses, I have tried to let one citation stand for several quotes taken from the same source that appear reasonably close to each other in the text.

References

Adams, R. R. 1959. "The Population Explosion." Records of the U.S. President's Committee to Study the United States Military Assistance Program (Draper Committee, 1958–59), container no. 15. Dwight D. Eisenhower Library, Abilene, Kans.

"The Administration Bell's Toll." 1966. *Time*, July 8, p. 18.

Agency for International Development. 1977. *Distribution of Personnel as of June 30, 1948, through 1976*. Office of Personnel and Manpower, Policy Development Division, Manpower Analysis Branch. Washington, D.C.: United States International Development Cooperation Agency.

———. 1982. *Congressional Presentation Fiscal Year 1982*. Main vol. Washington, D.C.: United States International Development Cooperation Agency.

Bachrach, Peter, and Elihu Bergman. 1972. "Participation and Conflict in Making American Population Policy: A Critical Analysis." In *Commission on Population Growth and the American Future, Research Reports*, vol. 6, *Aspects of Population Policy*, edited by Robert Park, Jr., and Charles F. Westoff, pp. 583–607. Washington, D.C.: U.S. Government Printing Office.

Becker, Howard, and Harry Elmer Barnes. 1961. *Social Thought from Lore to Science*. 3d ed. Vol. 3. New York: Dover.

Bell, David. N.d. "Summary." In *Third Bellagio Conference on Population*, Working Papers, pp. 91–93. New York: Rockefeller Foundation.

Bell, Karen N. 1984. "Collaborative Research Systems: The BOSTID Experience in Health to Date." Paper prepared for National Council for International Health Conference on Universities and International Health, University of North Carolina, Chapel Hill.

Berelson, Bernard. 1964. "National Family Planning Programs: A Guide." *Studies in Family Planning* 5:1–12.

———. 1975. "The Great Debate on Population: An Instructive Entertainment." Occasional Paper. New York: Population Council.

Berger, Peter L., and Thomas Luckman. 1967. *The Social Construction of Reality: A Treatise in the Sociology of Knowledge*. New York: Anchor Books.

Billy, John O. G. N.d. "Accounting for the Availability of Family Planning Services." Unpublished paper. Department of Sociology, University of North Carolina, Chapel Hill.

Bogue, Donald J. 1967. "The End of the Population Explosion." *Public Interest* 7:11–20.

Bogue, Donald J., and Amy O. Tsui. 1979. "A Rejoinder to Paul Demeny's Critique, 'On the End of the Population Explosion.' " *Population and Development Review* 5 (1):141–62.

Bolling, Landrum R., with Craig Smith. 1982. *Private Foreign Aid: U.S. Philanthropy for Relief and Development*. Boulder, Colo.: Westview Press.

Boserup, Ester. 1981. *Population and Technology*. Oxford: Basil Blackwell.

Boulier, Bryan. 1985. "Evaluating Unmet Need for Contraception." Staff Working Papers, no. 679. Washington, D.C.: The World Bank.

Bourne, Judith P. 1972. "Influences on Health Professionals' Attitudes." *Hospitals* 46 (14): 80–83.

Brady, Nyle. 1984. "Remarks." Presented at National Council for International Health Conference on Universities and International Health, University of North Carolina, Chapel Hill (author's notes).

Brandt, Vincent S. R. 1971. *A Korean Village: Between Farm and Sea*. Cambridge, Mass.: Harvard University Press.

Brecher, Ruth, and Edward Brecher. 1953. "Disease Detectives." *Saturday Evening Post* 225:24–25, 90–92.

Bundy, McGeorge. 1984. "Remarks." Paper prepared for presentation at the annual meeting of the Population Association of America, Minneapolis.

Bush, George H., Jr. 1973. Foreword to *World Population Crisis: The United States Response*, by Phyllis T. Piotrow, pp. vii–ix. New York: Praeger.

Caldwell, John C. 1969. "Family Planning in Korea." Notes by J. C. Caldwell on interviews conducted with John Ross.

Camp, Sharon L., and Cynthia P. Green. 1981. "Legislative and Policy Update." Population Crisis Committee, Washington, D.C., May 15.

Central Intelligence Agency. 1974. "Political Implications of Trends in World Population, Food Production and Climate." Mimeo, OPR-401.

———. 1981. "Population Growth and Sociopolitical Tensions: Five Case Studies." Washington, D.C.: National Foreign Assessment Center.

Chamie, Joseph. 1981. *Religion and Fertility: Arab Christian Muslim Differentials*. New York: Cambridge University Press.

Chang, Yunshik. 1982. "Personalism and Social Change in Korea." In *Society in Transition*, edited by Yunshik Chang, Tai-Hwan Kwon, and Peter J. Donaldson, pp. 29–43. Seoul: Seoul National University Press.

Chang, Yunshik; Tai-Hwan Kwon; and Peter J. Donaldson, eds. 1982. *Society in Transition*. Seoul: Seoul National University Press.

Chirot, Daniel. 1977. *Social Change in the Twentieth Century*. New York: Harcourt Brace Jovanovich.

Cho, Hyoung. 1975. "The Kin Network of the Urban Middle Class Family in Korea." *Korea Journal* 15:22–33.

Chomitz, Kenneth M., and Nancy Birdsall. 1985. "Incentives for Small Family Size: Concepts and Issues." Draft manuscript. Population, Health, and Nutrition Department, The World Bank, Washington, D.C.

Choucri, Nazli. 1978. "The Pervasiveness of Politics." *Populi* 5:30–44.

Chung, Bom Mo; James A. Palmore; San Joo Lee; and Sung Jin Lee. 1972. *Psychological Perspectives: Family Planning in Korea*. Seoul: Korean Institute for Research in the Behavioral Sciences.

Coale, Ansley J. 1974. "The History of the Human Population." *Scientific American* 231:40–51.

———. 1978. "Population Growth and Economic Development: The Case of Mexico." *Foreign Affairs* 56:415–29.

———. 1983. "Recent Trends in Fertility in Less Developed Countries." *Science* 221:828–32.

Coale, Ansley J.; Lee-Jay Cho; and Noreen Goldman. 1980. *Estimation of Recent Trends in Fertility and Mortality in the Republic of Korea.* Committee on Population and Demography, Report no. 1. Washington, D.C.: National Academy of Sciences.

Coale, Ansley J., and Edgar M. Hoover. 1958. *Population Growth and Economic Development in Low Income Countries: A Case Study of India's Prospects.* Princeton: Princeton University Press.

Comptroller General of the United States. 1978. "Reducing Population Growth through Social and Economic Change in Developing Countries—A New Direction for U.S. Assistance." Washington, D.C.: ID-78-6.

Consuega, Jose. 1974. "Birth Control as a Weapon of Imperialism." In *The Dynamics of Population Policy in Latin America*, edited by T. L. McCoy, pp. 163–81. Cambridge, Mass.: Ballinger.

Corsa, Leslie, and Deborah Oakley. 1979. *Population Planning.* Ann Arbor: University of Michigan Press.

Cowell, Alan. 1984. "Drought Spreads to Kenya, Stirring Fear of Food Crisis." *New York Times*, July 16, pp. 1, 7.

Crane, Barbara B., and Jason L. Finkle. 1981. "Organizational Impediments to Development Assistance: The World Bank's Population Program." *World Politics* 33:516–53.

Davis, Kingsley. 1967. "Population Policy: Will Current Programs Succeed?" *Science* 158:730–39.

———. 1982. "Population Control Cannot Be Painless." *People* 9:26–27.

de Arellano, Annette B. Ramirez, and Conrad Seipp. 1983. *Colonialism, Catholicism, and Contraception: A History of Birth Control in Puerto Rico.* Chapel Hill: University of North Carolina Press.

Delacroix, Jacques, and Charles Ragin. 1978. "Modernizing Institutions, Mobilization, and Third World Development: A Cross-National Study." *American Journal of Sociology* 84 (1): 123–50.

Demeny, Paul. 1975a. Letter to the editor. *Scientific American*, May.

———. 1975b. "On the Program of the Demographic Division and the Population Council." Text of comments delivered at a Population Council staff meeting, New York City, April.

———. 1979. "On the End of the Population Explosion." Working Papers, no. 39. New York: Population Council Center for Policy Studies.

———. 1982. "International Aspects of Population Policies." Working Papers, no. 80. New York: Population Council Center for Policy Studies.

———. 1983. "International Development and Population Policy." Paper prepared for the Harvard-Draeger Conference on Population Interactions between Poor and Rich Countries, Cambridge, Mass., October.

————. 1984. "Bucharest, Mexico City, and Beyond." *Population Notes*, no. 55. New York: Population Council Center for Policy Studies.

Demerath, Nicholas J. 1976. *Birth Control and Foreign Policy: The Alternatives to Family Planning*. New York: Harper and Row.

"Division on Birth Control: Pope Paul's Advisory Commission." 1965. *Time*, April 2, p. 80.

Donaldson, Peter J. 1981. "Evolution of the Korean Family Planning System." In *Economic Development, Population Policy, and Demographic Transition in the Republic of Korea*, by Robert Repetto, Tai-Hwan Kwon, Son-Ung Kim, One Young Kim, John E. Sloboda, and Peter J. Donaldson, pp. 222–58. Cambridge, Mass.: Harvard University Press.

Dore, Ronald. 1982. "Groups and Individuals." In *Society in Transition*, edited by Yunshik Chang, Tai-Hwan Kwon, and Peter J. Donaldson, pp. 13–27. Seoul: Seoul National University Press.

Dwight D. Eisenhower Library, Abilene, Kans. 1977. Records of the U.S. President's Committee to Study the United States Military Assistance Program (Draper Committee, 1958–59). Accession 67-9.

Entwisle, Barbara. 1981. "CBR versus TFR in Cross-National Fertility Research." *Demography* 18 (4): 635–43.

Entwisle, Barbara, and William M. Mason. 1985. "Multilevel Effects of Socio-economic Development and Family Planning Programs on Children Ever Born." *American Journal of Sociology* 91:616–49.

Evans, Peter B., and Michael Timberlake. 1980. "Dependence, Inequality and the Growth of the Tertiary: A Comparative Analysis of Less Developed Countries." *American Sociological Review* 45:531–52.

Fairbank, John K.; Edwin O. Reischauer; and Albert M. Craig. 1973. *East Asia Tradition and Transformation*. Boston: Houghton Mifflin.

Farnsworth, Clyde H. 1983. "Foreign Trade Becomes a Local Issue." *New York Times*, July 3, p. 43.

Finkle, Jason L., and Barbara B. Crane. 1975. "The Politics of Bucharest: Population, Development and the New International Economic Order." *Population and Development Review* 1 (1): 87–114.

Fitzgerald, C. P. 1964. *The Birth of Communist China*. Middlesex, England: Penguin Books.

FitzGerald, Frances. 1972. *Fire in the Lake: The Vietnamese and the Americans in Vietnam*. Boston: Atlantic Monthly Press/Little, Brown.

Freedman, Ronald, and Bernard Berelson. 1976. "The Record of Family Planning Programs." *Studies in Family Planning* 7 (1): 1–39.

Freedman, Ronald, and John Y. Takeshita. 1969. *Family Planning in Taiwan: An Experiment in Social Change*. Princeton: Princeton University Press.

Freedman, Ronald; Pascal K. Whelpton; and Arthur A. Campbell. 1959. *Family Planning, Sterility and Population Growth*. New York: McGraw-Hill.

Gardner, Richard N. 1968. "Toward a World Population Program." *International Organizations* 22 (1): 332–61.

————. 1973. "Population Growth, Economic Development, and the United Nations." *Department of State Bulletin* 48 (January 7).

Gendell, Murray. 1986. "Stalls in the Fertility Decline in Costa Rica and Korea." Unpublished paper. Department of Demography, Georgetown University, Washington, D.C.

Gereffi, Gary. 1983. *The Pharmaceutical Industry and Dependency in the Third World*. Princeton: Princeton University Press.

Gille, Halvor. 1979. "Recent Trends in International Population Assistance." In *International Population Assistance: The First Debate*, by Rafael M. Salas, pp. 379–93. New York: Pergamon Press.

————. 1982. "International Population Assistance." In *International Encyclopedia of Population*, edited by John A. Ross, pp. 374–82. New York: Free Press.

Goshko, John M. 1984. "Inside: State Department." *Washington Post*, June 12, p. A15.

Gray, R. H. 1974. "The Decline of Mortality in Ceylon and the Demographic Effects of Malaria Control." *Population Studies* 28:205–29.

Greeley, Andrew M. 1977. *The American Catholic: A Social Portrait*. New York: Basic Books.

Greer, Germaine. 1984. *Sex and Destiny: The Politics of Human Fertility*. London: Secker and Warburg.

Hall, R. 1977. *Marie Stopes*. London: Andre Deutsch.

Han, Dae Woo. 1970. "Korea." *Country Profile*. April. New York: Population Council.

Harkavy, Oscar; Lyle Saunders; and Anna L. Southam. 1968. "An Overview of the Ford Foundation's Strategy for Population Work." *Demography* 5 (2): 541–52.

Harrington, Michael. 1962. *The Other America: Poverty in the United States*. Baltimore: Penguin Books.

Hass, Ernest B.; Mary Pat Williams; and Don Babai. 1977. *Scientists and World Order: The Uses of Technical Knowledge in International Organizations*. Berkeley: University of California Press.

Hauser, Philip. 1963. *The Population Dilemma*. Englewood Cliffs, N.J.: Prentice-Hall.

————. 1967. "Family Planning and Population Programs: A Book Review Article." *Demography* 4 (1): 397–414.

Hernandez, Donald J. 1981a. "The Impact of Family Planning Programs on Fertility in Developing Countries: A Critical Evaluation." *Social Science Research* 10 (1): 32–66.

————. 1981b. "A Note on Measuring the Independent Impact of Family Planning Programs on Fertility Declines." *Demography* 18 (4): 627–34.

————. 1984. *Success or Failure? Family Planning Programs in the Third World*.

Westport, Conn.: Greenwood Press.

Hess, Peter N. 1982. "Demographic Factors in South Korean Economic Development: 1963–1977." Unpublished Ph.D. dissertation, Department of Economics, University of North Carolina, Chapel Hill.

Himes, Norman E. [1936] 1963. *Medical History of Contraception*. New York: Gamut Press.

Hirschman, Charles. 1983. "America's Melting Pot Reconsidered." *Annual Review of Sociology* 9:397–423.

Hodgson, Dennis. 1983. "Demography as Social Science and Policy Science." *Population and Development Review* 9 (1): 1–34.

Hong, Sawon. 1978. *Population Status Report: Korea*. Seoul: Korea Development Institute.

Hong, Sung-Bong, and Walter B. Watson. 1976. *The Increasing Utilization of Induced Abortion in Korea*. Seoul: Korea University Press.

Howard, Lee M. 1970. "Key Problems Impeding Modernization of Developing Countries: The Health Issues." Washington, D.C.: Agency for International Development, Office of Health, Technical Assistance Bureau.

Isaacs, Stephen L. 1983. "Reproductive Rights 1983: An International Survey." *Columbia Human Rights Law Review*. 14:311–53.

Johnson, W. E.; R. T. Ravenholt; W. E. Haroldson; and E. B. Perrin. 1965. "Some Relationships of Smoking to Teenagers' Achievements." *Washington Education* 77 (2): 11–13.

Jones, Gavin W. 1979. "Forms of Aid: Population Control." In *International Aid: Some Political, Administrative and Technical Realities*, edited by R. T. Shand and H. V. Richter, pp. 212–34. Canberra: Australian National University, Development Studies Center Monograph no. 16.

Kaiser, Irwin H. 1975. "Alan Guttmacher and Family Planning in Cuba, 1966 and 1974." *Mount Sinai Journal of Medicine* 42 (4): 300–307.

Kelly, William R., and Phillips Cutright. 1983. "Determinants of National Family Planning Effort." *Population Research and Policy Review* 2:111–30.

Kennedy, David M. 1970. *Birth Control in America: The Career of Margaret Sanger*. New Haven: Yale University Press.

Kim, Taek Il; John A. Ross; and George C. Worth. 1972. *The Korean National Family Planning Program: Population Control and Fertility Decline*. New York: Population Council.

Kirk, Dudley. 1944. "Population Changes and the Postwar World." *American Sociological Review* 9:28–35.

Kiser, Clyde. 1981. "The Role of the Milbank Memorial Fund in the Early History of the Association." *Population Index* 47 (3): 490–94.

Knodel, John. 1979. "From National Fertility to Family Limitation: The Onset of Fertility Transition in a Sample of German Villages." *Demography* 16 (4): 493–521.

Knodel, John; Napaporn Havanon; and Anthony Pramualratna. 1983. "A Tale of Two Generations: A Qualitative Analysis of Fertility Transition in

Thailand." Ann Arbor: University of Michigan, Population Studies Center, Research Reports, no. 83-44.

Knodel, John, and Etienne van de Walle. 1979. "Lessons from the Past: Policy Implications of Historical Fertility Studies." *Population and Development Review* 5 (2): 217–45.

Knowlton, Charles. 1980. *Fruits of Philosophy*. Reprint of the 1832 text. Austin, Tex.: American Atheist Press.

Koh, Kap Suk; Hee Soon Hahm; and Jong Hwa Byun. 1980. *1979 Korea Contraceptive Prevalence Survey Report*. Seoul: Korea Institute for Family Planning.

Kolata, Gina Bari. 1974. "!Kung Hunter-Gatherers: Feminism, Diet and Birth Control." *Science* 185:932–34.

Koo, Hagen. 1981. "Centre-Periphery Relations and Marginalization: Empirical Analysis of the Dependency Model of Inequality in Peripheral Nations." *Development and Change* 12:55–76.

Krannich, Ronald L., and Caryl Rae Krannich. 1980. *The Politics of Family Planning Policy: Thailand—A Case of Successful Implementation*. Berkeley: Center for South and Southeast Asia Studies, University of California, Berkeley.

Lamb, David. 1984. *The Africans*. New York: Vintage Books.

Lapham, Robert T., and W. Parker Mauldin. 1972. "National Family Programs: Review and Evaluation." *Studies in Family Planning* 3 (3): 29–52.

———. 1984. "Contraceptive Prevalence: The Influence of Organized Family Planning Programs." Paper presented at annual meeting of Population Association of America, Minneapolis, May 3–5.

Leathard, Audrey. 1980. *The Fight for Family Planning: The Development of Family Planning Services in Britain 1921–74*. New York: Holmes and Meier.

Lee, Byung-Moo. 1967. "Impact of Population Changes on Economic Growth in Developing Countries" (in Korean). *Journal of Population Studies* (Seoul) 5:36–50.

Levin, Sander; Stephen Joseph; and J. Joseph Speidel. 1980. "Statement on the Agency for International Development's Population Assistance Program." Prepared for presentation before the Foreign Relations Committee, United States Senate.

Lippes, Jack, and Maria Zielezny. 1975. "The Loop Decade." *Mount Sinai Journal of Medicine* 42:353–63.

Littlewood, Thomas B. 1977. *The Politics of Population Control*. Notre Dame, Ind.: University of Notre Dame Press.

Lorimer, Frank. 1981. "How the Demographers Saved the Association." *Population Index* 47 (3): 488–90.

Luker, Kristen. 1984. "The War between the Women." *Family Planning Perspectives* 16 (3): 105–10.

Lunde, Anders S. 1981. "The Beginning of the Population Association of America." *Population Index* 47 (3): 479–84.

McPherson, M. Peter. 1985. "International Family Planning: The Reasons for the Program." Remarks presented to American Enterprise Institute, Washington, D.C., November 25.

Macura, Milos. 1968. "The Long-Range Outlook—Summary of Current Estimates." In *World Population—The View Ahead*, edited by Richard N. Farmer, John D. Long, and George J. Stolnitz, pp. 15–42. Bloomington: Bureau of Business Research, Indiana University, International Development Research Series, no. 1.

Mahler, Halfdan. 1983. "Address to an International Conference on Oral Rehydration Therapy." Washington, D.C., June 7–10. *Proceedings*, pp. 6–8.

Maine, Deborah. 1981. *Family Planning: Its Impact on the Health of Women and Children*. New York: Center for Population and Family Health, College of Physicians and Surgeons, Columbia University.

Management Services for Health, Inc. 1973. First Quarterly Report. Korean Family Planning Program Management Project, Seoul.

Marcoux, Alain. 1975. "The Ford Foundation/Population Council North African Population Program in Retrospect: 1963–1975." Unpublished paper. Ford Foundation, North Africa Field Office.

Matthiessen, Peter. 1979. *The Snow Leopard*. New York: Bantam Books.

Mauldin, W. Parker, and Bernard Berelson. 1978. "Conditions of Fertility Decline in Developing Countries, 1965–1975." *Studies in Family Planning* 9 (5): 90–147.

Mauldin, W. Parker, and Robert J. Lapham. 1984. "Conditions of Fertility Decline in LDCs: 1965–80." Paper presented at annual meeting of Population Association of America, Minneapolis, May 3–5.

Merrick, Thomas, and D. G. Graham. 1979. *Population and Economic Development in Brazil*. Baltimore: Johns Hopkins University Press.

Morgan, Dan. 1979. *Merchants of Grain*. New York: Viking Press.

Morris, Charles R. 1980. *The Cost of Good Intentions: New York City and the Liberal Experiment, 1960–1975*. New York: W. W. Norton.

Mosher, William D., and Calvin Goldscheider. 1984. "Contraceptive Patterns of Religious and Racial Groups in the United States, 1955–76: Convergence and Distinctiveness." *Studies in Family Planning* 15 (3): 101–11.

Mosher, William D., and Gerry E. Hendershot. 1984. "Religion and Fertility: A Replication." *Demography* 21:185–91.

Moskowitz, Karl. 1982. "Korean Development and Korean Studies—A Review Article." *Journal of Asian Studies* 42 (1): 63–90.

Mothner, Ira. 1976. *Understanding Population*. New York: Ford Foundation.

Mumford, Stephen D.; Pouru P. Bhiwandiwala; and I-cheng Chi. 1980. "Laparoscopic and Minilaparotomy Female Sterilization Compared in 15,167 Cases." *Lancet*, November 15, pp. 1066–70.

Murray, John Courtney. 1960. *We Hold These Truths: Catholic Reflections on the American Proposition*. New York: Sheed and Ward.

Nam, Duck-Woo, and Kong-Kyun Ro. 1981. "Population Research and Population Policy in Korea in the 1970s." *Population and Development Review* 7:651–69.

National Academy of Sciences. 1971. *Rapid Population Growth: Consequences and Policy Implications*. Vol. 1, *Summary and Recommendations*. Baltimore: Johns Hopkins University Press.

National Bipartisan Commission on Central America. 1984. *Report of the National Bipartisan Commission on Central America*. New York: Macmillan.

National Research Council. Working Group on Population Growth and Economic Development, Committee on Population. 1986. *Population Growth and Economic Development: Policy Questions*. Washington, D.C.: National Academy Press.

———. Working Group on Family Planning Effectiveness, Committee on Population. 1987. *Organizing for Effective Family Planning Programs*. Washington, D.C.: National Academy Press.

———. Working Group on the Health Consequences of Contraceptive Use and Controlled Fertility. 1989. *Contraception and Reproduction: Health Consequences for Women and Children in the Developing World*. Washington, D.C.: National Academy Press.

National Security Council. 1980. "United States International Population Policy." *Population and Development Review* 6 (3): 509–20.

Nemeth, Roger J., and David A. Smith. 1982. "Toward a Political Economy of Urbanization in South Korea and the Philippines: A Preliminary Analysis." Unpublished paper. Department of Sociology, University of North Carolina, Chapel Hill.

Ness, Gayl D. 1979. "Organizational Issues in International Population Assistance." In *World Population and Development: Challenges and Prospects*, edited by Philip M. Hauser, pp. 615–49. Syracuse, N.Y.: Syracuse University Press.

———. 1983. "The Impact of International Population Assistance." In *The Development Impact of Economic Assistance to LDCs*, prepared by Anne O. Krueger and Vernon W. Ruttan, pp. 8.1–8.35. Minneapolis: Economic Development Center, University of Minnesota.

Ness, Gayl D., and Hirofumi Ando. 1984. *The Land Is Shrinking: Population Planning in Asia*. Baltimore: Johns Hopkins University Press.

Ness, Gayl D.; J. Timothy Johnson; and Stan J. Bernstein. 1983. "Program Performance: The Assessment of Asian Family Planning Programs." Ann Arbor: Center for Population Planning, University of Michigan.

Ness, Gayl D.; Willa Pressman; and Jane Hutchings. 1982. "Foreign Assistance for Population Planning." Unpublished paper. Center for Population Planning, University of Michigan, Ann Arbor.

"1963—The Beginning of the Road." 1982. *Asian-Pacific Population Programme News* 2:27–28.

Nixon, Richard M. 1969. "Problems of Population Growth." *Department of State Bulletin*, August 11.

Noonan, John T., Jr. 1965. *Contraception: A History of Its Treatment by the Catholic Theologians and Canonists*. New York: New American Library.

Northcott, C. 1965. "Will Rome Take the Pill?" *Christian Century* 82:518.

Nortman, Dorothy L., and Ellen Hofstatter. 1978. *Population and Family Planning Programs*. 9th ed. New York: Population Council.

Nossiter, Bernard D. 1983. "U.N. Population Agency Assailed for Giving India and China Prizes." *New York Times*, July 24, p. 4.

Notestein, Frank W. 1933. "The Differential Rate of Increase among Social Classes of the American Population." *Social Forces* 12 (1): 17–33.

———. 1939. "Some Implications of Current Demographic Trends for Birth Control and Eugenics." *Journal of Heredity* 30:121–26.

———. 1945. "Population—the Long View." In *Food for the World*, edited by Theodore W. Schultz, pp. 36–57. Chicago: University of Chicago Press.

———. 1963. "Introduction." *Studies in Family Planning* 1:1.

———. 1968. "The Population Council and the Demographic Crisis of the Less Developed World." *Demography* 5 (2): 553–66.

———. 1971. "Reminiscences: The Role of the Foundation, the Population Association, Princeton University and the United Nations in Fostering American Interest in Population Problems." *Milbank Memorial Fund Quarterly* 49 (4, Part 2): 67–84.

———. 1982. "Demography in the United States: A Partial Account of the Development of the Field." *Population and Development Review* 8 (4): 651–870.

Office of Management and Budget, Executive Office of the President. 1988. *Budget of the United States Government: Appendix, FY 1988*. Washington, D.C.: U.S. Government Printing Office.

Office of Technology Assessment. 1982. *World Population and Family Planning Technologies: The Next 20 Years*. Washington, D.C.: U.S. Government Printing Office.

Omran, Abdel R. 1971. "The Epidemiological Transition: A Theory of the Epidemiology of Population Change." *Milbank Memorial Fund Quarterly* 49: 509–38.

Osborn, Frederick. 1933. "Characteristics and Differential Fertility of American Population Groups." *Social Forces* 12 (1): 8–16.

Park, Chai Bin. 1978. "The Fourth Korean Child: The Effect of Son Preference on Subsequent Fertility." *Journal of Biosocial Science* 10:95–106.

Parsons, Talcott. 1972. "Definitions of Health and Illness in the Light of American Values and Social Structures." In *Patients, Physicians and Illness: A Source Book in Behavioral Science and Health*, 2nd ed., edited by E. Gartly Jaco, pp. 97–117. New York: Free Press.

Pelotte, Donald E. 1975. *John Courtney Murray: Theologian in Conflict*. New York: Paulist Press.

Perkins, James A. 1966. "Report on Food and Population." Washington, D.C.: President's General Advisory Committee on Foreign Assistance Programs.

Piotrow, Phyllis Tilson. 1973. *World Population Crisis: The United States Response*. New York: Praeger.

Planned Parenthood Federation of Korea. 1982. "New Population Policy in Korea: A Summary of Explanation." Seoul.

Poffenberger, Thomas. 1969. "Report to the American Public Health Association: Family Planning Committee for AID-Korea." Unpublished paper.

Population Council. 1978. *The Population Council: A Chronicle of the First Twenty-Five Years, 1952–1977*. New York: Population Council.

Population Crisis Committee. 1983. "World Population Growth and Global Security." Washington, D.C.

Population Services International. N.d. (c. 1978). "The World Population Crisis and Social Marketing: A New Approach." New York. Brochure.

Potts, Malcolm. 1980a. "Barriers to Birth Control." *New Scientist* 8 (1224): 232–34.

———. 1980b. "Hope for the Living—Dacca 1979." *Network* 1:1–2.

———. 1982. "History of Contraception." In *Gynecology and Obstetrics*, edited by John W. Sciarra, pp. 1–22. Philadelphia: Harper and Row.

Potts, Malcolm, and I-cheng Chi. 1982. "Trip Report—People's Republic of China." Research Triangle Park, N.C.: Family Health International.

Potts, Malcolm, and Peter Selman. 1979. *Society and Fertility*. Estover, Plymouth: Macdonald and Evans.

Pradervand, Pierre. 1980. "People Are Precious—A Critical Look at the Population Control Movement." In *Poverty and Population Control*, edited by Lars Bondestam and Staffan Bergstrom, pp. 61–74. New York: Academic Press.

Preston, Samuel H. 1984. "Children and the Elderly: Divergent Paths for America's Dependents." *Demography* 21:435–57.

Rangan, B. Kasturi. 1985. "Population Services International—The Social Marketing Project in Bangladesh." Case no. 0-586-013, H.B.S. Case Services. Boston: Harvard Business School.

Rasky, Susan F. 1984. "Reagan Restrictions on Foreign Aid for Abortion Programs Lead to a Fight." *New York Times*, October 14, p. 6.

Ravenholt, Reimert T. 1964. "Cigarette Smoking: Magnitude of the Hazard." *American Journal of Public Health* 54:1923–25.

———. 1966. "Malignant Cellular Evolution: An Analysis of the Causation and Prevention of Cancer." *Lancet*, March 5, pp. 523–26.

———. 1968. "The AID Population and Family Planning Program—Goals, Scope and Progress." *Demography* 5 (2): 561–73.

———. 1969. "AID's Family Planning Strategy." *Science* 163:124, 127.

———. 1978. "Population Program Assistance, U.S. Agency for International Development: 1965–1978." Unpublished paper prepared for presentation to the Select Committee on Population, U.S. House of Representatives, April 25.

———. 1980. "The Population Jungle." Unpublished memorandum to "Population Colleagues," June 2.

———. 1984. "World Fertility Survey: Origin and Development of the WFS." Paper prepared for presentation to the WFS Symposium, London, England, April.

Ravenholt, Reimert T., and J. R. Applegate. 1965. "Measurement of Smoking Experience." *New England Journal of Medicine* 272:789–90.

Ravenholt, Reimert T.; M. J. Levinski; D. Nellest; and M. Takenaga. 1966. "Effects of Smoking upon Reproduction." *American Journal of Obstetrics and Gynecology* 96:267–81.

Reed, James W. 1978. *Private Vice to Public Virtue: The Birth Control Movement and American Society, 1830–1975.* New York: Basic Books.

Reeves, Richard. 1982. "Patriotism to Make the Heart Vibrate." *New York Times*, July 4, p. E15.

Repetto, Robert. 1985. "Review of the Resourceful Earth: A Response to Global Zoo." *Population and Development Review* 11:757–68.

Repetto, Robert; Tai-Hwan Kwon; Son-Ung Kim; Dae Young Kim; John E. Sloboda; and Peter J. Donaldson. 1981. *Economic Development, Population Policy, and Demographic Transition in the Republic of Korea.* Cambridge, Mass.: Council on East Asian Studies, Harvard University Press.

Rock, John C. 1963. *The Time Has Come: A Catholic Doctor's Proposals to End the Battle over Birth Control.* New York: Knopf.

Rockefeller, John D., III. 1966. "Opening Remarks." In *Family Planning and Population Programs: A Review of World Development*, pp. 1–4. Chicago: University of Chicago Press.

———. 1974. "Population Growth: The Role of the Developed World." Liège: International Union for the Scientific Study of Population. Lecture Series on Population.

Rockefeller, Nelson A. 1969. "Quality of Life in the Americas: Report of a U.S. Presidential Mission for the Western Hemisphere." Washington, D.C.

Rockefeller Foundation. 1982. "Report to the Rockefeller Foundation Trustees on the Population Program." Unpublished report. Rockefeller Foundation, New York.

Ruprecht, Theodore K., and Carl Wahren. 1970. *Population Programmes and Economic and Social Development.* Paris: Development Centre, Organization for Economic Co-operation and Development.

Salas, Rafael. 1985. "Remarks" delivered to the Fifth Annual United Nations Fund for Population Activities/Non-governmental Organizations Consultation, New York, April 25 (author's notes).

Sanger, Margaret. 1922. *The Pivot of Civilization.* New York: Brentano's.

Schlesinger, Arthur M. 1965. *A Thousand Days: John F. Kennedy in the White House.* Boston: Houghton Mifflin.

Schubert, James N. 1981. "The Impact of Food Aid on World Malnutrition." *International Organizations* 35 (2): 329–54.

Schultz, George P. 1983. Hearings, Committee on Foreign Affairs, U.S. House of Representatives. February 16, pp. 93–111.

Segal, Sheldon J. 1984. "U.S. Population Assistance to Developing Countries." Rockefeller Foundation, New York. Mimeo.

Shorter, Edward. 1982. *A History of Women's Bodies.* New York: Basic Books.

Simmons, Ozzie G. 1983. "Development Perspectives and Population

Change." *Papers of the East-West Population Institute*, no. 85. Honolulu: East-West Population Institute.

Simon, Julian L. 1981. *The Ultimate Resource*. Princeton: Princeton University Press.

Simon, Julian L., and Roy Gobin. 1980. "The Relationship between Population and Economic Growth in LDCs." In *Research in Population Economics: A Research Annual*, edited by Julian L. Simon and Julie DaVanzo, 2:25–34. Greenwich, Conn.: JAI Press.

Smeeding, Timothy; Barbara Boyle Torrey; and Martin Rein. 1986. "The Economic Status of the Young and the Old in Six Countries." In *Proceedings of a Workshop on Demographic Change and the Wellbeing of Children and the Elderly*. Washington, D.C.: National Research Council, Committee on Population.

Soloway, Richard Allen. 1982. *Birth Control and the Population Question in England, 1877–1930*. Chapel Hill: University of North Carolina Press.

Sommer, John C. 1977. *Beyond Charity: U.S. Voluntary Aid for a Changing World*. Washington, D.C.: Overseas Development Council.

Sorensen, Theodore C. 1965. *Kennedy*. New York: Harper and Row.

Steinberg, David I. 1982. "The Economic Development of Korea: Sui Generis or Generic?" Unpublished paper. Agency for International Development, Evaluation Special Study, no. 6.

Stopes, Marie C. 1923. *Contraception: Its Theory, History and Practice*. London: John Bale, Sons, and Danielsson.

Suh, Suk Tai. 1977. "Foreign Aid, Foreign Capital Inflows and Industrialization in Korea: 1945–1975." Working Paper no. 7712, Korea Modernization Study Series. Seoul: Korea Development Institute.

Symonds, Richard, and Michael Carder. 1973. *The United Nations and the Population Question 1945–1970*. New York: McGraw-Hill.

Teitelbaum, Michael S., and Jay M. Winter. 1985. *The Fear of Population Decline*. Orlando, Fla.: Academic Press.

Tendler, Judith. 1975. *Inside Foreign Aid*. Baltimore: Johns Hopkins University Press.

Thompson, Warren. 1929a. *Danger Spots in World Population*.

———. 1929b. "Population." *American Journal of Sociology* 34:959–75.

Thornton, Arland; Ming-Cheng Chang; and Te-Hsuing Sun. 1984. "Social and Economic Change, Intergenerational Relationships and Family Formation in Taiwan." *Demography* 21:475–99.

Tsui, Amy Ong. 1982. "Contraceptive Availability and Family Limitation." *International Family Planning Perspective* 8 (1): 8–18.

United Nations. 1984. *Fertility and the Family: Changing Conditions and Perceptions*. New York: United Nations.

United Nations Economic and Social Council. 1983. "Recommendations of the Expert Group on Fertility and Family." Preparatory Committee for the International Conference on Population, January 23–27, 1984.

United Nations Fund for Population Activities. 1982. *Republic of Korea: Report of Mission on Needs Assessment for Population Assistance,* Report no. 7, April. United Nations Population Division and Fund for Population Activities.

1979. "Nepal." *Population Policy Compendium.*

U.S. Bureau of the Census. 1981. *Demographic Estimates for Countries with a Population of 10 Million or More: 1981.* Washington, D.C.: U.S. Government Printing Office.

U.S. House of Representatives. International Relations Committee. 1975. Hearings, July 18, H 381-63.5:291.

———. Select Committee on Population. 1978. *Population and Development Assistance,* Serial D. 95th Cong., 2d sess. Washington, D.C.: U.S. Government Printing Office.

Van de Walle, Etienne, and John Knodel. 1980. "Europe's Fertility Transition: New Evidence and Lessons for Today's Developing World." *Population Bulletin* 34 (6).

Viel, Benjamin. 1976. *The Demographic Explosion: The Latin American Experience.* New York: Irvington.

Wagman, Paul. 1977. "U.S. Goal: Sterilize Millions of World's Women." *St. Louis Post-Dispatch,* April 22, pp. 1, 6.

Walsh, John. 1978. "President and Science Adviser Push for a Foundation for Development." *Science* 200:1252–53.

Warwick, Donald P. 1982. *Bitter Pills: Population Policies and Their Implementation in Eight Developing Countries.* Cambridge: Cambridge University Press.

Weiner, Myron. 1971. "Political Demography: An Inquiry into the Political Consequences of Population Change." In *Rapid Population Growth: Consequences and Policy Implications,* edited by Roger Revelle, pp. 567–617. Baltimore: Johns Hopkins University Press.

Westoff, Charles F., and Norman B. Ryder. 1970. "The Papal Encyclical and Catholic Practice and Attitudes: United States, 1969." *Studies in Family Planning* 50:1–7.

———. 1977. *The Contraceptive Revolution.* Princeton: Princeton University Press.

Westoff, Leslie Aldridge, and Charles F. Westoff. 1971. *From Now to Zero: Fertility, Contraception and Abortion in America.* Boston: Little, Brown.

Westphal, Larry E.; Yung W. Rhee; and Garry Pursell. 1981. "Korean Industrial Competence: Where It Came From." *World Bank Staff Working Paper,* no. 469, July.

"What Happened at Bucharest?" 1974. *Development Forum* 2 (7): 3–13.

Wickman, Stephen B. 1982. "The Economy." In *South Korea: A Country Study,* edited by Frederica M. Bunge, pp. 107–58. Washington, D.C.: U.S. Government Printing Office.

Williams, Doone, and Greer Williams. 1978. *Every Child a Wanted Child: Clarence James Gamble, M.D., and His Work in the Birth Control Movement.* Boston: Francis A. Countway Library of Medicine.

Wills, Garry. 1971. *Bare Ruined Choirs: Doubt, Prophecy, and Radical Religion.* Garden City, N.Y.: Doubleday.

_____. 1979. *Inventing America: Jefferson's Declaration of Independence.* New York: Vintage Books.

Wilson, John. 1973. *Introduction to Social Movements.* New York: Basic Books.

Wilson, Robert N. 1981. "The Courage to Be Leisured." *Social Forces* 60 (2): 282–303.

Winter, J. M. 1980. "The Fear of Population Decline in Western Europe, 1870–1940." In *Demographic Patterns in Developed Societies,* edited by R. W. Hiorns, pp. 173–97. London: Taylor and Francis.

Wolf, Margery. 1972. *Women and the Family in Rural Taiwan.* Stanford: Stanford University Press.

Wray, Joe D. 1971. "Population Pressure on Families: Family Size and Child Spacing." In *Rapid Population Growth: Consequences and Policy Implications,* Research Papers, National Academy of Sciences, 2:403–61. Baltimore: Johns Hopkins University Press.

Wright, Nicholas H. 1972. "Some Estimates of the Potential Reduction in the United States Infant Mortality Rate by Family Planning." *American Journal of Public Health* 62 (8): 1130–34.

_____. 1975. "Thailand: Estimates of the Potential Impact of Family Planning." *Journal of the Medical Association of Thailand* 58 (4): 204–10.

Wrong, Dennis H. 1961. *Population and Society.* New York: Random House.

Xinzhong, Qian. 1983. "China's Population Policy: Theory and Methods." *Studies in Family Planning* 14 (12): 295–301.

Index